# Mitchell Beazley Pocket Guides

# FORTIFIED AND SWEET WINES

John Radford and Stephen Brook

**Fortified and Sweet Wines by John Radford
and Stephen Brook**

First published in Great Britain in 2000 by Mitchell Beazley
an imprint of Octopus Publishing Company Limited
2–4 Heron Quays, London E14 4JP

A CIP catalogue record for this book is available from the British
Library

ISBN 1 84000 248 4

Commissioning Editor: Rebecca Spry
Executive Art Editor: Tracy Killick
Managing Editor: Lucy Bridgers
Editor: Hugh Morgan
Maps: Kenny Grant
Production Controller: Karen Farquhar

Typeset in Veljovic Book

Printed and bound by Toppan Printing Company in Hong Kong

# Contents

# How to use this book

This book is made up of two distinct halves. The first half, by John Radford is devoted to fortified wines and the second half, by Stephen Brook, sweet wines. Each half of the book has its own introduction which explores the methods used for making the wines. The styles of fortified and sweet wine are described here as they relate directly to the method of production. A selection of maps of the major fortified and sweet wine regions and countries can be found between these two chapters. The key fortified and sweet wines, such as Port, Sherry, Madeira, Sauternes and Tokaji have their own sections. Otherwise, wines are listed in their respective geographical areas.

Each region has an introduction describing its history, the grape varieties used, how the wines are made and explaining the classification system and any relevant terminology. Each entry has a bold-typed heading with the name of the producer, their address and an overall quality "star-rating" system (*see* below). The text profiles the producer, highlighting recommended wines. Some producers appear in both parts of the book as they make fortified and unfortified wines. To look up a specific wine or producer, find the page reference in the alphabetical index at the back of the book.

To save space, a number of abbreviations have been used. Vineyard areas are expressed in hectares (shortened to ha), and yields are given in hectolitres per hectare (hl/ha).

☆ decent
☆☆ above average, good
☆☆☆ excellent, much admired
☆☆☆☆ outstanding

# Storing and serving fortified wines

With the exception of vintage Port, there's no need to worry too much about storing fortified wines. They're ready to drink when you buy them and although there's a slight improvement in any wine if it's kept for a short time, it's unlikely to be substantial.

### Sherry and Montilla
'Dry', Manzanilla and Fino – drink within six months to a year of bottling, but once opened the bottle should be consumed within a couple of days. Serve chilled. All other Sherry and Montilla wines may be kept for as long as you like or consumed as soon as you wish. Some people prefer drier styles with a hint of a chill.

### Port and Málaga
White Port – drink within about a year of bottling. Serve chilled. Vintage Port – according to the year, these wines can come to maturity in less than ten years (eg the 1960) or more than twenty-five (eg the 1977). The wine magazines (or your wine merchant) should be able to advise but if the wine is good enough to be declared a

vintage, then the longer the better. Serve at room temperature.

All other Port and Málaga wines may be kept for as long as you like or consumed as soon as you wish. Lighter styles such as tawny Port are sometimes preferred with a hint of a chill.

## Madeira

These are the world's longest-lived wines, and even the basic "dry" Madeira should keep for a year or two. Vintage Madeiras are not released until they're twenty years old but these too may be kept: the greatest years are still going strong after two centuries. Drier styles can be served slightly chilled.

## Marsala

The better the wine, the longer it will keep. All Marsala wines are aged in wood and should keep well. Many people prefer the drier styles with a hint of a chill.

## Other sweet fortified wines

These should keep well although Muscats in particular may start to throw a sediment after a few years. This is harmless but charmless in the glass. White wines and Pineau des Charentes should be served chilled, but many people enjoy wines such as Banyuls and Fondillón with a hint of a chill.

# Storing and serving sweet wines

Sweet wines should be stored in exactly the same as dry wines. Although the sugar in the wine will help to conserve it, many sweet wines are just as prone to oxidation as dry ones. In Tokaji the bottled wine is often stored standing, but the circumstances are exceptional, since the bottles are kept in extremely humid underground cellars. As many sweet wines, especially from Sauternes, the Loire, and Germany, benefit from extended bottle-ageing, the wines should be stored, if possible, in a cool, dark untroubled environment and kept on their sides.

There's little need to decant sweet wines. If you plan to consume an entire bottle at one sitting, then the wine can be decanted for aesthetic reasons. There are few sights more pleasing on a dinner table than a decanter filled with golden wine!

Most sweet wines are best enjoyed on their own, the lighter ones as aperitifs, the richer ones at the end of a meal. There is a vogue for matching all manner of foods with all manner of wines, but sugar – and how many desserts are free of sugar? – does most wines no favours. Flavours such as chocolate will destroy a fine old Riesling or Sauternes, and the acidity of some fruit desserts may also affect a sweet wine adversely. From time to time combinations of sweet wines with sweet foods crop up that do work, but they tend to be the exception. Mild fruit tarts can be well matched by sweet wines. But it is better to play safe and enjoy a great sweet wine as a kind of supplementary dessert, so that you can give it the attention it deserves and derive the greatest possible enjoyment of the wine in the glass before you.

# Part one: fortified wines

## Why fortify?

"Quinquireme of Nineveh from distant Ophir,
Rowing home to haven in sunny Palestine,
With a cargo of ivory and apes and peacocks,
Sandalwood, cedarwood, and sweet white wine..."

Imagine that scene described by John Masefield: the apes and pea-cocks could, no doubt, take care of themselves, and the aromatic woods would probably have benefited from the warm sea breezes, but what of the wine? In Graeco-Roman times wine was stored in often poorly sealed clay amphorae, and for export the holds of ships were fitted with wooden slots to hold the jars securely and prevent them from falling over, spilling, or hitting each other with potentially disastrous results. The known world was the Mediterranean, and even the mighty military forces of Rome were not renowned for their expert seamanship, so we may assume that most trade was carried out during the clement summer months. The heat would have been intense for most of that time and, below decks, the wine must have reached blood heat on a regular basis.

Consider, then, the effects on that wine after several weeks' travel from the river ports of Assyria to, say, the pillars of Hercules. Only the sweetest and strongest would have survived the trip, and even they might have suffered some oxidation, pas-teurisation (although Pasteur would not be born for nearly 2,000 years) and maderisation before they were tasted by the eventual customer: a modern quality-control manager would have kittens.

Fortification is the addition of spirit – typically grape spirit but occasionally neutral ethyl alcohol – to wine to give it a robust resistance to oxidation and the thousand natural shocks the cargo is heir to... But whence that spirit?

There are reports that China discovered the distillation of fer-mented rice-wine in the 8th century BC, and there is anecdotal evidence of distillation of sugar cane, dates and other sweet sub-stances between that date and the fall of Rome in the 5th century AD, but the first written evidence of distillation comes from Pliny the Elder in the 1st century AD. Interestingly enough, he also reports the first major use of the barrel. Certainly we know that the Moors, who ruled parts of Spain from AD 711 to 1492, intro-duced distilling to the Iberian peninsula and that the wine we know as Sherry could have been fortified as early as the 10th cen-tury and was certainly fortified by the 15th.

Distilling and barrels and, indeed, sea voyages are the stuff of fortified wines. Perhaps the ancient Assyrians had learned how to strengthen the sweet Muscat wines of the Greek islands and the Middle Eastern hinterland to preserve them in their clay jars, but the era of fortified wine as we know it begins with the water-tight cask, made to exacting standards and allegedly invented in the Alpine regions of what is now the Swiss-Italian border. Casks of sweet, strong wine made the sea journey across the

Mediterranean and, later, the voyage to the East Indies and the Americas. In some cases the wines came back and were found to be better than when they had been embarked. There was no science of oenology and little knowledge of oxidative development, but for quite a few centuries barrels of wine which had been strengthened with grape spirit were sent across the equator and back to improve their character. The modern style of fruit-up-front, crisply acid, elegantly balanced wine would have been vinegar within a fortnight.

## How to fortify

There are three basic methods of making a fortified wine. The simplest is to run freshly pressed grape juice into a vat containing spirit and then to leave it to come to terms with itself for a (usually substantial) period of time. No fermentation takes place, and perhaps the best-known of this type of product is Pineau des Charentes, from the Cognac region of France. This method retains all the natural sweetness of the grapes but needs fairly long storage if it's to be anything more than a hefty, sweet, everyday beverage. It's known in French as *mistelle* and in Spanish as *mistela*.

The second method is fortification during fermentation, as exemplified by Port, Madeira, Málaga and Marsala. The wine-maker decides at what point to stop the fermentation in order to retain the desired residual sugar levels. The wine will be ready to drink earlier than a *mistelle*. Once again, the wine needs long and careful ageing in order to give of its best.

The third method is fortification after fermentation, in the manner of Sherry and Montilla. In this case the wine ferments fully dry (and undergoes a malolactic fermentation) and is fortified one or more times in the year following the year of vintage. This is the only way in which a truly dry fortified wine can be made.

## The role of the barrel

All good-quality fortified wines will have spent at least some time in a barrel, although this may vary in size from 225 to 1,000 litres or more and the wine may stay in one cask (static ageing) or several (dynamic ageing). Barrel ageing is oxidative – in other words, there's oxygen present, in the ullage (the space above the wine) and, molecule by molecule it seeps through the staves of the cask and the bung. This speeds up the ageing process tremendously compared with bottle- or vat-ageing and allows the wine and the spirit to "marry" comprehensively. Even more effective is dynamic ageing, in which a whole row of barrels of a particular vintage is fractionally blended with other rows of older vintages, thereby allowing new wines to take on the character of older ones. This is known as the *solera* system, and is explained in full in the section devoted to Sherry. Interestingly, all the barrels used for fortified wines are "old wood": they will have been used before (usually for beverage or low-quality wines) so that the oak and caramel characteristics don't dominate the wine.

# The importance of heat

All the best fortified wines come from hot countries. At first sight this seems rather paradoxical, but the historical reasons are simple enough. In the days before modern winemaking technology, hot countries produced overripe, low-acid grapes which fermented out to great alcoholic strength and tasted rather overpowering, not to say boiled to death. With the availability of grape spirit, however, these overheated wines could be tamed by adding spirit and, in the absence of anything else, they found a market in their home countries. They found an even bigger and more enthusiastic market in the cold countries of northern Europe, of course, where the encapsulated sunshine of a Mediterranean summer was trebly welcome on a cold winter's morning.

Heat is the second most important factor in the development of a fortified wine, after wood. Wherever fortified wines are made, they are aged in situations that take into account the ambient temperature. Port was traditionally taken down-river to Oporto or Vila Nova de Gaia for ageing, as the upper Douro was considered too hot; Sherry is kept in well-ventilated ground-level *bodegas* to emphasise the difference in temperature between winter and summer; Madeira may go through a process known as *estufagem*, in which the wine is put into a heated vat for three months, traditionally to replicate the passage of the barrel across the equator on its way to Formosa or Goa or Brazil and back. All of these use one of the basic laws of physics: that things expand as they get warmer. During the summer the wine expands and is forced into the caramelised layer of wood lining the barrel (in many cases coated with generations of wine deposits, as well), and in the winter it eases back out again. The result is a mellowing, maturing influence that helps the ageing process as well as providing overtones of vanilla, sugars, caramel and the other trace elements present in the wood.

# When, with what and with whom?

These always used to be known as "sideboard wines" and, as the name implies, would have been presented in crystal decanters on the sideboards of our Victorian forefathers to offer to guests. Typically, mid-morning was the time for Sherry, mid-afternoon for Madeira or Marsala and after dinner for Port. This was the respectable face of alcohol consumption in those days, and the blush it may have brought to even the most maidenly cheek could be attributed to tight corsets, a letter from abroad or an unspoken dalliance. Certainly, it was a million miles away from the squalor of the gin palaces, where common folk could get 'drunk for a penny – dead drunk for tuppence'.

Even in the late 1970s there was scarcely a home in Britain, Holland or Germany without its regulation bottle of "sideboard wine" for guests – usually Sherry of a particularly brown and nauseous sweetness, it has to be said. This market collapsed by the mid-1980s, and a number of large-scale producers went to the wall. Fortunately, salvation was already at hand thanks to some –

generally smaller – producers who had doggedly preserved the quality of their wines, accepted lower profits and maintained their reputations. These were the firms that not only survived but went on to create the brave new world of fortified wines which we are beginning to see in the first year of the 21st century. Port has survived almost unscathed, and goes from strength to strength. Sherry went through the fire of Hades in from 1989 to 1992 and emerged smaller, tougher, wiser, but better for the experience, Madeira is poised to expand outside its current enthusiast market, and Marsala... Well, good Marsala must rank as one of the most undervalued wines in the world.

Add to this the wide range of Vins Doux Naturels from France and beyond, the liqueur Muscats of California and Australia and the traditional fortified wines of South Africa, Cyprus and Greece, and you have a whole new world of sideboards groaning with good things. It would be a crime to waste them – it will be a pleasure to discover them.

# Port

"Firm and erect the Highland Chieftain stood;
Old was his mutton, and his claret good.
'Thou shalt drink Port!' the English statesman cried.
He drank the poison, and his spirit died." Anon.

## The history

The origins of Port wine were not, as the verse implies, an English plot against the Scots, although the first red wines from the Douro to be exported to England did coincide with three historical events which may have given that impression. The first was the War of the Spanish Succession (1701 to 1714), in which England and her allies were ranged against France and her allies. This meant that the supply of French wine – principally claret – which had flowed almost unhindered from Aquitaine to England since Eleanor married Henry II in 1152, dried up. Scotland, however, was not at war with France, and claret was still being shipped from Bordeaux to the Clyde, to the delight of the everyday Highland chieftain.

Meanwhile, Queen Anne had come to the throne in 1702, and her envoy to Portugal, John Methuen, negotiated the treaty that bears his name (in 1703) to ensure Portuguese support for England in the war. It also agreed reduced tariffs on Portuguese wines into England and English woollens into Portugal – one of the so-called "wool for wine" treaties that characterised this era of Anglo-Portuguese history.

So far so good, as Queen Anne, John Methuen and the Portuguese government felt they had struck a good deal – the Highland chieftain having little interest at this point, although he will reappear in a moment. The average Englishman, however, was less enthusiastic as his daily flagon of claret was replaced with a thick, soupy, overheated red beverage-wine from northern Portugal. Even this could have been merely a blip in the great panoply of vinous history but for the Act of Union. On 1 May 1707 England and Scotland became one nation to be called "Great Britain" (as opposed to "Britain", which comprised only England and Wales), and the Highland chieftain and everybody else in Scotland found themselves instantaneously at war with France as well. The supply of claret stopped and was replaced by wine shipped from Oporto. This was the chain of events which led to the making of what we know today as Port.

Something had to be done to make the red wine of Portugal palatable. There are endless stories of how this happened, including mixing the wine with herbs, spices, flavourings and even sea-water to reduce the heady, heavy, over-fermented style. (English) legend has it that it was an Englishman who first added brandy to the wine to keep back some of the natural grape sweetness and prevent the overheating, but other sources offer different interpretations. One that seems to hold more water (metaphorically speaking) than most is that, late in the 17th century, the Bishop of Lamego entertained an English wine merchant at his *quinta* in the Douro and served a red wine which had been "doctored" with brandy. The merchant reputedly bought his entire cellar and shipped it back to England.

Whoever it was, the combination of the Douro's native vines, schistose soils and unique microclimates managed then and now to produce grapes with rich natural sugar, powerful tannins and enormous extract which are just perfect for fortification during fermentation. The resulting wines have delighted Englishmen (and others) for ten generations.

## Grapes for Port

There's a good deal of freedom in the choice of grapes (nearly 90 varieties are grown), although most winemakers will be looking for a variety that offers good colour, plenty of natural sugar and enough tannin to sustain the wine through long ageing. Interestingly, all but one of best of them are Portuguese native varieties which are not grown elsewhere:

**Tinta Barroca** "Tinta" simply means "black" in this context, and this is an early-maturing variety widely used in wines which are to be drunk young.

**Tinta Cão** This literally means "black dog", although the reason why is not immediately apparent. This grape brings freshness and depth to the wine, and it thrives on high, cool sites in the Douro.

**Tinta Roriz** the only foreigner, this is the Tempranillo of Spain, named after the famous Quinta de Roriz where it was, supposedly, grown for the first time. It crops well in arid climates and produces wines of richness and colour.

**Touriga Francesa** not French at all, as far as anyone has been able to find out, this is a grape which provides good fruit characteristics even in hot, arid microclimates.

**Touriga Nacional** almost the perfect Port grape, with small berries and a thick, ripe skin to provide dense colouring material. In common with all the best grapes, its yield is very low.

Other varieties that show good Port-making characteristics include the Tinta Amarela, Tinta Barroca, Tinta Carvalho, Bastardo, Mourisco and Periquita, but there are many more.

White Port may be made from the classic Madeira grapes Malvasia (Malmsey), Gouveio (Verdelho), Boal and Cercial (Sercial) as well as the native Rabigato.

## How Port is made

Port is one of the few wines still – for the most traditional – actually trodden. The industry is divided on the benefit of old-fashioned foot-pressing in stone _lagares_, but those who believe in it do so with an almost religious passion. Those who insist that there's really no difference between the wine produced by the human foot and that made in a stainless steel vinifier tend to be the larger-scale companies; those who insist that the opposite is true tend to be the smaller companies. A fresh whiff of rationalism comes from Christian Seely of Quinta do Noval, who uses traditional _lagares_ using human feet, _lagares_ with mechanical, aluminium feet (which work for 48 straight hours without time off for food, cigarettes or toilet breaks), modern stainless steel tanks, and stainless steel tanks with mechanical aluminium feet inside them (no, honest). He's currently engaged in a long-term research project with neighbouring Taylor's to determine which of these various methods actually produces the best wine.

However the grapes are pressed, the Port process involves running off the fermenting juice – once it has achieved six to eight per cent alcohol by volume (abv) – into barrels already a quarter filled with grape brandy to "mute" the fermentation and retain grape sugars. The brandy may be bought on the open market by each individual Port producer and, apart from having been distilled from grape wine, its source is relatively unregulated.

The grapes for Port (*see above*) are grown over some 40,000 hectares of land in the upper Douro river valley, which is impossibly steep and ruggedly beautiful. The grapes are picked from mid-September onwards and, whether they're traditionally pressed in stone *lagares* to the accompaniment of singing and accordion music, or processed through stainless steel by computer, they end up in "pipes" or barrels of approximately 550 litres.

Originally, all Port wine was shipped down-river to the cooler climate of Oporto or Vila Nova de Gaia for ageing in the "Port Lodges", but the law changed in 1986 to allow those smaller producers who wished to do so to complete their ageing and maturation in the upper Douro, and many of them have taken advantage of this.

## Styles of Port

Once the Port is in the pipe it's likely to be classified by the winemaker of the *quinta* (or "wine farm") where it has been produced. To achieve the relevant appellation, samples of the wine must be deposited with the Instituto do Vinho do Porto (IVP) to be assessed for quality. Until the mid-1990s regulation of the Port trade was split between the IVP and the Casa do Douro but, after a scandalous episode in which a major share of one of the Douro's largest producers was sold to the Casa do Douro, most of its powers were removed and control is now firmly in the hands of the IVP.

Once a wine has been approved, special numbered seals will be issued which are attached over the cork of the bottle such that they are broken as the cork is withdrawn. The received wisdom (and this is something of a generalisation) is that firms with a Portuguese heritage are likely to make tawny and Colheita wines, while companies with a northern European heritage will major on vintage and vintage character. These are the principal styles:

**White Port** This is often described as "dry", but even the driest white Port is sweet by comparison with a dry Sherry or other dry white wine. However, they are dry by comparison with other Port wines, if nothing else.

**Vintage Port** The finest wine from the finest years. A Port shipper will "declare" a vintage two years after the harvest if the wine shows enough character and staying power. The wines spend two years in cask and the rest in bottle, and the greatest of them will live for more than 50 years.

**Single Quinta Vintage Port** Classic vintage Port, as described above, normally comes under one of the major brand names (eg Graham, Taylor, Sandeman) and will be a blend of wines from the same vintage year harvested from different vineyards or wine farms (*quintas*). Occasionally, a particular *quinta* will throw up grapes of quality worthy of a vintage wine, while the other suppliers do not, and in this instance the shipper may decide to produce an individual vintage Port made solely from the grapes of this *quinta*. Some *quintas* do this on a regular basis, and the best-known are probably Quinta de Vargellas (Taylor's), Quinta de Foz (Cálem) and Quinta de Bomfim (Dow's). There are, in addition, single-*quinta* producers which don't sell to or belong to the big-name houses but produce their own wine under their own name. The most prominent among these is probably Quinta do Noval.

**Colheita Port** This is old tawny wine of a single vintage, but one which has been stored in cask for most of its life and which is bottled just before being put on sale. In practice these are wines that don't quite have the majesty and individualism of vintage Port but which show an identifiable vintage style.

**Late Bottled Vintage Port (LBV)** Wine of a single vintage which, like Colheita, didn't quite make the grade to be vintage Port but which displays considerable vintage style. Typically, these wines are kept in cask for four years (as opposed to two) and are then bottled and released at perhaps five years old. The best may be second only to genuine vintage Port in taste, tannins and fruit.

**Vintage Character Port** These are blended wines which exhibit vintage style – perhaps from two or three years from which there wasn't sufficient quantity to make an LBV. The taste should be reminiscent of vintage Port, however far removed, and the price should be relatively modest.

**Aged Tawny Port** This is the tawny version of vintage character – wines from a number of years blended together to make a mature wine ready for immediate drinking. Typically, these will be named with an age – as "40-year-old" or "20-year-old" etc. The wine in the bottle will generally have an average age as expressed on the label, and may be very good indeed.

**Tawny Port** Budget-priced wines, typically of five to ten years old, which have been aged in oak and taken on some tawny character.

**Ruby Port** Young wines with up to about four years' barrel-age, usually fairly hot and heady, and in the budget price bracket.

**Other styles** "Crusted" Port is a vintage character Port bottled without filtration to give more of the character and style of a genuine vintage Port – it throws a crust and needs decanting. The quality varies according to the bottling company, and because of this inconsistency its days seem to be numbered. "Garrafeira" Port is wine aged in carboys or other large glass jars, with the idea that it will age as fast as Port in a barrel but with the gentleness and polish of Port aged in a bottle. Only one company (Niepoort) still produces wine in this way.

# When to drink Port

Tradition has cast vintage and vintage-style Ports as the ultimate post-prandial wines and, indeed, there are few happier marriages than that of a good Port with a well-matured cheese. In France tawny Port is considered an excellent apéritif, usually chilled or even over ice, and there are those in Portugal and beyond who enjoy white Port with tonic water served in the same way, perhaps also with a slice of lemon. For the most part, however, Port, whether Tawny, Ruby or Vintage, has a weight and sweetness which demands to come after food rather than before it.

# Principal shippers

## Barros Almeida & Cª Vinhos SA ☆☆

*Rua D Leonor de Freitas 180–182, Apartado 39, 4431-955 Vila Nova de Gaia*

Established in 1911, this company now owns many other Port producers, including Kopke (*see* entry). Best wines: Tawnies and Colheitas principally, some of them up to 50 years old. Also includes Hutcheson, Feuerheerd & Associados Vinhos SA, H & C J Feist Vinhos SA.

## Borges & Irmão — Sociedade dos Vinhos Borges SA

*Rua General Torres 923, 4400-164 Vila Nova de Gaia*

Established in 1884 but nationalised in the debacle of the 1974 revolution, this company almost drowned in bureaucracy before being saved by a management buyout. Potential is good – it owns three excellent properties in the Douro valley – but only time will tell if it is to return to its former prominence. Includes Garret & Cª Lda.

## Burmester – J W Burmester & Cª Lda ☆☆

*Rua de Belmonte 37, 4050-097 Oporto.*

Established in 1730, this is a (Gilbert) family-owned house with a direct succession back to the founders, something of a low profile and some surprisingly good wines. Best wines: Aged Tawnies can be excellent, especially 20-year-old and Colheitas. Look out for Quinta Nova. Also includes Gilberts & Cª Lda.

## Cálem – A A Cálem & Filho SA ☆☆→☆☆☆☆

*Av. Diogo Leite 26, Apartado 140, 4431-111 Vila Nova de Gaia*

Established in 1859 and still family-owned. Owns vineyards and buys in grapes from around Pinhão in the central Douro. Best wines: excellent Aged Tawnies and first-rate Quinta de Foz. Very reliable vintage wines. Welcomes visitors (by appointment) to newly restored accommodation at Quinta de Foz. Also includes Beira Rio Soc. Comercial de Vinhos Lda and Quinta do Sagrado Comércio de Vinhos Lda.

## Churchill Graham Lda ☆☆→☆☆☆☆

*Rua da Fonte Nova 5, 4400-156 Vila Nova de Gaia*

Established in 1981 by Johnny Graham, whose family firm (W & J Graham & Ca; *see* entry) had been sold to the Symingtons in

1970. He left Cockburn Smithes (*see* entry) to a certain amount of amusement from those who thought it mad to start a new venture in such a mature market. Nearly 20 years on, the company has its own Port Lodge and has just bought its first vineyard – the Quinta da Gricha near Pinhão. Best wines: good Vintage Character, excellent Quinta da Agua Alta, fine vintages.

## Cockburn Smithes & Cª SA ☆☆→☆☆☆
*Rua das Coradas 13, Apartado 20, 4431-951 Vila Nova de Gaia*
Established in 1815 and, since 1962, part of the group that has changed its name many times but is now known as Allied-Domecq. Throughout most of this time the company has been allowed a certain autonomy, although the vast success of Cockburn's Ruby and Cockburn's Special Reserve seems to have overshadowed the production of more individual wines. Best wines: the basic wines are good enough, and some vintages are excellent. Look out for Quinta dos Canais, which is developing well. Allied-Domecq also owns Gassiot (*see* entry).

## Croft ☆
*Via Gilbeys/IDV/Grand Metropolitan/Diageo*
Established in 1678, this once-proud stalwart of ancient Port tradition is now little more than a brand within the multinational conglomerate that is Diageo, formed from the merger of Grand Metropolitan and Guinness, and now the biggest drinks group in the known universe. Great vintages in the 1960s and 1970s petered out in the trend for brand-building, and although the name is widely known the wines have been disappointing in recent years. However, reports of the work done by Nick Delaforce (of that ilk) are encouraging. Best wines: Aged Tawnies, Quinta da Roeda. Also includes Delaforce.

## Dow – Silva & Cosens Lda ☆☆☆
*Trav. Barão de Forrester 85, Apartado 14, 4401-997 Vila Nova de Gaia*
Established in 1862 and named after James Dow, who joined the business in 1877. Since then it has become part of the Symington empire (*see* Warre, Graham, Smith Woodhouse, Quarles Harris), who got involved from 1912. Best wines: vintages, Quinta do Bomfim.

## Ferreira – A A Ferreira SA ☆☆→☆☆☆
*Rua da Carvalhosa 19, Apartado 1309, 4401-501 Vila Nova de Gaia*
Established in 1761 but sold to the Sogrape Group (famous for Mateus Rosé, and they also own Offley) in 1987. They make wine from four wholly owned *quintas* as well as from bought-in grapes. Very strong on aged tawny Ports but also an excellent vintage. Best wines: Duque de Bragança 20-year-old Tawny; vintages. Also includes Hunt, Constantino Vinhos Lda, whose brand name is Tuke-Holdsworth, and Forrester & Cª SA.

## Fonseca Guimaraens Vinhos SA ☆☆☆→☆☆☆☆
*Rua Barão Forrester 404, Apartado 13, 4401-501 Vila Nova de Gaia*
A family-owned and family-run company since 1822, this firm

has belonged to Taylor's (*see* entry) since 1948, although there has been almost no cross-fertilisation, and the two companies have rigidly maintained their individuality. Anyone who has ever met ebullient, heavyweight Bruce Guimaraens, winemaker extraordinary, is unlikely to forget him. Best wines: all this company's wines (under the Fonseca brand name) are very reliable, even the Vintage Character and younger Tawnies. Vintages can be exceptional (even matching and beating Taylor's occasionally), and in lesser years seek out value-for-money late-bottled vintages under the Fonseca-Guimaraens label. Also includes the Guimaraens brand name and Romariz Vinhos SA.

## Gassiot – Martinez Gassiot & Co Ltd ☆☆
*Rua das Coradas 13, Apartado 20, 4431-951 Vila Nova de Gaia*
Established in 1797, this is a sister company of Cockburn Smithes (*see* entry) as a member of the Allied-Domecq empire, which explains why its brand-name is seldom seen outside Portugal. Its role has been as the own-label supplier of Port to Allied-Domecq customers, but on its home patch you may see some wine under the company's own label. Best wines: Aged Tawnies, vintages and Quinta da Eira Velha.

## Graham – W & J Graham & Cª SA ☆☆☆→☆☆☆☆
*Ramiro 514, Apartado 19, 4401-997 Vila Nova de Gaia*
Established in 1826 but sold to the Symington group in 1970, Graham's is reckoned to be the softest of the Symington "trilogy" of Dow, Graham and Warre (*see also* Smith Woodhouse entry), with excellent wines from the Quinta dos Malvedos at Túa and the Quinta del Vesúvio. Best wines: in great years, the vintages; in lesser years, Quinta dos Malvedos, Quinta del Vesúvio; good Aged Tawnies.

## Kopke – C N Kopke & Cª Lda ☆☆
*Rua de Serpa Pinto 183–191, Apartado 42, 4431-901 Vila Nova de Gaia*
Established in 1638, this is the oldest remaining Port house, but has belonged to the Barros Almeida Group (*see* entry) since 1953, although, unlike other members of the group, Kopke has retained a measure of independence. Best wines: Aged Tawnies and Colheitas from the Quinta de São Luiz.

## Messias – Sociedade Agrícola e Comercial dos Vinhos Messias SA
*Rua de José Mariani 139, Apartado 1566, 4401-901 Vila Nova de Gaia*
This is a family-owned business dating back to the 1930s which owns vineyards at Quinta do Rei and Quinta do Cachão. Seldom seen outside Portugal. Includes Alberto de Castro Lança Lda.

## Niepoort (Vinhos) SA ☆☆→☆☆☆
*Rua do Infante D Henrique 16 2°ªft, 4051-801 Oporto*
Established in 1842, this is a seriously underrated, family-owned company with a range of excellent wines sold mainly on the

German and Scandinavian markets. It's also the one remaining producer of Garrafeira Ports (*see* above). Best wines: all the wines are of good general quality, with the Aged Tawnies perhaps just overshadowing the vintages. Look out for Quinta do Passadouro.

## Noval – Quinta do Noval Vinhos SA ☆☆☆→☆☆☆☆

*Avenida Diogo Leite 256, Apartado 1319, 4401-501 Vila Nova de Gaia*

Established in 1813 but owned by the French insurance group AXA Millésimes since 1993 and managed by Englishman Christian Seely and his Portuguese wife Maria, daughter of neighbour Joaquim Cálem (of that ilk). The magnificent Quinta has been rebuilt almost from scratch, and the wines divide into three groups: "Noval" is the brand name for wines made from bought-in grapes; "Quinta do Noval" are wines made from grapes grown on the estate; and "Nacional" is the vintage wines from a portion of the vineyard still growing ungrafted vines of, mainly, Touriga Nacional. Best wines: all very reliable; excellent Aged Tawnies and vintages. Nacional vintages outstanding (though very expensive). The 1994 LBV represents excellent value.

## Osborne Portugal, Vinhos, Distribuição e Serviços Lda ☆

*Rua Cândido dos Reis 670, 4400-071 Vila Nova de Gaia*

A relative newcomer to the Port business, Osborne's main market is Spain (*see* Sherry). The company produces vintage, Aged Tawnies and a basic Ruby and White. It's a little too soon to say what might develop here. Best wines: Aged Tawnies; vintage.

## Poças – Manoel D Poças Júnior Vinhos SA

*Rua Visconde das Devesas 186, Apartado 1556, 4401-901 Vila Nova de Gaia*

Established in 1918 and still in the original family hands, this company services the everyday market in France and Belgium and makes some pleasant but lightweight vintage Port. Best wines: Aged Tawnies.

## Quarles Harris & Cª SA ☆

*Trav. Barão de Forrester 85, Apartado 26, 4401-997 Vila Nova de Gaia*

An offshoot of the Symington empire (*see* Warre, Graham, Dow, Smith Woodhouse), this house was originally established in 1680 and taken over by the nascent Symington empire in the first quarter of the 20th century. Best wines: decent, early-maturing vintages.

## Ramos-Pinto – Adriano Ramos Pinto (Vinhos) SA ☆☆

*Avenida Ramos-Pinto 380, Apartado 1320, 4401-997 Vila Nova de Gaia*

Established in 1880 but bought in 1990 by the Louis Roederer group, and as well-known for its inspired advertising campaigns as for its wines. Best wines: mainly Tawnies, especially 20-year-old and Colheitas. Reliable (and improving) vintages. Includes J Carvalho Macedo Lda.

**Rosa – Quinta da Rosa Vinhos Porto Lda** ☆→☆☆
*Quinta de la Rosa, 5085-000 Pinhão*
Until 1988 this *quinta*'s grapes went to the house of Robertson,
now part of the Sandeman group (*see* entry). However, the father-
and-daughter team of Tim and Sophia Bergqvist decided to go
independent, and since then the *quinta* has been making a name
for itself. Winemaking has returned to the lagar and quality has
lifted. Best wines: Aged Tawnies, pre-Sandeman vintages.

**Royal Oporto – Real Companhia Vinícola do Norte
de Portugal SA** ☆
*Rua Azevedo de Magalhães 314, Apartado 58, 4431 Vila Nova de Gaia*
The oldest company within this extended group was founded by
the Marquês de Pombal as a regulatory body for the Port trade in
1756, but since then so many names and brands have come and
gone that it's difficult to step between them. The most recent
headline events in the company's history have been the sale of a
major share to an Italian finance house which sold it on to the
Casa do Douro, which was then a regulatory body for Port generally. Day-to-day running of the company, however, still rests with
the Silva Reis family, and the Real Companhia Velha, known as
Royal Oporto (the main brand name) for short, owns more land
than anyone else in the Douro – some 2,000 hectares over eight
*quintas* at the last count. The wines, however, are relatively modest in quality. Best wines: some good Aged Tawnies. Also includes
Companhia Geral da Agricultura das Vinhas do Alto Douro SA
and Manuel da Silva Reis & Cª Lda.

**Rozés Lda** ☆
*Rua Cândido dos Reis 526-532, Apartado 376, 4431-905 Vila Nova
de Gaia*
This rather modest company was founded in France in the 19th
century principally to supply "working" tawny Port to the vast
French market, where it is consumed enthusiastically as an apéritif. However, in 1987 the company was bought by Louis
Vuitton-Moët-Hennessy (LVMH), which is better known for pre-
mium-price luxury products than middle-of-the-road tawny Port.
Since then we have seen some good-quality aged tawnies and a
couple of decent vintage Ports, but there is a suspicion that Rozés
is up to something and there may be surprises to come when
wines in the Lodges at Vila Nova come to maturity. Best wines:
currently the 10-year-old Tawny, but watch this space.

**Sandeman & Ca SA** ☆→☆☆
*Largo de Miguel Bombarda 3, Apartado 1308, 4401-501 Vila Nova
de Gaia*
Established in 1791, this is the brand that – along with Cockburns
– probably springs to mind first in English-speaking countries
whenever Port is mentioned. The Sandeman family sold out to
Seagrams in 1980, after which brand-building became more
important than quality. While sales of "fighting" wines leaped
ahead, the reputation of Sandeman among Port enthusiasts dwin-

dled. However, in 1990 Seagrams had a change of heart and appointed George Sandeman to head up his old family firm, with a brief to reinvigorate Sandeman Port. Ten years on and into its 4th century, work is in progress and we may yet see a return to the greatness for which the company was known in its second century. In the meantime, best wines: improving vintages and Quinta do Vau; good Aged Tawnies.

### Silva – C da Silva (Vinhos) SA ☆→☆☆
*Rua de Felizardo Lima 247, 4400-901 Vila Nova de Gaia*
This is a Dutch-owned house in spite of its Portuguese name, best known for middle-range commercial wines for the Dutch, German and French markets. Best wines: some good Aged Tawnies and the occasional spectacular Colheita.

### Smith Woodhouse & Ca Lda ☆☆→☆☆☆
*Trav. Barão de Forrester 85, Apartado 26, 4401-997 Vila Nova de Gaia*
Established in 1784 and taken over by Symington in 1970 (see entries on Warre, Graham, Dow, Quarles Harris), Smith Woodhouse has no vineyards to its name and yet manages to produce attractive and good-quality wines, often at bargain prices. Best wines: vintages, LBV.

### Taylor Fladgate & Yeatman Vinhos SA ☆☆☆☆
*Rua do Choupelo 250, Apartado 1311, 4401-501 Vila Nova de Gaia*
If Cockburn's and Sandeman are names with which to conjure success in the mass market, then Taylor's is the equivalent in the enthusiasts' market. Established in 1692 and known by a bewildering array of different names, it achieved its present nomenclature in 1844. Almost throughout its existence Taylor's has been regarded as "the best" Port, and a good deal of this reputation centres on its property at Quinta de Vargellas. In great years the vintage Port is made from grapes grown here and at Quinta da Terra Feita, near Pinhão. In lesser years the two Quintas produced their own single-*quinta* vintages. Best wines: there are no second-class wines in the Taylor's range, but Quinta de Vargellas in off-years and the vintage in great years are almost unmatched. Also includes Fonseca (*see* entry) and Skeffington Vinhos Lda.

### Warre & Cª SA ☆☆☆→☆☆☆☆
*Trav. Barão de Forrester 85, Apartado 26, 4401-997 Vila Nova de Gaia*
Established in 1670 but renamed by William Warre in 1729. Taken over by Andrew Symington in 1905, whose descendants then went on to take over Quarles Harris, Dow, Graham and Smith Woodhouse by 1970, becoming the largest group in the Port business (*see* entries for all of these). Best wines: Quinta da Cavadinha; vintages.

## Other Producers
### Quinta do Crasto ☆☆
Promising wines from a company mainly engaged in making non-fortified wines under the Douro DOC.

**Quinta do Côtto** ☆☆☆
Excellent wines are made here by the maverick winemaker
Miguel Montez Champalimaud.

# Port vintages

This is always a matter for the individual shippers, suitably rati-
fied by the IVP. The following table attempts to show who among
the major players declared what during the 20th century and is a
general quality guide:

| Year | Taylor | Fonseca | Ferreira | Ramos-Pinto | Consensus |
|------|--------|---------|----------|-------------|-----------|
| 1900 | Yes | Yes | Yes | No | ☆☆☆ |
| 1904 | Yes | Yes | Yes | No | ☆☆☆ |
| 1906 | Yes | No | No | No | ☆ |
| 1908 | Yes | Yes | Yes | No | ☆☆☆ |
| 1909 | No | No | No | Yes | ☆ |
| 1912 | Yes | Yes | Yes | Yes | ☆☆☆☆ |
| 1916 | No | No | No | Yes | ☆ |
| 1917 | Yes | No | Yes | Yes | ☆☆☆ |
| 1920 | Yes | Yes | Yes | Yes | ☆☆☆☆ |
| 1921 | No | No | No | Yes | ☆ |
| 1922 | No | Yes | No | Yes | ☆☆ |
| 1924 | Yes | No | Yes | Yes | ☆☆☆ |
| 1926 | No | No | No | Yes | ☆ |
| 1927 | Yes | Yes | No | No | ☆☆ |
| 1928 | No | No | Yes | No | ☆ |
| 1931 | No | No | No | No | ☆ |
| 1934 | No | Yes | Yes | Yes | ☆☆☆ |
| 1935 | Yes | No | No | Yes | ☆☆ |
| 1938 | Yes | No | No | No | ☆ |
| 1940 | Yes | No | No | No | ☆ |
| 1942 | Yes | No | No | No | ☆ |
| 1945 | Yes | Yes | Yes | Yes | ☆☆☆☆ |
| 1948 | Yes | Yes | Yes | No | ☆☆☆ |
| 1952 | No | No | No | No | ☆ |
| 1955 | Yes | Yes | Yes | No | ☆☆☆ |
| 1960 | Yes | Yes | Yes | Yes | ☆☆☆☆ |
| 1963 | Yes | Yes | Yes | No | ☆☆☆ |
| 1964 | No | No | No | Yes | ☆ |
| 1966 | No | Yes | Yes | No | ☆☆ |
| 1970 | Yes | Yes | Yes | Yes | ☆☆☆☆ |
| 1975 | Yes | Yes | Yes | Yes | ☆☆☆☆ |
| 1977 | Yes | Yes | Yes | No | ☆☆☆ |
| 1980 | Yes | Yes | Yes | Yes | ☆☆☆☆ |
| 1982 | Yes | No | No | Yes | ☆☆ |
| 1983 | Yes | Yes | Yes | Yes | ☆☆☆☆ |
| 1984 | Yes | No | No | No | ☆ |
| 1985 | Yes | Yes | Yes | Yes | ☆☆☆☆ |
| 1986 | Yes | No | No | No | ☆ |
| 1987 | Yes | No | No | No | ☆ |
| 1988 | Yes | No | No | No | ☆ |
| 1991 | Yes | No | No | Yes | ☆☆ |

| 1992 | Yes | Yes | Yes | No | ☆☆☆ |
| 1994 | Yes | Yes | Yes | No | ☆☆☆ |
| 1995 | Yes | Yes | Yes | Yes | ☆☆☆☆ |
| 1996 | Yes | Yes | No | No | ☆☆ |

# Madeira

## The history

History glosses over the suggestion that João Gonçalves Zarco (known as "the blue-eyed" or "the squinter") was supposed to be exploring the west coast of Africa – or looking for the Americas, depending on which set of legends you believe – when in 1418 he came upon this volcanic rock in the Atlantic off the coast of what is now Morocco. In the event, however, the island probably earned more money for Portugal than the average African or American venture, as it became an important entrepôt and provisioning stop for shipping not only from Lisbon to Rio de Janeiro and points west but also from Southampton to Durban and points east. Even though the capital, Funchal, is heavily built up with tourist development nowadays, there's still a slightly colonial feel to the old town areas, and the interior and the north coast are as rugged and subtropical as ever.

In 1418 the island was reportedly so thickly wooded that it was almost impossible to come ashore, and Captain Gonçalves Zarco and his crew solved the problem with a fine disregard for the environment by setting fire to the forest – a fire that burned, according to legend, for seven years, layering the soil with wood ash that would provide the perfect compost for the vine.

Whether or not this is true, the island quickly became a centre for vine-growing, and by Shakespeare's time was sending "Madeira-Sack" to northern Europe to compete with the Sherris-Sack, Málaga-Sack and Canary-Sack which had become a staple of celebration in England, Holland, Germany and much of Scandinavia, as well as to the Americas. Shakespeare it was who propagated the legend that the late Duke of Clarence, who was executed in 1478 for allegedly scheming against the king, his brother Edward IV, had been "drowned in a butt of Malmsey wine", although Madeira at this time would most probably have not been fortified.

The really big success period for the wine was, however, much later. The Victorians adored Madeira – which now definitely was a fortified wine – and, along with Port, Sherry and Marsala, it became one of the most respectable of wines, at home on the sideboards of aspiring families everywhere and usually sipped with a slice of plain cake (thereafter known as "Madeira cake") at four o'clock in the afternoon. The biggest markets were Britain, the US and Russia and, in the early part of the 19th century, the wine's future seemed assured.

It couldn't last. Madeira's pivotal position in the world of shipping brought the first great vine plague of oïdium (powdery mildew) to the island in the early 1850s, destroying some 98 per cent of the vines. They had scarcely managed to restore the vineyards before the second great vine plague of phylloxera struck, in the mid-1870s, devastating them yet again. During this 25-year period many of the old Madeira wine shippers simply sold up their stocks and left the island, and many farmers uprooted their vines and planted the islands' second most important crop – sugar cane. Others planted American vines and produced something of borderline acceptability (indeed, there are still those who claim that perfectly good Madeira was made for 100 years using grapes from *Vitis labrusca* vines), but most simply went bust.

However, by the turn of the century, grafting on to American roots had become commonplace, and the business began to build back. The next great setback was the Russian revolution, after which Madeira was seen (along with cigars, interestingly enough) as one of the worst symbols of capitalist oppression, and the loss of this market was quickly followed by Prohibition in America, which did for a large slice of the remainder. On the credit side, France, Belgium and Britain were buying quite large quantities of fairly basic Madeira wine for use in cooking, and this has been the slow, halting, but perceptible basis for the wine's renaissance.

## Grapes for Madeira

This is where the big change has taken place in the last few decades. Originally, Madeira wine was known by the names of its four "noble" grapes – Malmsey (Malvasia), Boal (Bual), Verdelho and Sercial – and these have informed the hierarchy – sweet, medium- sweet, medium-dry, dry – which now governs the style of all but the finest (ie old vintage) Madeira wines. Around 95 per cent of the vineyard is now planted with Tinta Negra Mole, and this is vinified to fit in with this sweet/dry hierarchy at the bottom of the price range. Other grapes which are hanging on include Terrantez (almost extinct until replanting began in the 1980s), Bastardo (similarly close to extinction) and Moscatel. There is a school of thought which suggests that if the Tinta Negra Mole were given the same kid-glove treatment as the "noble" varieties then it would produce wines of similar breeding and class. However, at the moment economic necessity makes this unlikely, if not impossible.

## How Madeira is made

Like Port, Madeira is fortified during fermentation, and the moment of fortification governs how much residual sugar is left in the wine. As a guideline, the degree of sugar left in the finished wine after fermentation, expressed in degrees Baumé ($^\circ$Bé), is as follows:

"**Dry**" wines (in the style of Sercial): up to 1.5 $^\circ$Bé

"**Medium-Dry**" wines (in the style of Verdelho): from 1–2.5 $^\circ$Bé

"**Medium-Sweet**" wines (in the style of Bual): from 2.5–3.5 $^\circ$Bé

"**Sweet**" wines (in the style of Malmsey): over 3.5 $^\circ$Bé – up to 7 typically, although great wines may achieve 10–11 $^\circ$Bé (by comparison, the ripest Port achieves 15 $^\circ$Bé).

If the winemaker wants to make a sweet wine, he will fortify early; if a "dry" wine (no Madeira is ever truly dry), he will fortify late during the fermentation to conserve greater or lesser amounts of the grapes' residual sugar. The fortification is done with (usually French) grape alcohol at 96 per cent, and this is introduced into the fermenting vessel (compare Port, where the wine is run off into vessels with standing spirit already inside them). The fermented wine will than have about 18 per cent alcohol and be ready for the next stage.

Tradition has it that casks of Madeira were taken around the world as ballast and that the rolling of the ship and the crossing of the equator twice (with attendant rising and falling of ambient temperatures) gave the wine a rich, mellow maturity which found it much approved on its return to Funchal. When the era of round-the-world sailing ships ended, the process was replicated by a process called *estufagem* ("heating"), which heats the wine to about 45°C for a period of about six months, after which it goes into cask. There is an alternative method of using heat to help age the wine called *canteiro*, in which the wines are stored in tall, well-ventilated warehouses and simply take advantage of the varying temperatures of the season – although the daily temperature in Madeira seldom exceeds 25°C in the summer or drops below 18°C in the winter.

There are mixed opinions on the value of *estufagem*, from those who refuse to have anything to do with it, to those who believe that, used correctly, it's the key to making magnificent Madeira wine. The old method was simply to have a heating element within a traditional concrete vat, through which hot water or steam was passed to raise the temperature to the appropriate level. A variation on this was to raise the temperature from ambient to 45°C in two degree stages, and then to reduce it in the same way, with two cycles over a six-month period to replicate the crossing of the equator twice. Some producers went a step further and pumped the wine around inside the vat to reproduce the rolling and pitching of the ship.

Those who favour *estufagem* say that it was crumbling old concrete vats and leaky heating systems which destroyed the reputation of the method, and that using new, stainless steel tanks, it can be so delicately controlled that it makes a real contribution to the ageing, development and longevity of the finished wine. While the rest of the world pumps chilled water into the double skin of its tanks to cool down the must and perform a carefully controlled fermentation, in Madeira they pump in hot water to raise the temperature and perform a carefully controlled *estufagem*. At the last count, at least one winemaker refuses to use the method at all, at least one uses it for all his wines, and nearly all the rest use *estufagem* for "TNM" wines (ie made from Tinta Negra Mole) but not for the "noble" wines.

The wines are blended and sold after a minimum three years in the cellars, although the greatest wines, of course, spend much longer than this in maturation.

## Styles of Madeira

Most producers now have two or three ranges of wines: those called simply "Madeira" and made very largely from the Tinta Negra Mole (TNM) and classified as "sweet", "medium-sweet", "medium-dry" and "dry"; those appended with the name of one of the traditional noble grapes – Sercial, Verdelho, Bual and Malmsey; and finally single-vintage wines, often of great antiquity. Madeira can be the longest-lived of all the wines in the world – examples from vintages in the 1790s are still available (to the moneyed) and are still full of vigour.

Some of the "medium" styles are labelled "Rainwater" for reasons which are unclear. There is a legend that a wine was once described by an American importer's advertising agency as being "as soft as rainwater" and it sold so well that the name stuck. There is an addition to the legend which records that the importer's name was the splendidly American "Rainwater Habisham" but this too may be apocryphal. Then there's the story that some casks once let some rainwater seep in and... But you've probably heard enough legends.

"TNM" wines will have one of the four levels of sweetness on the label and have been aged for a minimum of three years and more usually five, of which typically six months will have been spent undergoing *estufagem*. They range in quality from pleasant to very pleasant and are the economic mainstay of the industry.

"Noble" wines must be made from at least 85 per cent of the specified variety – Malvasia (Malmsey), Bual (Boal), Verdelho, Sercial and, more rarely, Terrantez. Most (though not all) producers age these solely by the *canteiro* method (ie no *estufagem*), and they are typically offered for sale as five-year-old and ten-year-old wines, although there are some fifteen-year-old examples on the market.

Vintage Madeiras are forbidden to use the word "vintage", as this is, believe it or not, a registered trademark for Port within Portugal. However, they are permitted to use the word "Colheita", but most simply stick the date on the bottle and allow the customers to draw their own conclusions as, for example "1900 Malvasia". In any case, wine of a single harvest must be aged in oak for a minimum of 20 years and then a couple of years in bottle before it may be released, which makes all of it rare and expensive. For this reason, a good deal of fine old Madeira has been matured in *soleras* (*see* the section on Sherry for a full description) in which younger wines blend imperceptibly with older wines to produce a dynamically aged wine of considerable quality rather more quickly than waiting for the vintage wines to become legally available.

*Solera* wines may carry the date of foundation of the *solera*, as, for example, "Solera 1900 Malvasia". This is very different, of course, from the vintage example quoted above, as there will be wine in the mix from most vintages since 1900, and the average age may be as young as 20 or 30 years old rather than the perceived 100.

Future developments: there are some proposals to redefine and expand the Colheita style of wine, and to market "single quinta" Madeiras but, given the length of time it takes for good wine to develop, these may be some considerable way into the future.

# Principal shippers

**Barbeito – Vinhos Barbeito (Madeira) Lda** ☆☆→☆☆☆
**(Vintages** ☆☆☆☆**)**
*Estrada Monumental 145, 9000 Funchal, Madeira*
Established in 1946 but now Japanese-owned and with a big export market to Japan as well as Korea and China. Most of the everyday production is split between modestly priced TNM wines and a goodish range of 5-year-old nobles. They also have a range of fabulous old vintages which long predate the company's foundation. Best wines: the vintages!

**Blandy's – Madeira Wine Company SA** ☆☆☆→☆☆☆☆
*Rua dos Ferreiros 191, Ap. 295, 9003 Funchal, Madeira*
Established in 1913, but it has taken over so many other companies that its origins are many. Names to conjure with in this outpost of the Symington empire (*see* Graham's Port) include Blandy, Leacock, Rutherford and Miles, Cossart Gordon – some 27 old firms in all make up today's Madeira Wine Company. The Symingtons took control after taking a shareholding in 1988 and have put a great deal of investment into the company. The best wines age under the *canteiro* system, in cask, using waste heat from the *estufagem* as well as the natural ambient heat of the seasons. Best wines: 10-year-old range of noble grapes, Colheitas from the 1980s, anything with a vintage date on it.

**Borges – H M Borges, Sucrs, Lda**
*Rua 31 de Janeiro 83, PO Box 92, 9001 Funchal, Madeira*
Established in 1877, this is a small family firm doing most of its export business in the US and Japan with bulk wine sales to Scandinavia. Best wines: mostly average to good quality.

**Henriques & Henriques Lda** ☆☆☆→☆☆☆☆
*Caminho Grande e Preces, Sítio de Belém, 9300 Câmara de Lobos, Madeira*
Established in 1850, this is one of the few Madeira wine producers which owns vineyards, and it recently moved out of Funchal to a spanking new winery. Winemaker is John Cossart (of that ilk; *see* the Madeira Wine Company), and he is an unreconstructed enthusiast for "the right kind of *estufagem*", ie done in steel tanks in the modern way. All H&H wines go through three months of this process, and the range is certainly impressive: TNM wines are well made and very pleasant. Noble wines at 10 years old are outstanding and the 15-year-old range is stunning. All of these, however, pale by comparison with the old vintages, which go back beyond 1800. Best wines: very reliable range, but especially Monte Seco dry; 10-year-old range, especially Bual; 15-year-old range, especially Malmsey; anything with a vintage date on it.

**Justino Henriques – Vinhos Justino Jenriques, Filhos, Lda** ☆→☆☆ **(Vintages** ☆☆☆☆**)**
*P I Cancela, 9125 Portugal*

Established in 1830, this is a big company – almost as big as the Madeira Wine Company (*see* entry) – and until relatively recently its main market was for bulk wines to the US and Japan. From 2000, however, the company plans to sell only in bottle and is developing a range of wines for this purpose. TNM wines are the mainstay, including one branded Broadbent for sale by the eponymous California-based wine merchant and scion of the former head of Christie's wine department in London. Best wines: 50-year-old Terrantez, anything with a vintage date on it.

**Oliveira – Pereira d'Oliveira (Vinhos) Lda** ☆
**(vintages** ☆☆☆→☆☆☆☆)
*Rua dos Ferreiros 107, 9000 Funchal, Madeira*
A beguiling family-run lodge in the centre of Funchal, with a retail area selling everything from souvenirs of Funchal to the most ancient vintages of Madeira wine. Even casual visitors are invited to taste one wine of their choice, and prices are remarkably modest. Most of the grapes are bought in from around Câmara de Lobos, and the wines are largely made "up country" and brought to Funchal to mature. Best wines: vintages and other very old wines.

**Silva Vinhos** ☆→?
*Sitio da Igreja, Estreito de Câmara de Lobos, 9325 Câmara de Lobos, Madeira*
Established in 1990, this is a spanking new winery making wines only from TNM harvested in the region of Câmara de Lobos. The Silva family formerly grew grapes and sold them to the Madeira Wine Company (*see* entry) and have finally achieved their life-long ambition to make their own wine. All wines except the TNM sweet go through *estufagem*. Best wines: TNM sweet, but it's a bit early to judge what potential this company has.

# Other Portuguese fortified wines

Probably the most famous fortified wine from Portugal which is not Port or Madeira comes from the Setúbal peninsula, southeast of Lisbon, but there are Moscatel-based wines produced in the Douro and, in a rather different style, there are wines of Carcavelos, west of the capital. One thing the wines from Setúbal and Carcavelos have in common is that Lisbon's suburban development continues to threaten the vineyard areas as building returns higher profits than winemaking. Nevertheless, some companies struggle ever onward, regardless.

## Moscatel de Setúbal

The Muscat grape (in this case the Muscat of Alexandria, but known locally as the Moscatel de Setúbal) is one of the oldest in viticulture, dating back to pre-Roman times. Its natural, rich, musky sweetness and tendency to ferment out to high alcoholic levels made it a very tradable commodity from the ancient Greek islands to the vineyards of Málaga.

There is in addition another Muscat called Moscatel Roxo, and other grapes that may be used in the wine include Arinto, Boal, Fernão Pires, Malvasia, Rabo de Ovelha, Roupeiro and half a dozen others. Wines labelled "Moscatel de Setúbal" must be made from a minimum of 85 per cent of the eponymous grape. Wines labelled "Setúbal" must be made from a minimum of 70 per cent of either or both Muscats, and in each case the remainder may be made up of any cocktail of the other grapes chosen by the producer.

The wine is fortified in the same way as Port, by stopping the fermentation with grape spirit, giving a resulting wine of 18 per cent alcohol. Unlike Port, however, the wine is left on its lees over the winter to take on the characteristic muskiness of the grape skins and pulp. Once this period is complete, the wine is run off into 600-litre casks. Meanwhile, the grape pulp is pressed – this must be the only wine in the world in which the grapes receive their first pressing some six months after the vintage – and the resulting wine is run off into separate casks for blending purposes.

The wine spends three to four years in cask, stored at ground level in well-ventilated cellars to take advantage of the changing seasonal temperatures. This concentrates and matures the wine, which takes on a walnut shade with spiky, spicy aromas and a fresh Muscat-flavoured sweetness. Most wines are bottled and sold at this point, but some of the best may be set aside for special treatment and aged for anything up to or even more than 20 years. These become deep, raisiny and powerful, yet never lose their characteristic Muscat style. There are some vintage wines – indeed, vintage Setúbal seems to be making something of a comeback. Very old vintages can be very great wines indeed.

## PRINCIPAL SHIPPERS
### José Maria da Fonseca Succrs., Azeitão ☆☆☆☆
Established in 1834 as a maker of Moscatel, part of the company separated from the original in 1968 and ended up under the IDV umbrella. However, the two halves came together again in 1997 and are now run by the brothers Soares Franco, who are descended from the original José Maria da Fonseca. The company has dominated the production of Moscatel de Setúbal for many years and still has vintages in its cellar dating back to the 1880s. Best wines: everything from here is very reliable; vintages from the 1980s; older vintages (especially from the 1950s and 1960s) are magnificent.

### J P Vinhos, Pinhal Novo ☆☆☆☆
Established in 1922 under the name João Pires, in recent years this company has found fame with inspired winemaking for its non-fortified wines from the Australian Peter Bright and is now run by António Avillez, who is related to the Soares Franco

brothers (*see* entry above). The company's Setúbal is a 100 per cent Moscatel de Setúbal and is aged, like some Madeira wines, in a heated warehouse to aid maturation. They also make vintage wines. Best wines: all wines are very reliable; vintages.

## Moscatel do Douro

There is some small production of Muscat-based wine as part of the growing interest in non-port wines from the Douro region. The best among them is probably that produced by the house of Niepoort (☆☆☆). Some older vintages are available and showing very well (*see* the Port section for contact details).

## Carcavelos

This region was first demarcated in 1908 and by the 1930s was turning out large quantities of wine, but it has suffered more than most from encroachment by building development as Lisbon expands inexorably outwards. Historically, the region was founded by the Marquês de Pombal, Prime Minister and virtual ruler of Portugal from 1750 to 1777, because he had his country estate in the region and he needed a market for the grapes from his vineyards. As a result, the permitted varieties for Carcavelos are legion – well, nine, anyway – probably reflecting what he happened to be growing at the time, including Galega Dourada (the principal grape), Arinto and Boais (white); and Trincadeira, Espadeiro, Periquita and Tinta Negra Mole. The black grapes are vinified *en blanc* to avoid any colouring of the wine.

The wine is fortified after or in the very last stages of fermentation, when it will be on the verge of becoming a dry white wine. Grape spirit and some *vinho abafado* (a *mistelle* of grape juice and spirit) will be added, to about 18 per cent alcohol, at the level of sweetness which the winemaker thinks appropriate, and the wine is run off into large clean casks, typically of 600 litres but often larger than that. The wine is aged for about five years and has a rather nutty medium-sweet character.

### PRINCIPAL SHIPPERS
#### Quinta do Barão, Carcavelos ☆☆→☆☆☆
This estate closed effectively in the early 1990s, having resisted development for many years, but a new road through the last remaining vineyards finally finished it off. Some few of its wines can still be found in the shops, however. Best wines: the older the better.

#### Quinta dos Pesos, Caparide ☆→☆☆
This is a new venture by Manoel Bulhosa, an oil millionaire who has set himself the task of preserving Carcavelos for the nation and the world. With help from the Australian winemaker Peter Bright, he planted a new vineyard which includes some Cabernet Sauvignon and produced his first harvest in 1987. The wine is aged for a minimum of three years in second-year red-wine casks and promises well. Best wines: the older the better.

# Other wine

## Adega Cooperativa da Lagoa, Lagoa ☆→☆☆

Another lone attempt to recapture past glories is this co-op, which is trying to re-create the heyday of Sherry-type fortified wines that used to be made all along the southern coast of the Iberian peninsula. The winery makes its money out of large-scale, cool-fermented lightweights for the beachfront market in the Algarve, but its heart is in the cask-aged, post-fortified past. Best wines: Afonso III, a dry Amontillado-style at 15 per cent alcohol.

# Sherry

"Now keep ye from the white and from the red,
And namely from the white wine of Lepe
That is to sell in Fish street or in Chepe.
This wine of Spain creepeth subtilly
In other wines, growing fast by,
Of which there riseth such fumositee
That when a man hath drunken draughtes three
And weneth that he be at home in Chepe,
He is in Spain, right at the town of Lepe,
Not at the Rochgelle, nor at Bordeaux town."

# The history

Geoffrey Chaucer (c.1342–1400 ) wrote the above words more than 600 years ago, when the wine of Lepe (which is in neigh-bouring Condado de Huelva) was routinely shipped to Jerez to bolster the burgeoning export trade. His use of the word "fumosi-tee" implies that Sherry was already fortified at that time, as well as being popular in Fish Street (London EC3) and Cheapside (London EC2) and probably everywhere else in England, but a mere six centuries pales by comparison with the wine's history.

There are older wines in the world than Sherry – indeed, the early Greeks who colonised what is now the province of Cádiz in the 6th and 5th centuries BC brought vines and winemaking skills with them from their own country, and their forebears in turn had learned the trade from Egypt or Persia or Asia Minor, so wine was an old culture even before the first vine was planted in what is now the "golden triangle" of the Sherry country. However, Sherry was the first wine to be heavily traded beyond the Mediterranean, as its geographical position at the pillars of Hercules was too good an opportunity to miss for traders from what we now call the Middle East, who founded the city of Gadir (Cádiz) in about 1100 BC. An entrepôt at this point would have halved the distance needed to travel from Phoenicia (modern-day Syria) to trade the three staples of the ancient world – wheat, olives and wine – up the west coast of Europe and down the west coast of Africa. At some point, some-one must have had the bright idea to plant vineyards, cereals and olive groves at Gadir itself, although they soon realised they were better off rather further inland away from the hot, dry Levanter wind which blasts the coastline throughout much of the summer, around the town of Xera. These are believed to be the origins of what we know today as Jerez and the Sherry country.

As empires came and went – Phoenicia, Carthage, Rome, the Vandals, the Visigoths – the business of growing grapes and making wine continued to expand. Amphorae of what we may assume to be naturally strong, sweet wines were shipped to Damascus, Carthage and Rome and traded throughout the known western world. The periodic changes of government would no doubt have caused considerable problems, but the trend was expansionist, and even the most hidebound conquering armies understood the value of a flourishing export industry. In these times the wine must have had a variety of names but, for the sake of consistency, we shall use the modern term throughout this section.

The next phase in the development of Sherry came with the invasion of the Moors in AD 711. They came from what is now Morocco, under the authority of the Caliphate of Damascus (interestingly enough, the capital of what had once been Phoenicia). The Moorish forces quickly took control and established an occupation which covered most of the Iberian peninsula south of the mountains of Cantabria. What this meant for the Sherry industry was almost-effectual prohibition, although individual provincial rulers had different ways of approaching the subject of alcoholic drink. Some were plainly quite happy to see wine made and sold to Christian infidels for hard cash and others encouraged the continued growth of grapes for the table, so it seems likely that at least some wine was made throughout Moorish rule in at least some parts of the region.

The most important contribution made by the Moors was, however, the secrets of distillation, which they had acquired from the Phoenicians who, according to legend, had acquired them from the Chinese. Distillation was used for pharmaceuticals and cosmetics by the invaders, whose interest was often more in the dry extract (*al-kohl* or "the ashes" in Arabic) created by the process than in the heady liquid that was its by-product. The local Andalusians adopted the Arabic name for it, as they did for the pot-still in which it was made – *al-ambiq*.

No one knows for sure when the first Sherry wine was fortified with grape spirit, although it could have coincided with the first cracks starting to appear in the Moorish occupation after AD 910, when factions in Damascus seceded from the Caliphate there and established a new authority in Tunis. Abd-ar-Rahman III, who was the ruler of Moorish Spain under the constitution of Damascus, switched to the new order, and in AD 929 proclaimed himself the Caliph of Córdoba. This got the Moorish provincial rulers fighting among themselves, allowing the armies of the princes of Castile, León, Catalonia, Aragón et al (when they weren't busy squabbling with each other) to fight their way down from the north, and the armies of Andalusia to take up arms from the west. Even so, progress was very slow, and it wasn't until 1264 that the decisive battle for Jerez was finally won. It took a further 228 years before the last Moorish forces were vanquished at Granada in 1492, and for much of that period the Sherry country was the frontier between Muslim and Christian Spain – hence Jerez de la Frontera.

It was probably in this climate that the winemakers of Jerez started to improve their business. With the eyes of their Moorish rulers elsewhere, there was much more opportunity to experiment, and it seems likely that some wine producers would have added grape spirit to their wines to "fortify" them against the heat and rough handling that they would experience for weeks at a time in transit to their final destination. The transition from naturally sweet and strong wines transported in clay amphorae to fortified wines transported in casks was a piecemeal process that could have taken several hundred years. Not every wine producer decided to switch methods at the same time.

The Moors were finally expelled in 1492 – the year in which Spain acquired its first American colonies – and Sherry boomed again in the Old World and the New. In 1587, during the war between England and Spain which culminated in the Spanish Armada, the famous occasion on which Sir Martin Frobisher – one of Drake's captains – "singed the King of Spain's beard" had a significant effect on the export market. Frobisher set the Spanish fleet alight in Cádiz harbour and also looted 2,900 pipes of Sherry which he subsequently delivered to an appreciative England. Sherry became the most fashionable drink in the 16th-century equivalent of trendy bars and restaurants, Shakespeare wrote about it, polite society adopted it and, war or no war, Sherry boomed yet again.

The epicentre of the wine was Victorian England, where no civilised home was without a decanter of Sherry, and in the 1870s more wine was shipped than ever before. It seemed as if the world's love affair with Sherry would go on for ever – indeed, give or take two world wars and the Spanish Civil War, it did... Until 1983.

In 1983 the Spanish government moved to take the giant company RuMaSA – owned by the Ruiz-Mateos family – into public ownership. RuMaSA controlled so much of the Sherry business by that time, as well as other wine companies, industrials and banks, that its collapse sent a shock wave through the industry. This, combined with a sudden drop in exports, caused the Sherry bubble to burst for the first time in living – or, indeed, any – memory. The industry went through a period of "reconversion", grubbing up vineyards, laying off staff, facing up to the reality that the business had become overstretched and over-confident. It took ten years or more to regroup and rebuild the sector, and even now, in the year 2000, there is still unfinished business in the market-place.

However, Sherry has been around for long enough to weather even the boom-and-bust economics of the close of the 20th century and, if the export quantity is less than it was 20 years ago, then the quality, value, range and choice is as good as ever, if not better.

# Grapes for Sherry

One grape dominates the Sherry business: the Palomino. It may be known as Palomino Fino, Palomino de Jerez, Listán Palomino or under half a dozen other names and, indeed, there are different clones, each of which has its aficionados, and the received wisdom is that the Palomino Fino offers the best combination of yield and quality. However, for the sake of clarity we shall refer simply to the Palomino. Other grapes grown in the region include Pedro Ximénez, which is sometimes sun-dried or otherwise reduced to give rich, dark, sweetening and colouring wines, and the Moscatel, which is normally vinified on its own.

The Palomino is a heavy cropper, but everywhere else in Spain it has proved to be a dull, uninspiring variety producing neutral wines with high strength with little varietal character. In Jerez, however, it comes into its own: the combination of climate, *albariza* soils (anything up to 80 per cent active chalk content) and a thousand years – and more – of trial and error and unremitting human endeavour has produced a wine unmatched in style, range or quality anywhere else in the world.

# How Sherry is made

Sherry is the result of the triumph of man's patience and labour over some fairly modest ingredients. It is the Sherry process that takes these ingredients and fashions them into one of the world's greatest wines. Over the years the best vineyard areas for growing Palomino grapes have been identified and classified, and among these – called *pagos* – the lower, cooler, more coastal vineyards will favour the production of Fino Sherry, while higher, hotter vineyards further inland will tend to produce grapes more suited to Oloroso (*see* Styles of Sherry below). Winemaking is, for the most part, thoroughly modern, in stainless steel at controlled – albeit high – temperatures. The Palomino is normally low in acid, and the old method of counteracting this was to spread *yeso* (gypsum, or plaster of Paris) over the grapes before fermentation. Nowadays, many *bodegas* will probably use a commercial acidulant to add tartaric acid to the must, but in either case the grapes are so ripe that some 70 per cent of the juice can be collected without pressing. Modern, fruit-up-front white wine is typically fermented at anything from 15–18°C, but the wine which will become Sherry is fermented at around 28°C to ensure maximum extract from the grapes: the winemaker wants a heavyweight wine which can withstand long ageing periods.

The wine is fermented through both alcoholic and malolactic fermentations, and by Christmas of the year of the harvest it will be a dry white wine of some 12–13 per cent alcohol. In January it will be inspected again and, assuming that it is correct in all the important details, it will be fortified to 14.5 per cent alcohol and run off into clean casks filled about 80 per cent full. At this point the wines are known as *sobretablas*.

In the following spring the wine (now some six months old) is inspected again, this time for the growth of *flor*. This is a yeast-cell growth that occurs naturally in the Jerez region. It's not unique to the Sherry country, but this is almost the only area where it's seen as beneficial – in other areas it's a wine fault (rather as botrytis is welcomed in sweet-wine producing areas and dreaded elsewhere). The yeast grows on the surface of the wine, feeding on residual components within it, and the strength of the growth will determine which direction the finished wine will take. If *flor* growth is strong and healthy, it will be re-fortified to a strength of about 15.2 per cent alcohol, which is the perfect level for more *flor* to develop. These are wines that will eventually become Finos. If *flor* growth is weak or non-existent, the wine will be fortified to 16.5 per cent, which is too strong for the yeast to grow. These are wines that will become Olorosos. At this stage, these are still wines of a single year (known as *añadas*) and they're likely to be left to their own devices for a year or more before they're needed for the *solera*.

The *solera* system is the great triumph of the Sherry production process. It achieves four things: maintenance of stock levels to ensure a consistent quantity of mature wine; refreshment of older wines by the addition of new ones; dynamic ageing of new wines by fractional blending with older wines; and a precise and self-governing quality-control system.

The *solera* itself is a row of barrels containing fine old wines. When a customer wants to buy some, it's withdrawn in equal measure from each barrel (to a maximum of one-third of the *solera's* contents in any one year). These barrels are then topped up, in equal measure, from another row of barrels containing younger wine, known as the first *criadera* ("nursery"). The process is repeated for increasingly younger wines from the second *criadera* to the third – indeed, as many *criaderas* as there are, which may be up to seven or more for a top-class Fino Sherry. This leaves the final *criadera* in need of topping up, of course, and this is done with *añada* wines from the most recent vintage. Wines must legally stay in the *solera* for a minimum of three years and one day, but anything any good will stay for very much longer than that.

In this way, the *solera* is continually refreshed with younger wines, and those younger wines, by mingling with older wines, take on the characteristics of the *solera*. It's a simple yet brilliant low-technology quality-control process that explains, in some measure, how Sherry achieved the reputation it did by the end of the 19th century.

Most wines offered for sale will be a blend of various different *soleras*: the *Capataz* (cellarmaster) is expected to know his cellar intimately enough to be able to put together a *cabeceo* (or formula – a Frenchman would say *assemblage*) to match the customer's requirements, whether that customer is seeking a modestly priced blend to match a price point or a no-holds-barred quality wine for the premium market.

# Styles of Sherry
## Natural styles

**Fino** describes Sherry which has grown *flor* to a large extent – strongly in spring and autumn and less so in summer and winter. Generally, the grapes will have come from lower, cooler, coastal vineyards and have a crisp, yeasty, bone-dry character and are likely to have been aged for six to nine years. If the wine has been made and matured in the cooler climate of the town of Sanlúcar de Barrameda, on the estuary of the river Guadalquivír, it will have grown *flor* all the year round and have a paler, fresher character, and will be known (three to six years old) as Manzanilla (Fina) or (five to nine years old) Manzanilla Pasada.

**Oloroso** (the word means "aromatic") describes wines that grew little or no *flor* in their early stages and were fortified to a higher level to mature in Oloroso *soleras*. Young Olorosos are pungent, spirity and mainly used for blending. Older wines take on a rich, raisiny, nutty character with great aromatics and a powerful, lingering palate, but are still bone dry. Dry Olorosos come on to the market at, perhaps, 15 years old and can live for anything up to 50 years or even more.

**Amontillado** wines started life as Finos, but instead of being withdrawn at the usual age have been passed to an older *solera* containing aged Fino wines, where they can develop for a very long time. Wines withdrawn at, say, 12–15 years old will be walnut-tinted and labelled Amontillado-Fino (or Fino-Amontillado). Sanlúcar Finos aged for this length of time may be called Manzanilla Amontillada, but these are very rare. Wines older than this will be simply Amontillado and can age impressively. However, rather too much wine for the export market labelled Amontillado is merely a *cabeceo* of low-price dry wine blended with sweetening wine designed to provide a "medium" style at a rock-bottom price for the mass market.

**Palo Cortado** is an unusual wine. Having grown *flor* vigorously when young, it will have been fortified as a Fino (ie to 15.2 per cent alcohol) and started to take on the nutty, yeasty Fino character. However, before reaching the *solera* the *flor* will have died, and the wine will be rerouted to a Palo Cortado *solera*, which, to all intents and purposes, then continues to develop along Oloroso lines. The result (at 15-plus years old) is one of the most complex and delicate of wines with overtones of Fino character attached to the voluptuousness of an Oloroso body. Quite rare and often expensive.

**Pedro Ximénez or PX** is made only from the grapes of the same name, often dried in the sun before pressing and, at its oldest, is thick, black and as rich as treacle. It may be used in small quantities to make up a *cabeceo* for one of the styles below or (expensively) as an old wine in its own right.

**Moscatel**: there are those who wish this grape had not been granted the DO Sherry, since it's usually bottled unblended (ie no *solera*), and is made – like Port – by stopping the fermentation with spirit. It has little similarity to the other wines of the region and yet has a beguiling richness (and often a modest price) which makes it much better value for money than most of the blended "Cream" Sherries (*see* below).

## Blended styles

**Cream Sherry** is typically a basic Oloroso sweetened with PX and/or another colouring wine – perhaps boiled-down grape juice (known as *arrope*). If a "Pale Cream" style is required, rectified grape must (which is colourless) is used to sweeten a young Fino without too much *flor* character to produce a fairly bland result: ironically, this category is the best seller in export markets. Cream Sherries may also be described as "East India", "Brown", "Milk" or by many other fanciful names, but they are all variations on the same theme. All Sherry made from the Palomino grape is naturally dry, and any sweetness has to be added by blending.

### Vintage sherries

In theory, these haven't existed for a century or more, but one or two houses do have the odd vintage wine lying about – most notably Williams & Humbert (*see* below) – and a vintage from González Byass (*see* below) came top in a magazine tasting in London in 1998. There is very little wine in this category, but there are whispers that more than one *bodega* is thinking about the prospect of the occasional vintage Sherry in an outstanding year – *à la* vintage Port, perhaps? No news yet, but watch this space.

## When to drink Sherry

This is the most versatile of wines. Light, fresh, bone-dry, young Manzanillas and Finos are not only the world's finest *aperitivo* but are also consumed with gusto throughout the meal in the seafood restaurants of the province of Cádiz and beyond, especially those in El Puerto de Santa María and Sanlúcar de Barrameda. Grand old sweetened Olorosos, PXs and the finest old Creams are the most sublime dessert wines, especially with heavyweight puddings containing chocolate, honey, marzipan and baked sugars (*tarte tatin* is an example) and including Christmas pudding and rich, real dairy ice cream (in Jerez they pour the PX into the ice cream). The finest old, rich Olorosos also fill every corner of the post-prandial niche, often enhanced by a good cigar.

The middle range – older Finos, Amontillados, Palos Cortados and naturally dry Olorosos – do duty in the *aperitivo* sector or when a glass is appropriate for no better reason than pure enjoyment: elevenses (*almuerzo* in Spain) or at teatime (*merienda*) with a slice of plain cake, a poached egg on toast or even cucumber sandwiches. These are very old-fashioned wines for very old-fashioned occasions. But they have been around for a very long time.

## Principal shippers

### Allied-Domecq

Giant multinational which owns Domecq, Harveys (*see* entries), de Terry, La Riva and Blázquez (*see* entry) in the Sherry country. Rationalisation of "brands" within the group has meant that many good wines have been elbowed aside by famous names, sometimes regardless of quality. The top Sherry brands from Allied-Domecq are Harveys Bristol Cream (☆☆), Harveys Club Amontillado (☆), and Fino La Ina (Domecq ☆☆☆). All the members of the group produce better wines than these, but we seem to live in an era in which fame rules.

**Argüeso – Manuel de Argüeso SA** ☆☆☆☆
*Pozo Olivar 16, 11403 Jerez de la Frontera; also at Sanlúcar de Barrameda*
A small firm that now belongs to Valdespino and turns out Manzanilla wines in Sanlúcar and Pedro Ximénez in Jerez. Best wines: all reliable, but the PX is outstanding (don't be put off by the awful label).

**Argüeso – Hrdos. de Argüeso SA** ☆☆☆→☆☆☆☆
*Mar 8, 11540 Sanlúcar de Barrameda*
Established in 1822 and no relation to the above. This is mainly a Manzanilla company, although it does produce Amontillado and an excellent Moscatel. Best wines: San León Manzanilla, Moscatel Fruta, Amontillado Viejo.

**Barbadillo – Antonio Barbadillo SA** ☆☆☆☆
*Luís Eguilaz 11, 11540 Sanlúcar de Barrameda*
Established in 1821 and a company that combines fine quality with large quantity – one of the biggest in the Sanlúcar area. It also makes the best-selling unfortified, Palomino-based wine of Jerez, Castillo de San Diego. Best wines: PX, Cuco dry Oloroso, Solear Manzanilla, EVA Cream, Principe Amontillado.

**Blázquez – Agustín Blázquez** ☆☆☆
*San Ildefonso 3, 11404 Jerez de la Frontera*
Established in 1795 and now part of the Allied-Domecq empire (*see* entry). Best wine: the Fino Carta Blanca, which has the courage to print its bottling date on the back label.

**Caballero – Luís Caballero SA** ☆☆
*San Francisco 24, 11500 El Puerto de Santa María*
Established in 1830 and owner of the famous Burdon's brand, this company has successfully specialised in the own-label market. In 1990 it bought the house of Lustau (*see* entry) and most quality-wine production moved there. Best wine: Lerchundi Moscatel.

**Croft Jerez SA** ☆☆→☆☆☆
*Ctra. Madrid-Cádiz, 11407 Jerez de la Frontera*
Established in 1970 as – before this date – wines were shipped through the Croft offices in Oporto. Now a part of the giant multi-national Diageo and famed worldwide for its sweetened Fino Croft Original. Best wines: Croft Palo Cortado, Croft Classic Amontillado.

**Cuevas Jurado – Manuel Cuevas Jurado** ☆☆☆☆
*Comisarios 6, Sanlúcar de Barrameda*
This is a Bodega de Almacen (a brokerage which buys young wines direct from the producer and stores them until they are ready to be sold back into the market). It provides one of the wines for the Lustau "Almacenista" range. Best wine: Manzanilla Amontillada, one of the rarest, most delicate and outstanding wines of the region.

**De Soto – José de Soto SA** ☆☆
*M Antonia Jesús Tirado 6, 11401 Jerez de la Frontera*
Well-known in Spain, this producer was taken over by the Nueva
RuMaSA company in 1991, and does mainly national but some
export business. Best wine: Don José María Cream. The RuMaSA
Nueva group also includes Garvey (*see* entry).

**Delgado Zuleta SA** ☆☆☆
*Ctra. Sanlúcar-Chipiona Km 1,5, 11540 Sanlúcar de Barrameda*
Established in 1744, this is a medium-sized business specialising
in Manzanilla wines and young, fresh table wines without the
Sherry DO but with a good mid-range selection including
Amontillados called ¿Quo Vadis? and Zuleta. Best wine: La Goya
Manzanilla.

**Domecq – Pedro Domecq SA** ☆☆☆→☆☆☆☆
*San Ildefonso 3, 11404 Jerez de la Frontera*
Established in 1730 and one of the major contributors to the
Sherry boom, which lasted almost unhindered from the 16th century until the 20th. The Domecq family has pervaded every
aspect of Andalusian life for more than 200 years, but only one
member – Beltrán Domecq – remains in a senior position, and
the company is now wholly owned by the giant multinational
Allied-Domecq (*see* entry).

The company launched a new "look" for its basic range of
Fino, Manzanilla, Isis Pale Cream and Celebration Cream
wines in 1999 and still leads the field in the mid-range with
Fino La Ina and Río Viejo Amontillado. Best wines: Venerable
PX, Sibarita Old Oloroso, Capuchino Palo Cortado, and
Amontillado 51-1a.

**Ferris – Bodegas J Ferris M, CB** ☆☆☆
*Avda. San Fernando 116 (Rota), 11500 El Puerto de Santa María*
Established in 1975, a smaller *bodega* with a focus on sweeter
wines, the basic range is called Las Tres Candidas and comprises
a Fino, an Amontillado and an Oloroso. Best wines: the J Ferris M
range: a PX and a Moscatel.

**Garvey BV** ☆☆☆→☆☆☆☆
*Ctra. Circunvalación – Bellavista, 11407 Jerez de la Frontera*
Established in 1780, this is a major exporting company which has
gone through several changes of ownership and now belongs to
the RuMaSA Nueva group. Its fame has been built on the Fino San
Patricio. Best wines: PX Gran Orden, Ochavico Oloroso, Flor de
Jerez Dulce.

**Gil Luque – M Gil Luque SA** ☆☆☆☆
*Edif. Jerez 74 – Esc. 6, 11407 Jerez de la Frontera*
Established in 1984 but situated in a beautifully refurbished old
*bodega*. The company also owns Rainera Pérez Marín (*see* entry).
Best wines: all are very good indeed, the best possibly
Amontillado de Bandera.

### González Byass SA ✩✩✩✩
*Manuel M González 12, Jerez de la Frontera*

Established in 1835, this is one of the biggest of all the Sherry companies but is still under family control. González Byass claim to have marketed the very first Fino, in around 1850. The founder, Manuel María González Angel, was guided in his early days by his uncle, José Angel de la Peña, who had a partiality for young wine when the general practice was to allow it to mature into Amontillado before sale. José had odd butts put aside for him, and these eventually developed into a small *solera*. In order to prevent the *bodegueros* from using any of this peculiar wine, Manuel chalked the words "Tío Pepe" on to the barrels, as they were destined for his "Uncle Joe". Manuel's English agent and later business partner, Robert Blake Byass, tasted the wine and asked why Manuel was not shipping it to England, and a star was born.

Even today, the world's best-selling Fino is still distinctly strong on quality and regularly performs well in blind tastings. The rest of the *bodega's* output is similarly quality-orientated. Best wines: the entire range is very reliable, but especially Noë PX, Matúsalem sweet Oloroso, Apostoles dry Oloroso, Amontillado del Duque, Viña AB Amontillado-Fino and Tío Pepe. The very best wines of all are old and rare vintage wines... for the moneyed.

### Harvey – John Harvey BV ✩✩
*San Ildefonso 3, Jerez de la Frontera*

Established in 1970 in Jerez but 1769 in England, whence all shipping was controlled until 1970. Now a member of the Allied-Domecq stable (*see* entry), which is a pity because there used to be some superb wines shipped under the "1769" label and, even further back, an excellent "Bristol Fino" and old-bottled Bristol Cream. Production has been rationalised so as not to interfere with major brands from other members of the group, and Harveys is left with the rather feeble Club Amontillado and the not much more exciting Bristol Cream in its ghastly blue bottle. Best wines: Bristol Cream (sob).

### Hidalgo – Vinícola Hidalgo y Cia SA ✩✩✩→✩✩✩✩
*Banda de la Playa 24, Sanlúcar de Barrameda*

Established in 1792, current head of the family Javier Hidalgo was a *dissidente* who resolutely ploughed his own furrow in the Sherry business and remains an independent spirit with a passion for Manzanilla. His wines reflect that throughout the range. Best wines: Napoléon PX, Napoléon Oloroso, La Gitana Manzanilla, Amontillado viejo, Palo Cortado.

### Hidalgo – Emilio Hidalgo SA ✩✩✩→✩✩✩✩
*Clavel 29, Jerez de la Frontera*

Established in 1874 and no relation to the above. Traditional Jerez style is the key to this *bodega's* wines, most of which are seldom seen outside Spain. Best wines: Gobernador Oloroso, Morenita Cream.

### Infantes Orleans-Borbón SAE ☆☆☆→☆☆☆☆
*Luís Eguilaz 11, Sanlúcar de Barrameda*
Established in 1943 and jointly owned by Barbadillo and the
Spanish Royal Family. The most interesting wine is the
Manzanilla Torre Breva, whose grapes come entirely from the
*pago* of the same name. Best wines: Fenicio Oloroso, Orleans 1884
PX, Manzanilla Fina, Torre Breva Manzanilla, Atlandida Moscatel.

### Lustau – Emilio Lustau SA ☆☆☆☆
*Plaza del Cubo 4, Jerez de la Frontera*
Established in 1896 as a Bodega de Almacen – buying wine from
producers and storing it to be sold back into the market later – the
founder's son-in-law put the firm on a commercial footing, and
his name was Emilio Lustau. The company was taken over in
1990 by Luís Caballero amid worries that it would be marginalised
by Caballero's mass-market empire, but the reverse happened
and Lustau has been able to dump its own-label business and
rebuild its range with an attention only to quality. The "*solera*"
range comprises traditional series of excellent quality; the
"Almacenista" range has some of the finest wines in the region
(including one from Cuevas Jurado; *see* entry). Best wines: all
very reliable but especially PX, Moscatel, Península Palo Cortado,
Manzanilla Amontillada Almacenista (Cuevas Jurado) and,
indeed, anything at all from the "Almacenista" range. Also
includes Marqués de Irun SA and Viña Herminia.

### Marqués del Real Tesoro ☆☆→☆☆☆
*Ctra. N-IV Km 640, 11407 Jerez de la Frontera*
Established in 1860 and named after the legendary sea captain
who, bringing back bullion for himself and the king from
the Americas, was set upon by pirates. The cannonballs ran
out and he was forced to smelt silver into shot to defeat
the pirates, but he used his own silver, not that destined for the
king. He was rewarded with the title of Marquess of the Royal
Treasure as a result. The company was dormant for many years
but was revived by the Estévez family in the early 1990s in a
sparkling new *bodega* on the Jerez ring road. They bought the
entire solera of Tío Mateo (formerly of Palomino y Vergara) from
Harveys, and this forms the nucleus of their stocks. In September
1999 they also bought the house of Valdespino (*see* entry). Best
wines: Amontillado del Principe, Tío Mateo.

### Osborne – Bodegas Osborne SA ☆☆☆☆
*Fernán Caballero 3, El Puerto de Santa María*
Established in 1772, this is the firm with the famous bull silhou-
ette trademark. Completely family-owned, it's the leading *bodega*
of Puerto de Santa María – and one of the most beautifully
maintained – and also owns Bobadilla in Jerez. Best wines:
all wines are very reliable, but especially (Osborne) AOS
*solera* Amontillado, Alonso El Sabio Oloroso, P Triangulo P
Palo Cortado, Bailén Oloroso, Fino Quinta, PX 1827; (Bobadilla)
Romántico PX.

### Rainera Pérez Marín – Hijos de Rainera Pérez Marín SA ☆☆☆☆

*Ctra. Lebrija Km 2 – Viña el Telégrafo, Sanlúcar de Barrameda*

Established in 1825 and now belonging to Gil Luque (*see* entry), this firm has made its name with the excellent La Guita, which comes as a 15 per cent alcohol Manzanilla and a slightly stronger Manzanilla Pasada. Best wine, indeed, only wine: La Guita.

### Sanchez Romate Hnos. SA ☆☆☆

*Lealas 28, Jerez de la Frontera*

Established in 1781, a company perhaps best known for its Brandy de Jerez (Cardenal Mendoza) than its wines, but it has its own vineyards and a range of Sherries of fine quality. Best wines: Amontillado NPU, Don José Oloroso, De Gloria PX.

### Sándeman-Coprimar SA ☆☆☆→☆☆☆☆

*Pizarro 10, Jerez de la Frontera*

Established in 1790, this is a company which, like Croft (*see* entry), used to ship its Sherry wines through its Port business in Oporto. Still very active in both markets, it has recently launched a new range around its established Oloroso "Royal Corregidor", marking a determination to return to the top end of the market. Best wines: Don Fino, Armada Oloroso, (premium range) Royal Corregidor Oloroso, Royal Esmeralda Amontillado, Royal Ambrosante PX.

### Valdespino – A R Valdespino SA ☆☆☆☆

*Pozo Olivar 16, Jerez de la Frontera*

Established in 1837, one of the most individual of the Jerez *bodegas*, family-owned and with a fine disregard for the vagaries of fashion: Miguel Valdespino has resisted the current trend to ship Fino wines at 15 per cent alcohol, and his own remain resolutely 16–17 per cent. "For six months, they will tell me that other Finos are fresher than mine," he avers, "but after a year mine will still be fresh." The company owns seven *bodegas* in the Sherry country (including Manuel de Argüeso; *see* entry) and its mainstream wines are exemplary. The *bodega* was sold in 1999 to the owners of Marqués de Real Tesoro (*see* entry) which has promised to continue it as a separate entity. Best wines: all wines are very reliable, especially Fino Inocente (Ynocente in Spain – one of the few remaining wines to be fermented in oak), Solera 1842 Oloroso, PX Solera superior.

### Williams & Humbert Ltd ☆☆☆

*Nuño de Caña 2, Jerez de la Frontera*

Established in 1877, this was another company which started out majoring on Fino-style wines while the rest of the market was still interested in Olorosos and Amontillados. The company's Pando Fino *solera* dates from that time. In 1995 it was taken over by Luís Paez SA, which, in turn, is owned 50 per cent by the Spanish family-owned Medina Group and 50 per cent by Royal Ahold of Holland (whose main brand is Bols liqueurs). W&H has a stunning "library" of old vintage wines going back to the 1920s, none of which are ever shipped but which are occasionally made available to visitors. Its international fame was built on the brand "Dry Sack", which once dominated the Amontillado market and still shows well in this category. Best wines: Pando Fino, Alégria Manzanilla, Dos Cortados Oloroso, Canasta Oloroso, Dry Sack Amontillado.

## Wisdom & Warter Ltd ☆☆
*Pizarro 7, Jerez de la Frontera*
Established in 1854, this company has belonged to González Byass (*see* entry) for a long time, although it has been allowed to go its own way in terms of wines, marketing and public profile. The range is generally good without being spectacular and includes La Canoa Manzanilla and Wisdom Dulce. Best wines: Very Rare Solera Amontillado, Viale PX.

# Málaga
## The history

Once upon a time Málaga was as important as Sherry. Indeed, in the Victorian era, when Sherry was at the height of its seemingly endless boom, no morning-room sideboard was complete without an additional decanter of "Mountain Wine" to offer to guests who might prefer something a little sweeter. As a post-prandial delight it rivalled Port and Madeira, and there seems little enough reason that it should have faded away quite so completely as it has.

Perhaps the main difference between Málaga and the other fortified wines of Andalusia is simply that it was too proud of its own reputation. After Sir Martin Frobisher "singed the King of Spain's beard" and stole 2,900 pipes of Sherry in 1587, the demand in England and much of northern Europe became phenomenal. English, Irish, Dutch and German businesses were established in the Jerez area, and whereas the Condado de Huelva and Montilla cheerfully buried their individuality and made up the shortfall of wine for the Sherry producers, Málaga stuck to its guns in the (at the time, quite reasonable) hope that it would continue to be recognised as a unique wine in its own right.

It was not to be, however, and despite a resurgence in the late 19th century, the 20th dealt its own mortal blows. First came the phylloxera epidemic, which destroyed most of the vineyard, then the Civil War, then the Second World War, and then tourism became southeastern Spain's major industry, and the coastal areas where the best grapes had been grown were swallowed up by the development of resorts, hotels, apartment blocks and holiday villages. Although there are now only about eight *bodegas* left in the Málaga business, they still have to buy grapes in under a special dispensation from neighbouring Montilla-Moriles to compensate for the vineyards which have been lost.

## Grapes for Málaga

One grape dominates production here, and that's the Pedro Ximénez (PX), although there are small amounts of Moscatel, Doradilla, Airén and Vidueño. However, the great Málaga wines are pure PX, grown in two areas: along the coast around and behind Estepona, and around the city of Málaga itself and back up into the hills towards Montilla. There is a vast acreage of vines, but less than a tenth of them (some 1,000 hectares at the last count) are registered to the Málaga DO. The rest turn out cheap and cheerful everyday wines for the Costa, or go to the distillery.

## How Málaga is made

Málaga wine differs from the other fortified wines of Andalusia in that it is fortified during fermentation to stop the process and retain natural grape sugars – and these can be substantial. The grapes are "sunned" by lying them out on mats to dry in the sun (a process known as *soleo*). By the time they reach the press they're shrivelled and sticky and fermentation is slow. Once the winemaker has decided that enough of the sugars have been fermented, grape spirit at 25 per cent alcohol is added and the wine goes for ageing. This may be static in individual oak casks or in a variant of the *solera* system (as described in the section on Sherry). The law recognises four grades of maturity: Málaga (up to two years), Málaga Noble (two to three years), Málaga Añejo (three to five years) and Málaga Trasañejo (more than five years). The regulations also permit the making of light table wines (usually with Airén) and varietal Moscatel. All wines must be matured within the city limits of Málaga itself.

There have been experiments with a dry (ie fully fermented) style, and there are young, lighter-coloured, lower-strength medium styles as well as some excellent "dry Oloroso" wines. However, the classic Málaga is a sweet, strong PX wine, the older the better. It tastes of rich, old, bonfire toffee and cream with dried apricots, raisins and a hint of nuttiness which is quite unique. The richest and oldest versions may have anything up to 600 grammes per litre of natural, concentrated grape sugar, and are among the most awe-inspiring wines on earth. No one who has tasted one will ever forget it.

## Principal producers

### Larios SA☆☆→☆☆☆

*César Vallejo 24, 29004 Málaga*

Established in 1863, this is a large company now belonging to the Pernod-Ricard Group, which pervades most aspects of the drinks business in Spain and is particularly famous for its gin. It keeps the Málaga flag flying, however, and its main brand is called simply Málaga Larios. Best wine: Benefique, which is in the dry "Oloroso" style.

### López Hermanos SA ☆☆→☆☆☆☆

*Canadá 10, Pol. Ind. El Viso, 29006 Málaga*

Established in 1885 and the biggest of the surviving *bodegas* in the region. They still use big old redwood vats here to make the wines, and although the *bodega* is in a charmless industrial estate its wines are very much traditional Málaga. Best wines: Malaga Virgen, Trajinero dry "Oloroso".

### Mollina – Tierras de Mollina (formerly Coop. Agricola Virgen de la Oliva)☆

*Ctra. Alameda 35, 29532 Mollina*

Established in 1977, this *bodega* hedges its bets by producing *joven afrutado* wines (ie light white table wines made from PX, Doradilla and Airén) under the Montespejo brand name as well as the more traditional style of Málaga. Best wine: Carpe Diem.

### Manilva – Vinos y Bodegas de Manilva ☆→☆☆

*Rel. 83, 29680 Estepona*

Established in 1996 – is there hope for the future after all? This *bodega* has made its early approach to the market with lighter wines, none of which has the Málaga DO, but, after all, that's how a number of wine regions have changed their spots. If it helps to provide the infrastructure so that the classic wines can continue to be produced, then it's probably a good thing. There's a sweet white, Sol de Estepona, made from Moscatel, and a red wine made from Garnacha (both at a natural 15 per cent alcohol). Best wine: Manilva, a dry white made from fully fermented Moscatel.

# Montilla

## The history

Ask most people about Montilla and they'll probably say "Oh, it's like Sherry, isn't it?" This has been the region's greatest triumph and subsequently biggest problem – the two-edged sword which won it mighty export markets in past centuries but at the same time submerged the wine's identity. So, once the rules changed and wines made in Montilla-Moriles, to use the area's full name, were no longer permitted to be shipped down to Jerez and quietly relabelled as Sherry, Montilla was left with a bit of an image-vacuum.

To make matters worse, a badly handled court case in the UK shortly after the Second World War deprived Montilla of the right to use the terms "Fino", "Oloroso" and even "Amontillado" (which means "in the style of Montilla"). The court ruled that Jerez had "first use" and the terms must be restricted to wines from there destined for the UK export market. Meanwhile, of course, Jerez was fighting to win back exclusive rights to the name "Sherry", which had become a generic term for all kinds of pastiche drinks, so there was little sympathy from that quarter. Jerez finally won its case in Europe in 1996, and, after a 1999 ruling from the European parliament endorsing the use of classic regional names for all wines, Montilla is now, at last, shipping fortified wines to the UK using the traditional names, for the first time in fifty years. Elsewhere the terms have always been perfectly legal.

Montilla set about reinventing itself, reacquainting its market with the wines, but most of all reminding people that, while some of its wines may be similar in style to Sherry, the majority are not, and that the region produces wines in three categories: *joven afrutado* (young, fresh light whites at 10–12 per cent alcohol); *solera* wines without fortification, which achieve a natural strength of 13–15 per cent; and the fortified *generoso* wines, which are 15 per cent-plus, aged in the *solera* and which may be very old and very grand indeed.

A helping hand in the UK export market was provided by the tax barrier at 15 per cent alcohol. Below this strength, wine pays only "table wine" duty; above 15 per cent it pays "liqueur wine" duty, which is substantially more – certainly enough to make a big difference on the supermarket shelf. Some Fino and Manzanilla Sherries will survive for six months or so at that strength, but if these are any good they tend to be from the better producers and are therefore rather expensive. Montilla, however, has an excellent range of (unfortified) wines which naturally fall just under 15 per cent alcohol. This opportunity was grasped with both hands, and Montilla started to appear, filling the spaces once occupied by the ersatz "Cyprus Sherry" and "British Sherry" with a consummate increase in quality for the customer.

A gentle programme of information, promotion and development is gradually starting to make a difference, spearheaded by two of the region's largest *bodegas*, Alvear and Pérez Barquero (*see* entries below). These sworn rivals in the Montilla business have, nevertheless, come together for the greater good of Montilla wine as a generic whole, and the message is getting through – not quickly, but drip by drip, bottle by bottle – that Montilla is making new friends.

## Grapes for Montilla

This, like Málaga, is Pedro Ximénez (PX) country. The vast majority of the wines are 100 per cent PX, and there is a small amount of Airén. There are even smaller amounts of (whisper it!) Sauvignon Blanc, Riesling and Chardonnay for some of the *joven afrutado* wines. The *solera* wines, both fortified and unfortified, however, will tend to be made exclusively from PX.

## How Montilla is made

As we have seen, there are three basic styles of wine which carry the Montilla-Moriles DO but, from a winemaking point of view, they all start the same way, although a good cellarmaster will have a pretty good idea in advance as to which grapes are likely to go to make up which styles of wine. However, the grapes are pressed and fermented in the normal way and, after alcoholic fermentation is completed, they're inspected. Those showing the most freshness, acidity and fruit are selected to become *jovenes afrutados*, filtered and racked off into tanks before bottling.

The rest of the wines will be allowed to undergo full malolactic fermentation and, once they are fully fermented (and completely dry), they are racked into tanks to await the formation of *flor* (*see* the Sherry section for details). Unlike Sherry, the Montilla PX base-wines will have had enough natural sugar to achieve 15–15.5 per cent alcohol (the perfect level for *flor* growth) without any artificial fortification, and those that have the requisite residual nutrients will grow the cap of *flor* just as Fino Sherry does. The wines (still unfortified) are divided into those that have and those that have not developed vigorous *flor* and put into static ageing casks or separate *soleras*, which are called Fino and Oloroso respectively. After this, they mature according to the normal processes which occur (described in detail in the section on Sherry). It's important to remember that these wines are still not fortified, and will eventually emerge from the cask or *solera* at around 15 per cent alcohol, which has been achieved by natural fermentation.

Some of the wines, however, will demonstrate greater potential, and these may be selected for the *generoso soleras*. Most of the best Finos remain unfortified and go to the market at 15 per cent, but if the cellarmaster decides that a Fino wine has the potential to become an Amontillado, or that a non-Fino will make a classic Oloroso, then he may decide to fortify, typically to 16–18 per cent alcohol, but this may become as high as 20–22 per cent alcohol prior to dispatch. After this, the wines will progress to the appropriate *solera* and age for any number of years until the producer decides that they are ready for blending, bottling and sale.

## Styles of Montilla

The regulations admit to a bewildering array of styles, including Fino, Amontillado (Montilla in the style of Montilla? What next?), Oloroso, Palo Cortado (something that looked as if it was going to be a Fino but then decided to become an Oloroso), Raya (an Oloroso which didn't quite make the grade), Ruedo (a young wine in the old style: ie not fresh, crisp and fruity but an unfortified dry white base-wine). What's more there is Pedro Ximénez (varietal wine from partially sunned grapes achieving a minimum of 272 grammes per litre of unfermented natural grape sugar), Blanco *sin envejecimento* (white without ageing – *joven afrutado*) and Blanco *con envejecimento* (white with ageing, which has achieved a minimum 13 per cent alcohol and been aged for a minimum of one year in oak casks of 1,000 litres or less).

What this means in real terms is:

1) Young, fruity, dry white wines made mainly with PX but maybe also Airén, Sauvignon, Chardonnay et al, unfortified, 10–12 per cent alcohol.

2) Classic Montilla styles of dry, medium and sweet wines at up to 15 per cent alcohol, unfortified but often aged in a *solera*. These can become very fine old wines.

3) Classic Montilla styles of Fino, Amontillado and Oloroso, fortified to 17–18 per cent alcohol and aged in a *solera* (*generosos*). These may achieve 20–22 per cent alcohol eventually and are the greatest wines of the region.

## Principal producers

**Alvear SA** ☆☆☆☆
*Av. María Auxiliadora 1, 14550 Montilla*
Established in 1729, this is one of the two companies that have

done more than most to advance the cause of Montilla wine in the last decade of the 20th century (the other is Pérez Barquero; *see* entry), as well as maintaining solid quality in all its wines. The winemaker is Bosco de Alvear y Zubiria, who was one of the pioneers of the *joven afrutado* sector with Marqués de la Sierra and has never compromised on quality. Alvear also owns Conde de la Cortina (*see* entry). Best wines: the entire range, but especially PX 1830 Dulce, *solera* Fundación Amontillado, Pelayo Oloroso, Carlos VII Amontillado, CB Fino, Asunción Oloroso and PX 1927.

### Aragón y Cia SA ☆☆→☆☆☆
*Ancha 31–33, 14900 Lucena*
Established in 1946, a rather old-fashioned firm although none the worse for that, doing business over the bodega gate as well as by mail order. Best wines: Paccorrito Amontillado, Araceli Dulce.

### Compañía Vinícola del Sur ☆☆→☆☆☆☆
This is the parent company that owns Pérez Barquero and Gracia Hermanos (*see* entries) as well as Tomás García in Montilla.

### Conde de la Cortina SA ☆☆
*Contact details as for Alvear (see entry above)*
Established in 1973, this company now belongs to Alvear and has the same winemaker, but its wines and markets are completely independent. Best wines: Cortina Fino CC, Gran Vino Dulce.

### Crismona SA ☆
*Baena 25, 14860 Doña Mencía*
Established in 1904 but recently modernised to a large extent, this bodega does mainly national (some 60 per cent) business but exports to the UK and Holland. Best wine: Dulce Crema PX.

### Cruz Conde – Bodegas Cruz Conde ☆→☆☆
*Ronda Canillo 4, 14550 Montilla*
Established in 1902, this is an old-fashioned *bodega* trading mainly in the Spanish market, with a good selection of *generosos* alongside the usual non-fortified wines. Best wines: PX Cruz Conde, Mercedes Oloroso.

### Delgado Hermanos SL ☆→☆☆
*Cosano 2, 14500 Puente Genil*
Established in 1874, this is a modernised *bodega* but one that uses epoxy-concrete as well as new stainless steel fermentation vessels. Most of the production is sold inside Spain. Best wine: Anacreonte Amontillado.

### Gracia Hermanos SA ☆☆☆ (Part of Compañía Vinícola del Sur)
*Av. Marqués de la Vega de Armijo 103, 14550 Montilla*
Established in 1962, this is a modern *bodega* with a good reputation throughout its range. Most production is sold in Spain but there are significant exports. It belongs to the same group as Pérez

Barquero (*see* entry) and shares the same winemaker – Juan Márquez Gutiérrez. Best wines: all are reliable, especially Montearruit Amontillado, Gracia Oloroso, Gracia PX Dulce Viejo.

## Navisa Industrial Vinícola Española ☆→☆☆
*Ctra Montalbán, s/n, 14550 Montilla*
Established in 1950, this company also owns Cobos, Montúlia, Montebello and Velasco Chacón and, although these *bodegas* still exist as entities, their wines have been assimilated into the parent group's output and their names survive mainly as brand names for the individual wines. Best wine: Fino Cobos.

## Pérez Barquero SA ☆☆☆☆ (Part of Compañía Vinícola del Sur)
*Av. Andalucía 27, 14550 Montilla*
Established in 1905, this bodega has spearheaded the new wave of Montilla marketing alongside Alvear (*see* entry) and with the help of winemaker Juan Márquez Gutiérrez turns out some classic Montilla wines. The bodega is well equipped with modern kit, and the wines are among the best of the region. Best wines: all very reliable, but especially the Gran Barquero range: PX, Amontillado, Oloroso, Fino.

## Toro Albalá SA ☆☆☆☆
*Ctra Málaga 1, 14920 Aguilar de la Frontera*
Established in 1922 on the site of an old heating plant (guess the origin of the brand name Eléctrico!), this is a relatively small producer but its wines (including a *joven afrutado*) are splendid and the labelling very original. Best wines: Don PX Gran Reserva 1972, Veijisimo Solera 1922, Don PX Dulce, Fino Eléctrico del Lagar.

## Torres Burgos SA ☆☆→☆☆☆
*Ronda San Francisco 1, 14900 Lucena*
Established in 1965 in a beguiling old *bodega*, this is a small house selling locally and nationally, but has some very good wines. Best wine: Moriles 1890 Amontillado.

# Condado de Huelva

## The history
"Condado" means "County" in the sense of an area of land ruled by a Count. In England it would be an Earldom, in France a *Comté*, in Germany a *Grafschaft* but the Spanish province of Huelva contains the town of Lepe, immortalized by Chaucer in the 14th century as a source of strong wines (*see* the section on Sherry). As it happens, Lepe is not included within the boundaries of the Condado de Huelva DO nowadays, but the history of its wine has passed into legend.

Rather like Montilla, the Condado de Huelva made wines and shipped them to Jerez in the boom years of the 16th–19th centuries, during which they were quietly assimilated into the Sherry *soleras*. Also like Montilla, once the Sherry country banned "imports" in the 1930s, Huelva had to find a recourse for the wines it produced. This has taken a threefold path. First, the region's native grape, the Zalema, is now being vinified fresh, crisp and early-picked to make _joven afrutado_ styles of wine. The quality is modest; the Zalema, in common with almost all principal Andalusian grape varieties, makes for a fairly neutral basic wine – but so are the prices, and this is a market for the tourist trade.

Secondly, the _Pálido_ wines of the Condado parallel the "_solera_" wines of Montilla – naturally high-strength, unfortified or very lightly fortified wines from dry to sweet, the latter using natural grape sugar. The best wines of the region are, however, Condado _Viejo_ – wines fortified after fermentation in the Sherry manner, up to 18 per cent alcohol and aged for a minimum of two years (and often much longer) in oak casks of no more than 650 litres (known in the trade as _bocoyes_). An additional source of income for the region is the seasoning of oak casks for the Scotch Whisky industry: two years with a Condado _Viejo_ "Oloroso" in a new barrel which is then racked off, and the empty barrel sold to Scotland, can earn almost as much for the bodega as the value of the wine used in the process. Many Scotch whiskies which claim to be "aged in a Sherry cask" have actually been in contact with wood from the Condado de Huelva.

In practical terms, what this means is that the _joven afrutado_ wines jostle for position with those from around the Mediterranean rim, at bargain-basement prices; the lighter (_Pálido_) wines of the Condado have joined _solera_ Montilla on the shelves of UK supermarkets, taking the place of ersatz non-Spanish former "Sherries"; and the heavyweight (_Viejo_) wines are sold mainly locally or shipped to South America, where a significant export market still exists.

# Principal producers

**Andrade – Bodegas Andrade** ☆→☆☆
_Av. Coronación 35, 21710 Bollullos Par del Condado_
Established in 1942, this is a partly modernised _bodega_ with some stainless steel equipment as well as traditional concrete vats lined with epoxy resin. It is family-run and makes all three styles of wine. Best wine: Doceañero Oloroso (_Viejo_).

## Vinícola del Condado - Soc. Coop. Vinícola del Condado ☆☆→☆☆☆
_San José 2, 21710 Bollullos Par del Condado_
Established in 1955, this is, on the face of it, a standard, giant, southern Spanish co-op with nearly 2,000 members turning out make-weight, workmanlike wines of no particular significance. Nothing could be further from the truth – these are some of the Condado's best wines, put together with real style by winemaker Juan Ojeda Tovar. Best wines: Misterio (_Pálido_), Mioro Fino (_Pálido_).

**Iglesias – Bodegas Iglesias** ☆
_Teniente Merchante 2, 21710 Bollullos Par del Condado_

Established in 1937, this is a partly modernised company making wines in all three categories, largely for the local and national market. Best wine: Rica Hembra Dulce (*Pálido*).

## Oliveros – Jaime Oliveros Macías
*Rábida 12, 21710 Bollullos Par del Condado*
Established in 1940, this is a fairly large producer selling wines in all three categories mainly in bulk in the local area. Here at Oliveros, the owner is the winemaker. Best wine: La Bolita Fino (*Pálido*).

## Sauci – Bodegas Manuel Sauci Salas
*Doctor Fleming 1–11, 21710 Bollullos Par del Condado*
Established in 1925, this *bodega* specialises in Finos and Olorosos, selling locally and into Spanish markets. Best wine: Vino Dulce Sauci (*Viejo*).

# Other Spanish fortified wines

Outside the four DO regions of Andalusia it's sometimes hard to distinguish between sweet and fortified wines, since in many places the winemaker is not averse to adding a little fortification if they think the wine needs it to come up to strength. The actual strength of all wines is given in this section to simplify matters. Star ratings given are for the fortified/sweet wines only of each *bodega*. In addition, other terms that are used are:

*Rancio*: this is a wine that has been kept, typically, in glass carboys with a loose bung and left out in the sun to mature for many years. The wine becomes almost black in colour and very concentrated and tends to be drunk as a *digestivo* after a meal.

*Fondillón*: mainly found in the Valencia region, it is typically made from Monastrell, fortified to about 16 per cent alcohol and aged for a minimum of eight years, sometimes in a *solera*-type system. The wine tends towards a tawny/brown colour with a nutty, delicate sweetness.

## Andalucía – Andalusia
### Country wines
Outside the main DO regions are eight Table Wine (TW) areas, some of which produce a fortified wine, usually in the style of Sherry but often aged statically in barrels rather than using the full *solera*. Quality is variable, and few *bodegas* are known outside their home area.

### Góngora – José Gallego Góngora ☆
*José-Antonio 59, 41808 Villanueva del Ariscal*
This small *bodega* in the TW area of Aljarafe uses the Garrido Fino grape to make locally respected dry and old wines, which it dignifies with the titles of "Fino" and "Amontillado". Best wine: Amontillado Muy Viejo Góngora (17 per cent alcohol).

# Aragón

This region is also known for *mistelas*, particularly in Campo de Borja, although these are not entitled to the DO.

## Campo de Borja DO

### Santo Cristo - Crianzas y Viñedos Santo Cristo Soc. Coop. ☆☆→☆☆☆
*Afueras s/n, 50570 Ainzón*

Established in 1956, this is a fairly big cooperative *bodega* and one of the two largest producers in the area. As well as the usual range of wines, they also produce a Dulce entirely from the Moscatel grape. Best fortified/sweet wine: Moscatel Ainzón (15 per cent alcohol).

## Cariñena DO

### Marín, Bodegas Ignacio ☆
*San Valero 1, 50400 Cariñena*

Established in 1903, this is another *bodega* with mainly local but some national and export trade, specialising in reds, whites and *rosados*. Best fortified/sweet wine: Barón de Lajoyosa Moscatel (15 per cent alcohol).

### Perdiguer – Bodegas Perdiguer ☆
*Av. Ejército 15, 50400 Cariñena*

Established in 1893, this small *bodega* majors on red wines and sells mainly within Spain. Best fortified/sweet wine: Perdiguer Requemado Dulce (Garnacha; 18 per cent alcohol).

### San Esteban - Bodega Coop. San Esteban ☆
*Camino Estación s/n, 50470 Encinacorba*

Established in 1946, this is a small *bodega* which sells mainly in the locality. Best fortified/sweet wine: Moscatel Virgen del Mar (15 per cent alcohol).

### Señorío – Bodegas del Señorío ☆
*Afueras s/n, 50108 Almonacid de la Sierra*

Established in 1936, this is a *bodega* which sells locally with some national and even occasional export business. The main stock in trade is red, white and *rosado* wines. Best fortified/sweet wine: Gran Paulet Rancio (Garnacha; 17 per cent alcohol).

# Canarias – the Canary Islands

In the 16th and 17th centuries "Canary-Sack" was almost as popular as "Sherris-Sack" for a time, but the sheer economy of scale provided by the Sherry country quietly edged out its island cousin. Furthermore, a series of volcanic eruptions in the 18th century destroyed many vineyard areas, most of the best of which were (and still are) on La Palma and Lanzarote (both of which are now DO wines). However, something similar to Canary-Sack is still being made, sweet, lightly fortified and usually made from Malvasía.

## La Palma DO

The north of La Palma is a wilderness of misty rift valleys and volcanic rills in which independent winemakers grow grapes and make wine in their own styles. None of these has the DO classification but, especially when tasted in the cellars, most of which have been hollowed out of the volcanic rock, they are an education. Mostly *Rancio* in style, they are very old, very concentrated and very popular with the islanders, but don't bother to look for them in the tourist areas. These wines all have the La Palma DO.

## Carballo SL ☆
*Ctra. Las Indias 44, 38740 Fuencaliente*

Established in 1990, this is a small *bodega* making wine only with its own grapes, bottling it on the premises and entirely family-run. Best fortified/sweet wine: Carballo Malvasía Dulce (Canary-Sack 15 per cent alcohol).

## El Hoyo – Bodegas El Hoyo ☆
*Callejones 60, 38738 Villa de Mazo*

Established in 1986, this is a firm with spanking-new equipment which also makes wine for smaller farmers in the central part of the island. It is one of those *bodegas* trying hard to reintroduce the old grape varieties of the Canary Islands which have died out on the mainland. Best fortified/sweet wine: Hoyo de Mazo Dulce (Canary-Sack Malvasía; 14.5 per cent alcohol).

## Llanovid Soc Coop Ltda ☆
*Los Canarios s/n, 38740 Fuencaliente*

Established in 1948, this co-op is the main producer in the south of the island of La Palma and makes wine with some of the old, unique Canary varieties. Its main sweet wine is, however, traditional enough. Best wine: Malvasía Dulce Teneguía (Canary-Sack 15 per cent alcohol).

## Lanzarote DO
## El Grifo – Bodegas El Grifo ☆☆
*Ctra. Masdache 121, 35550 San Bartolomé de Lanzarote*

Established in 1980 but based on the residuals of a company established in 1775, this family-owned enterprise promises great things, not just in rediscovering the roots of Canary viniculture but also in making crisp, fruit-up-front modern styles as well. Best fortified/sweet wines: El Grifo Semidulce (Malvasía; 11 per cent alcohol), El Grifo Dulce (Malvasía; 12 per cent alcohol), El Grifo Dulce Moscatel (Canary-Sack 17 per cent alcohol).

## Montaña Clara ☆
*Mozaga s/n, 35550 San Bartolomé de Lanzarote*

Established in 1970, this is a modern *bodega* and also one of those trying to maintain the continuity of the old grape varieties. Best fortified/sweet wine: Mozaga Dulce Malvasía (11.5 per cent alcohol).

### Valle de Güímar DO (Tenerife)

#### Bodega Comarcal Valle de Güímar ☆→☆☆
*Subida los Loros Km 4, 38550 Arafo*
Established in 1991, this is the only major *bodega* in this DO on
the west coast of the island of Tenerife. However, its wines show
increasingly well. Best fortified/sweet wine: Brumas de Ayosa
Semiseco (Listán Blanco; 12 per cent alcohol).

### Valle de la Orotava DO (Tenerife)

#### S.A.T. Union de Viticultores del Valle de la Orotava ☆→☆☆
*Ctra. La Orotava–Los Realejos Km 45, 38315 La Orotava*
Established in 1988, this is another very modern co-op *bodega*
whose wines show real promise. Best fortified/sweet wine: Gran
Tehyda Afrutado Semiseco (Listán Blanco; 11 per cent alcohol).

# Castilla-León – Old Castile
## Rueda DO

Uniquely in this part of northwestern Spain, Rueda has a long-
established and well-developed tradition of fortified wines,
made from (mainly) the Palomino grape and aged in the traditional style. When the Moors ruled southern Spain, and Sherry
and the other *vinos generosos* of Andalusia were not available,
the reconquering Castilian kings and their armies still
demanded supplies of the precious nectar. Rueda, where land
was cheap after the scorched-earth policies of the retreating
Moors, was ideal for this, and the high-producing Palomino (the
grape of Jerez) thrived in its soils.

Although much of this type of traditional winemaking
has been swept away by the new-wave, clean, crisp, fruit-up-
front dry white wines made from Verdejo and Sauvignon Blanc,
there is a small but enthusiastic market for the old wines of
Rueda. They are distinguished as "Pálido" – dry wines which
have grown *flor* (*see* the section on Sherry for details) and been
aged for at least three years – or "Dorada", which is a cross
between dry Oloroso and Rancio styles. The latter must be aged
for at least four years.

#### Castilla la Vieja – Bodegas de Crianza de ☆☆
*Ctra. Madrid–A Coruña Km 171, 47490 Rueda*
Established in 1976, this is a limb of the Sanz family, which runs
a number of very successful *bodegas* throughout Rueda and turns
out some of its best new-wave wines. But they also remember
their roots. Best fortified/sweet wine: "62" Dorada (Verdejo/
Palomino; 17.5 per cent alcohol).

#### Gutiérrez, Hijos de Alberto ☆→☆☆
*Ctra. Valdestillas 2, 47239 Serrada*
Established in 1949, this is part of a group that exports widely as
well as selling throughout Spain. Although its main thrust is the

new-wave fresh whites, it has not deserted the old styles. Best fortified/sweet wine: San Martín Dorada (Verdejo/Palomino; 17.5 per cent alcohol).

# Catalunya – Catalonia

This region has historically made Vino Rancio (*Vi Ranci* in Catalan) but has a major claim to historical fame in Tarragona Clásico. Known in England in the postwar years as "the poor man's Port", it has a distinguished history of its own. Typically made from Garnacha grapes, it must achieve a natural minimum of 13.5 per cent alcohol (and has been known to achieve 17 per cent alcohol) and be aged in oak for 12 years, by which time the alcohol level will probably have risen as the wine has concentrated (and if it hasn't, the hand of the winemaker can be relied on to help). These wines are rare these days because of simple economics: they don't command a very high price, and the cost of ageing them for the full 12 years is generally prohibitive. Wine of a similar type but aged for much shorter periods (and therefore much cheaper to produce) is called "Garnatxa", the most famous of which come from the Ampurdán-Costa Brava DO (Empordà-Costa Brava in Catalan). They may be made by drying the grapes in the sun before pressing in the style of Montilla and Málaga.

## Ampurdán-Costa Brava DO (Empordà-Costa Brava DO)

### CoViNoSA – Comercial Vinícola del Nordeste SA ☆
*Espolla 9, 17752 Mollet de Perelada*
Established in 1977, this is a joint venture company by Cavas del Ampurdán (best known for its Cava wines) and the local co-op in Mollet de Perelada. Best fortified/sweet wine: Garnatxa de l'Emporda (15 per cent alcohol).

### Fabra – Celler Martí Fabra ☆
*Vic. 26, 17751 Sant Climent Sescebes*
Established in 1913, a small firm making wine mainly from its own grapes and selling locally. However, it has a strong commitment to the sweet/fortified ethos and grows a lot of Moscatel. Best fortified/sweet wines: Garnatxa Masía Pairal Can Carreras (15 per cent alcohol), Muscat Masía Pairal Can Carreras (15 per cent alcohol).

### Guardiola, Pere ☆
*Centre 1, 17750 Capmany*
Established in 1989, this is a modern company aiming squarely at the new-wave Catalan market. Best fortified/sweet wine: Garnatxa Pere Guardiola (15 per cent alcohol).

## Priorato DO (Priorat DO)

### Costers del Siurana ☆☆☆☆
*Manyetes s/n, 43747 Gratallops*
Established in 1987 as part of the new-wave "Siurana project", this

*bodega* is the only one to have attempted a fortified/sweet wine, and it has boggled the minds of the international sweet-wine community, made as it is from overripe Garnacha, Cabernet Sauvignon and Syrah, and aged in oak for a minimum of 14 months. Best fortified/sweet wine: Dolç de l'Obac (16 per cent alcohol).

### Rottlan Torra – Vins d'Alta Qualitat ☆☆☆
*Balandra 8, 43737 Torroja del Priorat*

Established in 1984, this is a modern *bodega* mainly interested in red wines, but it also produces a sweet wine made from Garnacha, Cabernet Sauvignon, Cariñena and Syrah. Best fortified/sweet wine: Amadis Dolç (14.5 per cent alcohol).

### Vinícola del Priorat ☆☆
*Piró s/n, 43737 Gratallops*

Established in 1991, this is a modern semi-co-op *bodega* with the very latest equipment and shareholders who take an active interest in the business and the wines. In spite of the very modern aspect of its mainstream wines, its attention to tradition is exemplary. Best fortified/sweet wines: Cingle Rancio (Garnacha, Cariñena; 17 per cent alcohol), Cingle Mistela (ditto; 16.5 per cent alcohol).

## Tarragona DO

### De Muller ☆
*Camí Pedra Estela 34, 43205 Reus*

Established in 1851, this is a big old firm active elsewhere in Catalonia (*see* Terra Alta, below) and seen by many as traditional. Certainly, it doesn't neglect the traditional wines. Best fortified/sweet wine: Moscatel Añejo de Muller (15 per cent alcohol).

### Falsetença – Coop. Agrícola Falsetença S.C.C.L. ☆☆
*Miguel Barceló 31, 43730 Falset*

Established in 1917, this modernised co-op has a joint venture with Bodegas Pedro Rovira in Mora la Nova and with a little consultancy from some Australian "flying winemakers", the wines of both *bodegas* have been rather better than average. Best fortified/sweet wines: Garnatxa Negra (16 per cent alcohol), Garnatxa Blanca (made from the named grape; 16 per cent), Vi Ranci (Garnacha/Garnacha Blanca/Macabeo; 16 per cent).

## Terra Alta DO

### De Muller ☆
*Contact details as for De Muller, Tarragona (above).*
Best fortified/sweet wines: Pajarete (non-DO, Garnacha, Mazuela; 21 per cent alcohol), Vino de Misa Dulce Superior (Garnacha, Macabeo; 15.5 per cent alcohol).

### Gandesa – Celler Co-op de Gandesa S.C.C.L. ☆→☆☆
*Av. Catalunya 28, 43780 Gandesa*

Established in 1919, this is the biggest co-op in Gandesa (the capital of Terra Alta), housed in a splendid Gaudiesque main building with a sparkling modern shop attached selling all the *bodega*'s products and local food specialities. Best fortified/sweet wines: 1919 Rancio Semiseco (Garnacha Blanca; 21 per cent alcohol), Mistela de la Terra Alta (Garnacha Blanca; 16.5 per cent).

## Navarra DO

Navarra is not well-known for its sweeter wines (although sweet wines are made almost everywhere in northern Spain). However, it is well-known for its spirit of experimentation, and some of its leading *bodegas* have had some considerable success in the field.

### Castillo – Herederos Camilo Castillo ☆☆
*Santa Bárbara 40, 31591 Corella*

Established in 1856, this is a classic old *bodega* which has always made sweet and fortified wines, in the traditional style. Production may have switched direction, but the old wines still have their place. Best fortified/sweet wines: Goya (Moscatel; 15 per cent alcohol), Capricho de Goya Gran Reserva (Moscatel; 15.5 per cent).

### Chivite, Bodegas Julián ☆☆☆
*Ribera 34, 31592 Cintruénigo*

Established in 1647 and incorporated in 1860, this is the oldest company in Navarra and one of the oldest in Spain. The 125 Colección range was inaugurated in 1985 to celebrate the 125th anniversary of incorporation and has been continued ever since, selecting the best wines of each vintage. Best fortified/sweet wine: Chivite Colección 125 Moscatel (14 per cent alcohol).

### Ochoa, Bodegas ☆☆☆☆
*Alcalde Maillata 2, 31390 Olite*

Established in 1986, but the roots of this family company go much further back. Javier Ochoa, the chief executive and winemaker, also gives a good deal of time to EVENA, the local research establishment which has done so much to make Navarra an exciting and innovative region. Best fortified/sweet wine: Ochoa Moscatel (11.5 per cent alcohol).

### Piedemonte, Bodegas ☆☆☆
*Rua Romana s/n, 31390 Olite*

Established in 1993, this is a new-style *bodega* committed to reinventing the cooperative for the 21st century. Its major business is young red wines, but it has also been in the forefront of experimenting with sweet wines. Best fortified/sweet wine: Piedemonte Moscatel (10.5 per cent alcohol).

## Valencia

Valencia is best known today for its very successful budget-priced everyday wines, but there is a long tradition of sweet wines, especially *mistelas* made from Moscatel in the Alicante DO. In spite of the rush towards modern, squeaky-clean, state-of-the-art wineries turning out impeccably engineered wines for the world's supermarkets, the tradition for rich, old Fondillón and luscious Muscats continues. Moscatel de Valencia is also one of the stalwarts of the supermarket trade, usually a cheerful *mistela* made from Moscatel de Alejándria but occasionally a lovely old wine, delicately fortified and remarkably good.

## Alicante DO

### Alfonso – Bodegas Alfonso Crianza de Vinos ☆
*Casas de Rodrigo 79, 03650 Culebrón-Pinoso*

Established in 1872, this *bodega* is run by the sixth generation of the founding family and uses only the Monastrell grape for all its wines. Best fortified/sweet wine: Fondillón 64 (18 per cent alcohol).

### Gutiérrez de la Vega Bodegas ☆☆☆→☆☆☆☆
*Canalejas 4, 03792 Parcent*

Established in 1978, this is one of the few *bodegas* which has made a feature of sweet wines in its production, although it makes other wines as well. Best fortified/sweet wines: Casta Diva Cosecha Miel Moscatel (14 per cent alcohol), Viña Caballetta Moscatel (13.5 per cent).

### Mendoza – Bodegas Enrique Mendoza ☆☆→☆☆☆
*Partida El Romeral s/n, 03580 Alfaz del Pi*

Established in 1989, this is a very modern *bodega* mainly involved in the production of new-wave wines. Best fortified/sweet wines: Moscatel de Mendoza (15 per cent alcohol), Moscatel de la Marina (15 per cent).

### Nuestra Señora de las Virtudes Bodegas ☆
*Ctra. de Yecla 9, 03400 Villena*

Established in 1961, this is a giant co-op in the traditional style selling everyday wines, mainly within the region. Best fortified/sweet wine: Tesoro de Villena Fondillón Gran Reserva (Monastrell; 16.5 per cent alcohol).

## Valencia DO

### CVVE - Compañía Valenciana de Vins i Espirituosos ☆
*Pl. Maestro Serrano 3, 46380 Cheste*

Established in 1996, CVVE is a new company working with the traditional varieties of the region – in traditional styles. Best fortified/sweet wines: *solera* Cordiales Dulce Gran Reserva (PX/Moscatel; 15 per cent alcohol), CVVE Monastrell Rancio (15 per cent).

# Marsala

## The history

Well, an assortment of histories in actual fact: it is incontrovertible that the founder of the Marsala business as we know it was one John Woodhouse, an import–export merchant from Liverpool, England, and that he began shipping the wine to England in 1773. There are varying stories as to how this came about. In one version, Woodhouse had been annoyed and felt that he had been rebuffed by the Madeira producers when he had attempted to do business on the island and had left, vowing that he would find somewhere else to get his Madeira and that they would regret it. At some later date he was aboard one of his own ships heading for the Port of Mazaro del Vallo, on the Sicilian coast, in search of a cargo of washing soda when bad weather forced him to take shelter at Marsala, just north of Mazaro. At this time – indeed, for several centuries – Sicily had been at the crossroads of Mediterranean trade, and one of the most popular export commodities in Marsala was a locally made wine. He sampled it and, finding it to be remarkably like the base-wine for Madeira, bought a consignment and took it back to England, experimenting the while with the addition of Brandy, partly to help it survive the sea voyage and partly to see whether it might appeal to the current English taste, which was for powerful, sweet, fortified wines such as Madeira and Sherry.

In the event, he sold the first consignment easily and decided that there was a whole new market waiting to be discovered. He returned to Sicily in 1773 and set up in business as an exporter, subsequently establishing a winery and vineyards to supply it. By 1800 he was supplying the Royal Navy under Horatio Nelson, and Marsala wine had become a staple of respectably smart celebrations throughout Georgian England.

So successful was the trade that another Englishman, Benjamin Ingham, set up in business in Marsala alongside Woodhouse and, in 1833, the first Italian producer, Vicenzo Florio, built a winery between those of the two Englishmen. Many more followed, but it's important to remember that these were relatively lawless times: pirate ships still stalked the seaways, and Sicily itself was ruled by the Bourbon King Francis of Naples in defiance of Victor Emmanuel II, Savoy king of Piedmont-Sardinia, who had committed himself to a united Italy. This was the next opportunity for Marsala wine to play a part in history. The Italian military leader Giuseppe Garibaldi decided to capitalise on reports of a popular insurrection in Sicily by leading a motley army against the Bourbons. He arranged to travel to the island aboard ships of a merchant fleet whose main business was shipping Marsala to England, and it's also recorded that the British fleet was standing by, with dire warnings should anything happen to the wine supplies. Garibaldi and his forces landed on May 11th 1863 and marched on Palermo. In the event, popular support was such that Garibaldi and his 1,000 keen but scrappily trained troops defeated 20,000 professional Neapolitan soldiers and marched first to Palermo (June 6th) and then to Naples itself, in triumph, arriving on September 7th.

Aside from the standoff of the fleet, there are two versions of the part played by Marsala wine in the victory. In one, Garibaldi is astonished to discover the Woodhouse shop still open for business as his troops clatter through the streets of Marsala. He goes in and asks are they not aware that he and a thousand troops are about to drive the Bourbons out of Sicily? "In that case, sir", says the shop manager, "your men will be requiring a little fortification before their journey", and Garibaldi emerges from the shop having purchased several barrels of wine for his troops. The other (probably the true version) records that on arrival in Palermo, having defeated nearly all the Neapolitan army, he was offered a celebratory glass of Marsala to mark the event. He was not known as a wine-drinker but accepted out of courtesy and professed himself surprised and delighted with the taste of the wine. This was the sweetest of the wines, which came to be known as *Garibaldi Dolce* and went on to form part of the recipe for the curranty biscuits known as Garibaldis (quite how the family name of the defeated King Francis also came to be attached to a biscuit is not recorded).

The wine boomed in popularity as the stories of Garibaldi's heroic triumph were carried back to England and, along with Madeira and Sherry, a decanter of Marsala wine became de rigueur on society sideboards throughout the Victorian era.

Sadly, the late-19th-century plagues of mildew and phylloxera did as much damage in Sicily as they did in Spain, Portugal and Madeira. Lacking the economy of scale of these other regions, Marsala started to fade from view, kept alive by a few enthusiasts, as well as a considerable market in the Italian cookery business, which endures to this day. Good Marsala is still made, however, and now that the wine laws have been tightened up considerably, it's possible to get something closer to the original in the year 2000 than it has been for a century.

## Grapes for Marsala

Originally, the best Marsala was made entirely from the local Grillo grape variety, but the quantity proved inadequate and modern regulations permit the following principal varieties: (white grapes) Grillo, Cataratto, Inzolia, Ansonica, Damaschino; (red grapes) Perricone, Calabrese, Nerello Mascarese.

## How Marsala is made

Whether or not John Woodhouse was a refugee from an unwelcoming Madeira, the winemaking process certainly shows roots that link it with the wine from that island, as well as Oporto and Málaga as the fermenting must is stopped by the addition of grape spirit. Uniquely, however, a small quantity of the must is "muted" with spirit immediately after pressing to make what is called *sifone* or *mistella* (French *mistelle*, Spanish *mistela*) and set aside for later use as a colourless sweetening agent. Another way of doing this is to treat fresh grape juice with heat to provide a boiled-down, rich, sweet syrup. This is known as *vino cotto* (literally "cooked wine", although, rather beguilingly, it could also translate as "tipsy wine") and is very dark in colour.

The main wine is fermented for as long as the winemaker thinks appropriate before being fortified, typically to 17–18 per cent alcohol. After this, it progresses to large oak casks usually in above-ground cellars for maturing. Once the wine has settled, a decision will be taken as to where it's going next.

## Styles of Marsala

The rules about Marsala were revised in 1994 to tidy up a number of loose ends, and the result is a rationalisation of the styles of wine, as follows.

### Basic types of Marsala

**Marsala Fine** is the basic grade (in many cases not very "fine" at all) and very popular with Italian chefs all over the world. It must achieve 17 per cent alcohol and be aged for a minimum of one year in cask before release. Marsala Fine per Cremovo is a wine cordial flavoured with eggs, almonds or other aromatic ingredients and is very popular as a restorative for convalescent people, but need not concern us here.

**Marsala Superiore** must achieve 18 per cent alcohol and be aged for a minimum of two years in cask before release. Sweet versions are sometimes called Garibaldi Dolce.

**Marsala Superiore Riserva** must achieve 18 per cent alcohol and be aged for a minimum of four years in cask before release.

**Marsala Vergine** must achieve 18 per cent alcohol and be aged for a minimum of five years in cask before release, or be aged for that minimum period in a *solera* (*see* the section on Sherry), in which case it may be called "Marsala Solera".

**Marsala Vergine Stravecchio or Riserva** must achieve 18 per cent alcohol and be aged for a at least ten years in cask before release. These may also be wines of a single vintage.

### Epithets

All the wines above may, if they meet the appropriate criteria, add one from each group of the following epithets:

**Oro, Ambra, Rubino (gold, amber, ruby)**: descriptive of the colour of the wine.

**Secco, Semisecco, Dolce (dry, medium-dry, sweet)**: descriptive of the levels of residual sugar and/or sweetening wines (*sifone* or *cotto*) used in the final blend. Sweetening wines are not permitted in any Marsala Vergine wines, so sweeter versions of these wines may only have become so using the natural sugar in the original grapes which remains after fermentation.

## When to drink Marsala

Marsala Fine is aimed mainly at the culinary market and provides wonderful sauces and goes into excellent *tiramisù* at countless Italian restaurants throughout the world. It's unlikely that many people would want to drink it. Marsala Superiore is an everyday, low-priced wine that makes a modest *aperitivo* when dry and an agreeable mid-morning reviver when sweet; the *riserva* is obviously better. Marsala Vergine is the best wine, with dry versions offering the same style and power as a "dry" Madeira or Pale Cream Sherry or white Port – ie not very dry but quite grapey and often delicious. Rubino (red) wines are a new departure and offer a crisp hint of tannin at the drier end of the scale. However, Stravecchio versions of Marsala Vergine are the region's finest work, ranging from rich, sweet, raisiny *dolci* to some remarkably nutty, delicate and delicious *semisecco* wines. There is little single-vintage Marsala around, but what there is proves just how good Marsala can be. These are post-prandial wines *per eccellenza*, on a par with all but the finest from Spain or Portugal.

# Principal producers

These include other fortified/semi-fortified wines made by the same companies.

### De Bartolì – Marco de Bartolì & Co SRL ☆☆☆☆
*Contrada Fornara Samperi 292, 91025 Marsala*
An old family firm with a reputation for innovation and a maverick tendency to make wines, if necessary, at lower strengths than permitted by the DOC system – its Marsala wines are denied the name because they are unfortified. *See also* Other Fortified Wines of Italy (below). Best wines: Vigna la Miccia Superiore Oro (14.5 per cent alcohol), Vecchio Samperi 20 Anni Viene (15 per cent).

### Florio – SAVI Florio & Co SPA ☆☆☆→☆☆☆☆
*Via V Florio 1, 91025 Marsala*
Established in 1833, this company was taken over by Cinzano in 1929 and owns the residuals of the original Woodhouse and Ingham companies (they still appear as brands). Cinzano sold it on to the Saronno Group (of Amaretto fame) in 1998. It exports widely and specialises in older Marsala wines. Best wines: Terre Arse Vergine (pure Grillo; ten years old), any vintage wines.

### Pellegrino – Carlo Pellegrino & Co SPA ☆☆☆→☆☆☆☆
*Via del Fante 39, 91025 Marsala*
Established in 1880, this company is now the leading producer in Italy in terms of volume and makes all the major styles of the wine, including the red Rubino, which is relatively new in Marsala. Best wines: all reliable, but especially 1962 Vintage Vergine, Superiore Dolce and Secco.

### Rallo – Alvis SPA ☆☆→☆☆☆☆
*Via V Florio 2, 91025 Marsala*
The holding company masks the name of Diego Rallo i Figli, founded in 1860 and still family-run. They make a wide range of wine, but Marsala is where they started and, some would say, where their best work is still done. They used to have an ancient Solera Vergine called 1860, but this has been absent from their main list for some time. Best wines: Vergine Solera Riserva 12 Anni, Superiore Dolce and Secco.

# Other Italian fortified wines

Many Italian regions produce a *liquoroso* or sweet/semi-forti-fied/fortified version of their main wine. In the north, particularly, there are "portmanteau" DOC wines in which the same name may be appended to anything up to a dozen styles, from white to red, young to old, and sweet to fortified. In the south, the approach may be more deliberate and based on traditions going back to Mediterranean trade a thousand years ago. However, most of the wine styles may be found in most places.

Wine may be made *passito* (by allowing the grapes to shrivel on the vine before harvesting) or as Vin Santo (literally "holy wine", the grapes for which were traditionally dried in the loft from harvest-time until Christmas) or *liquoroso* (fortified). Often the grapes used will be those that naturally produce sweet musts: eg the Moscato, Malvasìa, Zibibbo (a type of Moscato) and others. Many of these are scarcely seen outside their home province, but they are listed here in a general canter through Italy's regions. Where there are notable producers in an area, their names are simply listed. In many areas, however, only local knowledge will reveal true quality. Alcoholic strengths are given as the minimum permitted by the DOC regulations.

## Emilia-Romagna
Colli Piacentini is a multiple DOC which offers a Vin Santo (16 per cent alcohol) mainly from Malvasìa (but also Sauvignon Blanc and Marsanne) and a Vin Santo di Vigoleno (18 per cent), which is largely Marsanne. They are aged for four and five years respectively.

## Lazio – Latium
Aleatico di Gradoli has a red *liquoroso* (15 per cent alcohol), made entirely from the Aleatico grape, which may be plain or *riserva* and aged for six months or two years respectively.

## Liguria
Golfo del Tigullio among its many incarnations has a *passito* (16.5 per cent alcohol), which may be made from any white varieties, and a Moscato *passito* (15.5 per cent), which must be made from Moscato Bianco. Both aged for a year.

## Lombardia – Lombardy
Oltrepò Pavese has many forms, two of them *liquoroso dolce* (17.5 per cent) and *secco* (18 per cent). Rare but highly prized.

Valcalepio is another portmanteau DOC and it, too, offers a red Moscato *passito* (15 per cent) and a different sub-variety of the grape in Moscato di Scanzo *passito*. Both must be aged for 14 months.

## Puglia – Apulia
Aleatico di Puglia is rather better than its namesake from Latium. At its best, the *liquoroso* version (aged four months) has some real character, and the *riserva* (aged three years-plus) is better still

(both 18.5 per cent). Best producer: Francisco Candido, but recent production has all been of the unfortified versions.

Gioia del Colle makes a very sweet Aleatico *liquoroso dolce* (16 per cent), but it doesn't really have the style of the wine above.

Moscato di Trani comes as a "natural" sweet wine and a *liquoroso* (16 per cent) with a year's ageing. Southern Italy in general – and Apulia in particular – does this type of lightly fortified Muscat very well. Best producer: Fratelli Nugnes at Bari, who are specialists in this wine.

Primitivo di Manduria is made entirely from the Primitivo grape, which turns out real heavyweights in this southern climate. There are two *liquoroso* versions: *dolce* (15 per cent) and *secco* (16.5 per cent), both aged for two years. Many examples simply overpower the senses, but a few producers balance heat and strength with ripeness and maturity. Best producer: Giordano.

Salice Salentino makes its fortified wines with Aleatico. *Liquoroso dolce* is aged for four months, and the *riserva* version for 26 months (both 16 per cent). There are good wines to be found, although this grape never quite performs anywhere as well as it does in the straight Aleatico di Puglia.

# Sardegna – Sardinia

Alghero *liquoroso* (18 per cent) is made from a mixture of local varieties and is aged for three years-plus. A *riserva* version ages for five years, and there is also an Alghero *passito* (white; 15 per cent) made mainly from Cabernet Sauvignon. Best producer: Sella e Mosca.

Cannonau di Sardegna comes *secco* (18 per cent) and *dolce naturale* (16.5 per cent), made from the grape of the same name. Best producer: Sella e Mosca.

Girò di Cagliari *liquoroso* covers a range of wines (15–16.5 per cent), which may or may not be fortified, according to the natural strength of the finished wine. Basic wines are aged for eight months, *riservas* for two years.

Malvasìa di Bosa *liquoroso* may be *dolce* (15 per cent) or *secco* (16.5 per cent) and must be aged for two years-plus.

Malvasìa di Cagliari *liquoroso* comes in three styles: *secco* (16.5 per cent), *dolce* (15 per cent) and *riserva* (17.5 per cent). The former two age for eight months, the last for two years.

Moscato di Cagliari *liquoroso* (15 per cent) must be aged for four months, the *riserva* version for a year. Quality can be good but is very variable.

Nasco de Cagliari *liquoroso* comes *dolce* (15 per cent), *secco* (16.5 per cent) and *riserva* (17.5 per cent). Nasco is a rustic heavyweight much prized locally. Ageing is eight months for the first two, a year for the last. Sella e Mosca make an unfortified version which does not have the DOC.

Vernaccia de Oristana comes plain (15 per cent), *superiore* (15.5 per cent), *liquoroso* (16.5 per cent) and *riserva* (17.5 per cent). The wine is aged for two years and five months except for the *superiore*, which gets an extra year. One of the best producers is Attilio Contini.

# Sicilia – Sicily

(*See* above for Marsala.)

Malvasia delle Lipari may be *passito* (18 per cent) or *liquoroso* (20 per cent) and must be aged for seven and six months respectively. Best producer: Carlo Hauner.

Moscato Passito de Pantelleria is something of a Mediterranean legend. The island of Pantelleria is administered by Sicily, some 120 kilometres away, but is actually closer to Tunisia, which is only 80 kilometres away. A staging post for shipping for centuries, place-names have an Arabic feel to them, and this wine originated in the splendidly named *contado*, or hamlet, of Bukkuram: the wine is sometimes so labelled. The wine is made from the Zibibbo grape (actually the Muscat of Alexandria) and may be *liquoroso* (15 per cent) or *extra liquoroso* (15.5 per cent), which must be aged for 14 months. Best producers: Marco de Bartoli, SAVI Florio (*see* Marsala, above).

# Toscana – Tuscany

Bianco dell' Empollese also make Vin Santo both *secco* (16 per cent) and *amabile* (15 per cent). Both are made mainly from Trebbiano and must be aged for at least three years.

Candia dei Colli Apuani make a lightish Vin Santo (16.5 per cent) largely from Vermentino. It is aged for three years.

Colline Luchesi include a white Vin Santo (16 per cent), which may be *secco* or *amabile*, and a *rosato* (pink) version called Vin Santo Occhio di Pernice ("partridge-eye"; 16 per cent). They age for four and three years respectively.

Vin Santo de Chianti has its own DOC, separate from the main wine. It's a *rosato* wine called Occhio di Pernice (16.5 per cent; aged for three years) or Occhio di Pernice Riserva (16.5 per cent; aged for four years). In addition, the same names may be preceded by one of the seven "districts" of Chianti (Colli Aretini, Colli Fiorentini, Colli Senesi, Colline Pisane, Montalbano, Rufina and Montespertoli) for wines made in those areas. The minimum strength is 17 per cent. All wines are made mainly with Sangiovese.

# France

## The history

France is not well-known for its fortified wines, probably because they are overshadowed by everything else the country produces. However, there are some excellent – and a few outstanding – wines made, particularly in the southwest, where the heritage is as much Catalan as French and the wines of Spain and France show great similarities. Broadly, the fortified wines of France can be divided into two groups: Vin Doux Naturel and Vin de Liqueur.

## Vin doux naturel

Vin Doux Naturel (VdN) is not, as its name implies, a natural sweet wine, although its sweetness does come from natural grape sugar. The must is fermented normally until it reaches about five to six per cent alcohol, and then it is fortified with grape spirit to preserve the sweetness, and often aged for long periods. In Roussillon (where Catalan influence is strongest) they also like it in the *rancio* style, which usually means ageing the wines in direct sunlight for several years. In France this is done in the barrel, whereas in Catalonia it's generally done in glass carboys. Although the *rancio* style is popular, it's not widely seen outside its home area. Much more popular are the sweet Muscats. The following is a list of the most important VdN appellations with a mention of the major producers where appropriate. Muscat varieties are listed as Muscat de Frontignan (MF) or Muscat d'Alexandrie (MA).

## Banyuls, Roussillon

This is France's most southerly appellation, and abuts the Spanish border. The wine is made from Grenache Noir, Gris and Blanc and topped up with ten per cent of other varieties. The wine must be aged for at least 30 months, and this may be in single-vintage barrels which are regularly topped up with new wine, or in a variant of the *solera* system (*see* the section on Sherry). Best producers: Domaine du Mas Blanc (Banyuls), Banyuls L'Étoile Cooperative (Banyuls), Château de Jau (Rivesaltes).

## Clairette du Languedoc, Languedoc

Fortification of this probably began because in its natural, dry form it's not very inspiring. Branded versions of it are the norm, and it may come in VdN and *rancio* styles. Best producer: Domaine de la Condamine (Paulhan).

## Grand Roussillon, Roussillon

In spite of its grandiose name, this tends to be a "dustbin" classification for Muscats from the other appellations of Roussillon: anything not good enough to be sold under its own name is "declassified" and sold as Grand Roussillon. Perhaps it should have been called Petit Roussillon (MF, MA).

## Muscat de Beaumes-de-Venise, Rhône

The most northerly outpost of VdN Muscat (MF), the soils and climate here make for one of the best Vins Doux Naturels in France. The wine has the happy ability to be enjoyed young or with a bit of bottle-age. Best producers: most is made by the Beaumes-de-Venise co-op, but there are some good small producers, including Domaines Durban, des Coyeaux and des Bernadins (all in Beaumes).

## Muscat de Cap Corse, Corsica

A relatively new appellation, and very small, this nevertheless makes an excellent Muscat (MF) VdN which seems likely to become very much better known in the future. Best producer: Clos Nicrosi (Rogliano).

## Muscat de Frontignan, Languedoc

This is the town which gave its name to the grape (known elsewhere as the Muscat à Petits Grains), although its fame has probably now been eclipsed by its cousin in Beaumes-de-Venise. The wines – MF, of course – are excellent, and may be VdN or Vin de Liqueur (*see* below). Best producers: the local co-op, Château de la Peyrade (Frontignan).

## Muscat de Lunel, Languedoc

A smaller version of Frontignan making similar good-quality (MF) wines but without the high public profile. Best producers: the local co-op, Château du Grès St-Paul (Lunel).

## Muscat de Mireval, Languedoc

Neighbouring Frontignan, making similarly good (MF) wines, although hardly seen outside its home area. Best producer: Cave de Rabelais co-op (Mireval).

## Muscat de Rivesaltes, Roussillon

Rivesaltes is better known for its red and white VdNs (*see* below) but it also makes Muscat (MA, MF) in a pleasant, early-drinking style. Best producers: Mont Tauch (Tuchan), Domaine Sarda-Malet (Perpignan).

## Muscat de St-Jean-de-Minervois, Minervois

Better known for its red wines, Minervois also produces a Muscat (MF) within this particular enclave. Quality can be extremely good. Best producers: the local co-op, Domaine Barroubio.

## Rasteau, Rhône

This is the northern outpost of Grenache-based VdN, although it can be either red or brown. The latter is generally acknowledged to be the better. Best producers: most is made by the Rasteau co-op.

## Rivesaltes, Roussillon

This is a major appellation producing very large amounts of VdN, including a Muscat (*see* above). However, its main stock in trade is red, pink and white wines made with all sorts of combinations of Muscat (MA, MF), Grenache and other southern French varieties. The reds quite possibly have the edge in terms of quality. Best producers: Domaine Cazes (Rivesaltes), Château de Corneilla (Corneilla-del-Vercol), Baixas co-op (Baixas).

# Vin de Liqueur

Vin de Liqueur differs from Vin Doux Naturel in that no fermentation takes place: the grape juice is mixed with grape spirit immediately after pressing (in other words, it's a *mistelle* rather than a wine) and then allowed to mellow in barrel. When young, these tend to be a bit "stalky" and "spirity", but some of them – particularly from the Cognac area – age very gracefully.

## Floc de Gascogne, Armagnac

This is the Armagnac equivalent of Pineau des Charentes (*see* below) and very rarely found outside the area. It does not have a recognised AC.

## Macvin du Jura, Jura

Grape spirit added to unfermented juice from Jura grapes, including Poulsard, Savagnin Trousseau etc. Quite why this has an AC and Floc and Ratafia do not is something of a mystery. It doesn't have the richness of Muscat or the delicious Cognac-style of Pineau des Charentes, but it does have its adherents. Best producer: Henri Maire is very reliable.

## Muscat de Frontignan, Languedoc

As well as the VdN version (*see* above), this wine is also made as Vin de Liqueur.

## Pineau des Charentes, Cognac

Pineau has the highest profile of any French Vin de Liqueur and its own AC. The story tells of a young winemaker working for a Cognac distiller in the town of Burie in 1589. By mistake he ran fresh grape juice into a barrel which still contained some Cognac, so instead of fermenting, the juice was "muted" and became what we know today as Pineau des Charentes. Unwilling to throw it away, he decided to forget about it until he could decide what to do with it, and there it stayed for several years. When it was rediscovered, they found it to be very good, and so a new drink was born. In practical terms, it's also a useful way of using up excess grape-production and acting as a "safety valve" for smaller Cognac producers. Only Cognac producers are permitted to make Pineau, and it may be white or red. The white is made mainly from the standard Cognac grapes: St-Émilion (Ugni Blanc), Folle Blanche and Colombard; red is made from Malbec, Merlot, Cabernet Franc and Cabernet Sauvignon. Because the grape juice has to be fresh, the process has to be carried out at vintage time using young Cognac distilled from the previous vintage. The resulting wine is then aged in old Cognac barrels for as long as the winemaker sees fit. When young it can be a touch "spiky", but it mellows with age and at ten years old can be splendid – rich with the redolence of old Cognac and as powerful as tawny Port. Best producers: there are so many, and some of the very smallest produce some of the very best wines, that it would be invidious to list a few and impossible to list them all. When buying outside the Charentes region, stick to the ten-year-old-plus wines; if you're in the Charentes, there are few greater pleasures than touring the tiny independent Cognac distilleries and sampling their Pineau. For further information, the regulatory body is always happy to supply information: Comité National du Pineau des Charentes, 112 Av. Victor Hugo, 16100 Cognac.

## Ratafia, Champagne

This is a mistelle made with grape spirit and unfermented Champagne must. Like Floc (*see* above) it has no AC and is rarely found outside its home region.

# Greece

## The history

The history of wine in Greece is impossibly long, muted in recent times by a long sojourn in the Ottoman Empire and coming to a new flowering in the years since 1990 with innovative wineries turning out bright, fresh, new-wave wines, but these do not concern us here. The history of sweet and fortified wines in Greece starts with the gods themselves, who ate ambrosia and drank nectar on Mount Olympus. Indeed, part of the reason why Greek wine history is shrouded in so much legend is that it goes so far back in time, to the days when the Mediterranean was the centre of the world.

It was the Greeks who took vines to southwestern Europe in the first millennium BC, but by that time they had been wine-makers for a thousand years or more themselves, having inherited the skills from the Babylonians and the Egyptians, who had been making wine for a thousand years before that.

## Muscat

The "nectar" in question was undoubtedly sweet Muscat aged by the *nama* system in large clay jars into which new wine was poured before the old wine had been completely exhausted – an early forerunner of the *solera* system. Great sweetness and natural alcoholic strength were the most important factors in an age when wine vessels were scarcely airtight and oxidation was the rule rather than the exception. Fortification came in at some time in the first few centuries AD and was adopted as a further way to preserve the wines" characteristics for longer. The sweet Muscats of Greece remain among the most primeval styles of wine in the world: rich, all-encompassing, endlessly sweet, they have instant appeal to the beginner and lasting appeal to the enthusiast. It might be fair to say that every Muscat wine subsequently produced throughout the world owes something to the style and heritage of these wines. The originals have changed, of course, and yet they still carry something of the magic of that distant past. They may be fortified, lightly fortified or unfortified, and some of them are made from the Muscat of Frontignan (MF) and some from Muscat of Alexandria (MA), under the rather complex Greek appellation system in the following regions.

### Cephalonia, Ionian Islands

This island is better known today for its production of new-wave wines, but the Muscat of Cephalonia (MF) is legendary in its own way and is still produced.

### Lemnos, Aegean Islands

Another island making its name with new-wave wines, this one also maintains its traditional Muscat (MA). Best producer: Achaia Clauss (but *see* entry below).

### Patras, Peloponnese

The Muscat of Patras (MF), from the north coast of the Peloponnese, is reckoned to be one of the finest in Greece. There's also a sub-classification Muscat Rion of Patras. Best producer: Achaia Clauss (but *see* entry below).

### Rhodes, Dodecanese Islands

This is another top-ranking Muscat (MF), in the same league as that of Patras. Best producer: the local cooperative, CAIR.

### Samos, Aegean Islands

Perhaps the greatest of all the classic Muscats of Greece (MF) is made here, and it's also where the famous Nectar is made by the Samos Union of Cooperatives (EOS). Best producer: EOS (*see* entry below).

# Mavrodaphne

This is something unique to Greece, created by Gustav Clauss, who founded his winery in the Achaia region in 1861. Legend has it that, newly widowed, he moved from Bavaria to Greece to restart his life and subsequently fell in love with a local woman whose name was Daphne. Unfortunately, she died shortly afterwards, and he vowed to create a wine in her name and her memory which he called Mavrodaphne, which means "dark (-eyed) Daphne". No one knows what the original grape variety was, but since then it has always been known simply as the Mavrodaphne grape.

The grapes are sun-dried and fortified after fermentation, and they pass into extremely large barrels and remain there for a very long time, although the wine can be drunk young. The best, however, is ancient. Most Mavrodaphne is made in the area of Patras, but there is some production on the Ionic island of Cephalonia. Best producer: Achaia Clauss (but *see* entry below).

# Other Greek fortified wines

Daphnes and Sitia, both on the island of Crete, include a fortified liqueur red wine made from the Liatiko grape. Santorini, one of the islands in the Cyclades, makes a sweet wine, Visanto, from sunned Assyrtiko grapes with a light fortification.

## PRINCIPAL PRODUCERS

Most Greek wine producers will have a range of wines, sometimes from the crispest, freshest, new-wave Sauvignon Blanc to the richest old Muscat. These are a couple of them:

### Achaia-Clauss ☆☆☆☆
*PO Box 1035, GR-26110 Patras*

Established in 1861 and, sadly, went out of business in 1999. However, much of the company's wine will be in the supply-chain for several years. Best wines: the original Mavrodaphne, Muscats of Lemnos and Patras.

**EOS Samos** ☆☆☆☆
*Malagari, GR-83100 Samos*

A cooperative union making some of the best Muscat wines on the island. Best wines: Nectar, Anthemis.

# Cyprus

## The history

The further east you go in the Mediterranean, the older the wine history becomes. Even if we assume that the Phoenicians who discovered what is now the Sherry country 3,000 years ago planted vines on their first visit, it still makes Sherry a late-comer compared with Cyprus, which had been in the wine business for a thousand years by that time. However, the chessboard of history has given Cyprus more checks than most and, whilst its position as yet another well-placed entrepôt on the shipping run from Latakia to Gadir brought it trade and prosperity, it also brought pirates and invaders.

The first wine of which we have real evidence is the famous Commandaria. Cyprus was conquered by the forces of the English King Richard Cœur de Lion (who, in spite of all the legends, only actually visited England twice in his life and spoke no English at all) during the Crusades, in 1191. He passed the island on to the Knights Templar (for money – they were an enormously rich order) and they established a Commanderie – a regional head-quarters – on the island. They were a political as well as a military force and wielded great power in the 12th and 13th centuries. Knightly aristocracy involved the usual round of good living, fine food, and the best wines, and those which were chosen by the order became known as the "wines for the Commanderie" and, by elision, "Commandaria". At this time, the wines would have been naturally sweet, probably made from sun-dried grapes and quite possibly fortified. Certainly they were made by the Nama system – an early forerunner of the *solera*. Grapes were sunned for anything up to a fortnight and then fermented and subsequently stored in large clay jars of the type that would be recognised by Ali Baba. The early winemakers quickly learned that if they left a proportion of wine in the bottom of the jar and then added new wine to it, the new wine took on many of the characteristics of the old. The modern *solera* system is widely used in Cyprus today, using oak and chestnut casks.

Like Greece, Cyprus became part of the Ottoman Empire and winemaking went into a decline for some three hundred years, but in 1878 came under British control, at that time on behalf of the Sultan of Turkey. During the First World War Britain and Turkey found themselves on opposing sides and the island was annexed by Britain, and it formally became a British Colony in 1925. Since then, of course, the island has become an independent state, and a good deal of military, political and religious effort has gone into making life rather more difficult than it needs to be, but that does not concern us here.

The British connection, from 1878, gave Cyprus two things which it had lacked almost since the time of the Crusaders - contact with an extensive shipping and trade network, and the vast market of the British Empire. As a Crown Colony, Cyprus enjoyed preferential duty rates, cut-rate shipping charges and an easy ride into the British market and beyond. This was the golden age of "sideboard wines" and Cyprus leapt to it with enthusiasm. Commandaria was (and still is) being made and enjoyed a small but enthusiastic following, but the big growth was in a fortified wine called (until 1996) "Cyprus Sherry" which owed little to the original but the name. In terms of cost, however, the benefits of being part of the British Commonwealth meant that Cyprus wines could undercut anything from Europe and business was good.

Business was so good, in fact, that Cypriot vineyards had become very conservative. Vine-growers had seen Europe devastated by phylloxera in the second half of the 19th century and corporately vowed that they would never allow the import of any vines from outside the island. This worked well, except that it meant that every wine made on the island ended up being a mix-and-match blend of just three major grape-varieties – Mavro (red), Xynisteri (white) and Muscat (of Alexandria). Some trials of other varieties were conducted, starting in the 1960s. In the 1990s, when it became clear that "Cyprus Sherry" was on a fairly long walk off a fairly short pier, commercial winemaking started using what we might describe as "western European" varieties to make new-wave, even New World-style wines. These, however, do not concern us here.

The most important thing from a fortified-wine point of view has been that Cyprus has taken another look at its minority varieties, just a few of which (such as the Maratheftico and the Ophthalmo) have survived since medieval times.

# Modern Cypriot fortified wines
## Commandaria

There are those who say that this wine is but a shadow of its former self. Quite how they know is something of a mystery, as we can never know how the wines of the Crusaders tasted. However, the wine was given legal status by the Cypriot government in 1993. The grapes are grown in the Troodos mountains and the best wines are likely to be a 50/50 mix of Mavro and Xynisteri, sunned, fermented, fortified with grape spirit and then matured in a *solera*. The best examples will be at least ten years old and some may carry a vintage date. They have a strength typically of 15-17 per cent alcohol but legally up to 20 per cent.

## Cyprus fortified wines

These are the Sherry- and Port-type wines which came to such prominence during the Commonwealth preference period and before Sherry won back the rights to its own name within the EU (Port had done so in the Edwardian era). Like all "me-too" wines they suffer by comparison with the original but, it has to be said, there are agreeable sweet fortified wines made in the *solera* system. The better wines tend to be the sweeter ones.

## Cyprus Muscat

The legendary Muscats of Greece were recreated in Cyprus and even today there are excellent wines made from sun-dried grapes and lightly fortified. Indeed, some producers favour unfortified Muscat wines, relying on the natural grape sugar – although the low strength (10 per cent alcohol or less) of these wines usually means they're mostly consumed early, and in Cyprus.

# Principal producers

Most Cyprus wine is made by half a dozen large companies in Paphos and Limassol, and most of the companies make all styles of Cyprus wine, including "new-wave" reds, whites and pinks. However, there are small firms unknown in export markets which are worth seeking out for the interested visitor. These are the big names, however:

### Etko Ltd ☆
*PO Box 261, Limassol*
This is the company which makes what used to be called EMVA Cyprus Sherry, although the wines are now known as Emva Cream, Emva dry, Emva ruby, etc. Their best wines range from average to good range across the board.

### Keo Ltd ☆☆
*PO Box 209, Limassol*
A large company making famous-name wines in the unfortified sector but it is active in the fortified market and makes Cyprus' best dry fortified wine. Best fortified wines: Commandaria St John, Keo Fino.

### Loel Ltd ☆☆☆
*PO Box 139, Limassol*
This company is a major distiller as well as a winemaker, so some of its products may end up in other companies' wines. Best fortified wines: Commandaria Alasia 1989, Muscat Limassol.

### Sodap Ltd ☆☆
*PO Box 314, Limassol*
Established in 1844, this is a cooperative of considerable size which turns out a lot of wine of all types. Best fortified wine – Commandaria St Barnabas.

# United States of America

Historically, California's production of sweet wines dramatically outweighed the production of dry wines until as recently as 1968. These included many poor imitations of Port and Sherry. Today, there remains a steady production of very undistinguished fortified wines, which need not concern us here, as well as some striking "Ports", both from Portuguese varieties and from Zinfandel. It is not all bad news though. There are some notable examples of these wines, the producers of which are listed below.

# Central Valley
## PRINCIPAL PRODUCERS
### Ficklin ☆☆☆
*Madera, CA 93637*
The Ficklins have specialised in Port-style wines ever since they planted Portuguese varieties in this extremely hot inland area in 1946. *Soleras* are the basis of their non-vintage blends, including a tawny matured in American oak, but there is also a very fine vintage Port-style from mostly Tinta Madeira.

### Quady ☆☆☆
*Madera, CA 93639*
Andrew Quady has real flair, both as an inventive winemaker and as a packager. His wines include the grandly named Essensia – a Muscat, fortified to give a sweet, fresh, tangy style. Elysium is his Black Muscat, vinified in the same way and displaying an intriguing rose-like aroma.

Quady also makes excellent Port-style wines, mostly from Sierra Foothills fruit, either Zinfandel or Portuguese varieties. The best-known of these is called Starboard. They are very sweet and can lack elegance.

# Napa Valley
## PRINCIPAL PRODUCERS
### Togni ☆☆☆
*St Helena, CA 94574*
Philip Togni specialises in Cabernet Sauvignon but also makes a tiny quantity of delicious Black Homburg, which is very lightly fortified before bottling. It's a flowery, grapey wine best enjoyed in its youth.

### Other fortified wines
Some appealing "Ports" are made from the Italian Grignolino grape and from Portuguese varieties by Heitz. Beaulieu have long produced a silky, honeyed Muscat, given long ageing in small barrels.

# San Luis Obispo County
Justin produce a Port from Cabernet Sauvignon called Obtuse, and Twin Hills Winery in Paso Robles specialise in Port- and Sherry-style wines made by the *solera* system.

# Sierra Foothills and Lodi
## PRINCIPAL PRODUCERS
### Mondavi Woodbridge ☆☆
*Acampo, CA 95258*

Mondavi's second, and less publicised, winery turns out some six million cases per year. Portuguese grape varieties were planted in 1988, and the outcome is Port-style Porto Cinco, first made in 1993 and showing distinct promise.

### Renwood ☆☆☆
*Plymouth, CA 95669*
Renwood offer a wide range of skilfully made wines, including "Ports", mostly from Zinfandel and made in a distinctive rich and powerful style.

### St Amant ☆☆
*Stockton, CA 95204*
Tim Spencer has replanted his Portuguese varieties, despite an onslaught of phylloxera, so he can continue to make his Port-style wines. His tawny is somewhat spirity, but the vintage style, made from Portuguese varieties planted in the Sierra Foothills, can be excellent.

### Shenandoah ☆☆
*Plymouth, CA 95669*
Although there are some decent "Ports" made mostly from Zinfandel that are produced here, the star turn here is the lush, peppery Black Muscat.

### Sonora Winery & Port Works ☆☆
*Sonora, CA 95370*
Founded in 1986, this winery specialises in Port-style wines made from Portuguese varieties.

# Australia

The great Australian sweet-wine style is the Liqueur Muscat or Tokay as it is also known. It is a speciality of the Rutherglen district in northeast Victoria, and the wines have been produced since the 1850s. The difference between the two is that Muscat is made from Muscat à Petits Grains Rouge, whereas Tokay is made from the white Muscadelle and has nothing whatever to do with Hungarian Tokaji (*see* sweet wines). Grapes are left on the vine through autumns that are usually long and dry to become raisined.

Harvesting dates vary, according to the ripeness levels and other factors that winemakers seek. After harvesting, the grapes are pressed and fermented, and the fermentation is arrested by the addition of brandy. Then the wines are classified, according to their potential quality, and decanted into older casks of various sizes for maturation.

Some producers opt for a *solera* system, while others prefer to blend on an *ad hoc* basis. Before bottling, the wines are refreshed by the addition of some younger wines. With age, of course, the wines evaporate and become more concentrated, and the trick is

to balance the intensity of the old wine with the exuberant fruitiness of the younger wine. Producers are jealous of their stocks of
old wine – they include barrels of treacly dark wine that may be
up to 90 years old – which need to be conserved to maintain consistency and quality, so only a small proportion of wine is bottled
each year. Consequently, some of the more prestigious wines,
with a higher percentage of very old wine, are made only in very
limited quantities and are sold at high prices. But this is a unique
style of wine, worthy of comparison with the very best from
Portugal or Roussillon.

Australia also produces a good range of other fortified wines,
including some creditable sherries and powerful, long-lived Ports,
which are usually made from Shiraz and Grenache. The style
known in Australia as Liqueur Port indicates a wine aged in barrels that have been placed beneath the winery roof, where the
fluctuating temperature, and considerable heat in summer, cause
evaporation and thus concentration of flavour. Madeira, as an
Australian style, usually signifies a dryish style of fortified wine
made from white grapes.

Overall, however, fortified wines are in decline. In the 1950s
they represented 80 per cent of production, although most of the
wines were sold in what Australians call the "brown paper bag"
segment of the market.

# New South Wales
## PRINCIPAL PRODUCERS
### De Bortoli ☆☆☆☆
*Bilbul, NSW 2680*

De Bortoli is best know for its startlingly concentrated botrytised
Semillon, Noble One (*see* sweet wines). Although another of their
specialities is Black Noble – sweet wine left in barrel for about ten
years without topping up; it is lightly fortified to protect the wine.
The outcome is intense and raisiny, not unlike a Pedro Ximénez
in flavour but less viscous.

# Queensland

Two producers stand out here. Ballandean produce a vigorous if
rather alcoholic white Muscat, and Roma Villa offer a range of
Port- and Madeira-style wines.

# South Australia
## PRINCIPAL PRODUCERS
### Chateau Yaldara ☆☆☆
*Lyndoch, SA 5351*

Most of the fortified wines here are of routine quality, but the
Lakewood Show Liqueur Port, with an average age of about 25
years, is outstanding.

### D'Arenberg ☆☆☆
*McLaren Vale, SA 5171*

The fortified wine produced by D'Arenberg is Nostalgia Very Old
Port, from Grenache and Shiraz.

### Penfolds ☆☆☆
*Nuriootpa, SA 5355*
Magill Tawny, made mostly from Barossa Valley Grenache, has a lovely nose of caramelised oranges, and a fresh lively palate. More serious and concentrated is the Grandfather "Port" from Shiraz and Mataro (Mourvèdre), which has an average age of 20 years.

### Seppelt ☆☆☆
*Seppeltsfield, SA 5352*
One of Australia's finest sources of fortified wines, Seppelt produce splendid Show Tawny from Barossa fruit, a wine averaging some 21 years in age, and some impressive sherries from Palomino, notably the Show Amontillado and Show Flor Fino. But Seppelt is best known for its century-old Para Liqueur Port, a costly rarity composed of wines from casks set aside for 100 years, a tradition that dates from 1878.

### Yalumba ☆☆☆
*Angaston, SA 5353*
This large company produces a wide range of Port-style wines, and some of the bottlings of very old wines, such as the Antique Tawny, can be magnificent.

Sherry-style wines are produced by Angoves, Peter Lehmann and McWilliams, and Ports by Jim Barry (Old Tawny), Bethany, Grant Burge, Chateau Reynella, Hardy's (Show Port, vintage Port), Manning Park, Normans, Rockford (Marion Tawny) and Wirra Wirra (Old Tawny).

# Victoria
The leading producers of old Muscats and Tokays, united under the umbrella of the Muscat of Rutherglen Network, have reorganised the hierarchy of quality levels. The long-term aim is to clarify this hierarchy for consumers; in the short term it adds to confusion, as styles being phased out, such as "Old" and "Special", are still on retailers' shelves. The basic style of any producer will be labelled as Rutherglen Muscat or Tokay. Then, in ascending order of concentration, rarity and cost, are Classic, Grand and Rare. Producers must establish their own criteria for each category, with peer pressure ensuring that quality is roughly equivalent across the board. "Rare" Muscats are released in tiny quantities, as they draw on some of the oldest wines; prices are very high.

## PRINCIPAL PRODUCERS
### All Saints ☆☆☆
*Wahgunyah, Victoria 3687*
All Saints went through a disappointing patch until 1991, when the company was acquired by Brown Bros (*see* entry). There are signs of improvement, and the Museum Release Muscat was outstanding. As well as dependable Tokays, there are also fine old Port- and Sherry-style wines.

### Baileys ☆☆☆☆
*Glenrowan, Victoria 3675*

My notes refer to a variety of styles, including Founders Award and Gold Label. Quality has varied, but the best wines are truly great, with fabulous intensity of flavour, and tremendous figgy, treacly richness.

### Brown Bros ☆☆☆
*Milawa, Victoria 3678*

The Reserve Muscat is, despite its name, a less serious blend than the Liqueur Muscat, which is a fine introduction to the style: Christmas pudding on the nose, and chocolatey on the palate, which is refreshed by vigorous acidity. The Tokays are made in a similar style; and the Very Old Tokay is superb, with no spiritiness to mar its intensity.

### Bullers ☆☆☆
*Rutherglen, Victoria 3685*

This very traditional producer was founded in the 1920s and remains in the hands of the third generation. The style of the best bottlings is somewhat lean but complex none the less, with overtones of burned sugar, liquorice, figs and coffee. The emphasis is on finesse rather than richness. There is also a vintage Port, made, unusually, from Durif and Touriga.

### Campbell's ☆☆☆☆
*Rutherglen, Victoria 3685*

These are wonderful wines at all levels. Naturally the top, and most expensive bottlings – the Isabella Tokay and the Merchant Prince Muscat – are the most concentrated and viscous, but the far less expensive Classic Muscat, with its nose of caramelised oranges and its intense creamy palate, is also extremely impressive. Merchant Prince is highly individual, with spicy tones of cinnamon and quite aggressive acidity.

### Chambers ☆☆☆☆
*Rutherglen, Victoria 3685*

Founded in 1858, Chambers is one of the few producers with access to stocks of pre-phylloxera wines – undrinkable in their pure, ultra-concentrated state, but invaluable as blending components. These are glorious wines, with hints of oranges, caramel, butterscotch and coffee, and the Rare Muscat, which contains wines up to 90 years old, is simply magnificent.

### Morris ☆☆☆☆
*Rutherglen, Victoria 3685*

Since 1970 Morris have been owned by Orlando, but the family remains in charge of winemaking. They have the good fortune to own stocks of very old wines, which give considerable weight and lushness to their bottlings. The Old Premium Muscat and Tokay are first-rate.

**Pfeiffer** ☆☆
*Wahgunyah, Victoria 3687*
Chris Pfeiffer, who worked for Lindemans (qv) before establishing this winery in 1986, is aware that as a relative newcomer he lacks the stocks of very old wines and *soleras* that give such richness and backbone to his more established neighbours' wines. But, nevertheless, there is an extensive range of Muscats and Port-styles, and the determination to produce wines of high quality.

**Seppelt** ☆☆☆
*Seppeltsfield, SA 5352*
Seppelt produce a fine Rutherglen Muscat, with a figgy nose, and on the palate rich, peppery and assertive.

**Stanton & Killeen** ☆☆☆
*Rutherglen, Victoria 3685*
This is one of the producers of Muscats that uses the *solera* system as the basis for its blends. The simpler bottlings can be rather aggressive, but the fruitier Premium and Collector's Muscats are richer, though less sweet and concentrated than many others from Rutherglen.

# Western Australia
Some well-aged fortified wines are produced by Talijancich at Herne Hill.

# New Zealand
There have long been fortified wines made here, with the emphasis on alcohol and sweetness more than finesse. "Sauterne" was produced mostly from hybrid varieties and Muscat. There is still a loyal clientele for the old-style fortified wines, some of which are of high quality.

Although fortified wine production is in decline, these old-fashioned wines continue to have a faithful following. Some of these wines, such as those from Mazuran in Auckland, are aged up to 20 years before being offered for sale, so there are Port- and Sherry-style wines of good quality to be found. In addition to Mazuran, other producers include Pleasant Valley (Auckland) and Esk Valley (Hawke's Bay), who still make a Liqueur Muscat.

# South Africa
## The history
South Africa is always seen as New World in its winemaking style, so it's something of a surprise to remind ourselves that wine has been made here since the 1650s. Fortified wine played a part from

the very start: the Dutch settlers were well acquainted with distilling, and the first attempts at winemaking produced wines of such miserable quality that it seems likely that brandy (Dutch *brandtwijn*) would have been added at an early stage.

The first big switch in South African wine came after 1910, when the Union of South Africa, as it then was, became a British colony. As with Cyprus, easy, fast and tax-beneficial access to the markets of the British Empire concentrated the minds of the winemakers, and the biggest items on the market at that time were Sherry and Port. The name "Port" was already protected by British law, but Sherry, in the middle of yet another boom, had failed to register its exclusive rights to the name. So it was that South Africa began shipping fortified wines to Britain under the names "South African Sherry" and "South African Ruby". Low tax rates and a ready market provided early success for both these wines, which were, for the most part, made by the methods used in Jerez and Oporto.

Meanwhile, South Africa was developing its own fortified-wine culture with something called Jerepigo. This is a *mistelle* (in French), in which freshly pressed grape juice is run off into a vessel containing fortifying spirit. No fermentation takes place, but the finished product matures in barrel and takes on a good deal of mellowness as it does so. However, Jerepigo is not widely seen outside South Africa. Another South African speciality is Hanepoot, otherwise known as Muscadel (Muscat of Alexandria). It's made unfortified in some areas (*see* Sweet Wines), but with the easily available "rebate" brandy (grape spirit distilled from excess wine production) fortification has become the norm. As we have seen in other countries, however, the actual amount of fortification may vary from almost none to quite a lot, and the final arbiter will be the winemaker (or the marketing men if the resulting wine is for export to one of those countries where tax rates vary according to alcoholic strength).

The second big switch in South African winemaking came in the 1990s, when the dismantling of apartheid and the coming of democracy meant that South African wineries at last had a chance to compete on equal terms with the rest of the wine world. The wines that are building their new reputation are almost exclusively unfortified and need not detain us here, but the old styles of wine are still available, and very popular within South Africa and in non-European markets. Some of the best are listed below as Port-style (P), Sherry-style (S), Jerepigo (J) and Muscadel (M).

# Principal producers

## Bon Courage, Robertson ☆☆

*PO Box 589, Robertson 6705*

Established in 1984, this firm belongs to the Brouwer family and has a good track record, with several winemaking awards under its corporate belt. Best fortified wine: M Muscadel.

## Boplass, Klein Karoo ☆☆☆

*PO Box 156, Calitzdorp 6660*

Established in 1981, this is a company that specialises in the "Port-type" wines and does it very well. Best fortified wine: P Vintage Reserve.

### De Krans Estate, Klein Karoo ☆☆
*PO Box 28, Calitzdorp 6660*
An old-stager this, specialising in fortified wines in the old Cape styles, and none the worse for that. Best fortified wines: P Vintage Reserve, J wines.

### Glen Carlou, Paarl ☆☆☆
*PO Box 23, Klapmuts 7625*
Another two-family house – Finlayson and Hess, this time with one of the families (that of Donald Hess) in California, enabling distribution and development. Generally very good wines. Best fortified wines: P wines.

### KWV International, Paarl ☆☆
*PO Box 528, Suider-Paarl 7624*
This was the giant cooperative of cooperatives which virtually ran the South African wine business in the years before democracy. It lost its constitutional status in 1995 but today, as a private company, it is still very much the biggest animal in the South African wine zoo. Past ascendancy means that its wines encompass most of the styles of the country. Best fortified wines: P all types.

### Nuy Cooperative, Worcester ☆☆
*PO Box 5225, Worcester 6850*
This is a cooperative winery of good reputation. Best fortified wines: M Muscadel red and white.

### Overgaauw Estate, Stellenbosch ☆☆→☆☆☆
*PO Box 3, Vlottenburg 7604*
Established in 1906, this is a family-owned concern based on a farm owned since the 18th century and credited with producing one of the best South African "Port-type" wines. Best fortified wine: P vintage.

### Robertson Winery, Robertson ☆☆
*PO Box 37, Robertson 6705*
This cooperative is making a name for itself in the dessert-wine market. Best fortified wine: M Muscadel.

### Rooiberg Winery, Robertson ☆☆
*PO Box 358, Robertson 6705*
A rather old-fashioned cooperative which turns out exemplary fortified wines in defiance of fashion. Best fortified wines: M Red Muscadel, J Rooi.

### Rustenberg Estate, Stellenbosch ☆☆
*PO Box 33, Stellenbosch 7600*
Established in 1891, this is a well-respected winery with a long

heritage of quality in all its wines. Although the focus is on new-wave wines, the old style has not been forgotten. Best fortified wines: P wines.

## Twee Jonge Gezellen Estate, Tulbagh ☆☆
*PO Box 16, Tulbagh 6820*

Established in 1947, this belongs to the Krone family, who have farmed here for two centuries. Best fortified wine: M Muscadel.

## Weltevrede Estate, Bonnievale (Robertson) ☆☆
*PO Box 6, Bonnievale 6730*

Established in 1974 and owned by the Jonker family (whence Lourens Jonker, chairman of the KWV), this is a well-respected company producing value-for-money wines. Best fortified wine: M Muscadel red and white.

Fine Muscats come from Douglas (N Cape), Grundheim (Klein Karoo), Jonkheer (Robertson) and Rietvallei (Robertson). Rich Hanepoots are produced by Bergsig (Worcester North), Botha (Worcester) and du Toitskloof (Worcester), and there's a singular Jerepigo made by Rooiberg (Robertson) from fortified Pinotage.

# Maps

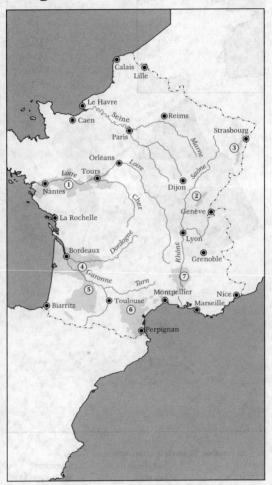

**Key to major French fortified and sweet wine areas:**

| | | |
|---|---|---|
| 1 Loire Valley | 4 Bordeaux | 7 Rhône |
| 2 Savoie and Jura | 5 Southwest | |
| 3 Alsace | 6 Roussillon | |

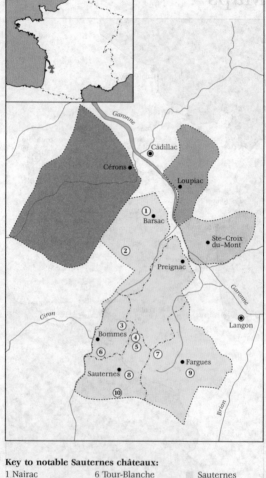

**Key to notable Sauternes châteaux:**

| | | |
|---|---|---|
| 1 Nairac | 6 Tour-Blanche | Sauternes |
| 2 Climens | 7 Rieussec | Ste-Croix-du-Mont |
| 3 Sigalas-Rabaud | 8 Guiraud | Loupiac |
| 4 Raymond-Lafon | 9 Fargues | Cérons |
| 5 Yquem | 10 Filhot | |

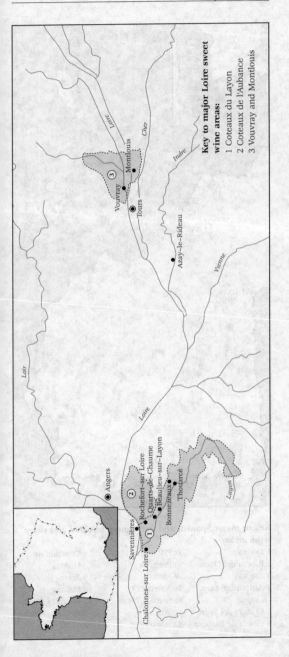

Key to major Loire sweet wine areas:

1 Coteaux du Layon
2 Coteaux de l'Aubance
3 Vouvray and Montlouis

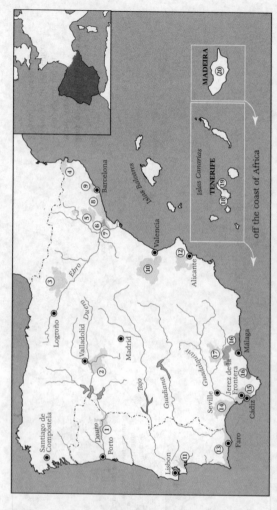

**Key to major Spanish and Portuguese fortified and sweet wine areas:**

1 Douro
2 Ribera del Duero
3 Rioja
4 Ampurdan Costa Brava
5 Costers del Segre
6 Conca de Barbera
7 Priorato
8 Penedès
9 Alella
10 Valencia
11 Setúbal
12 Alicante
13 Algarve
14 Condado de Huelva
15 Jerez
16 Málaga
17 Montilla-Moriles

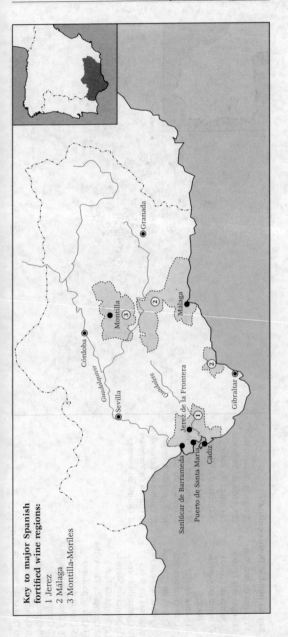

Key to major Spanish
fortified wine regions:
1 Jerez
2 Málaga
3 Montilla-Moriles

**Key to notable Douro quintas:**

1 Quinta de Boa Vista
2 Quinta dos Frades
3 Quinta do Crasto
4 Quinta do Castello Borges
5 Quinta da Foz
6 Quinta do Boavista
7 Quinta do Panascal
8 Quinta do Bom Retiro
9 Quinta do Seixo
10 Quinta do Porto
11 Quinta do Sagrado
12 Quinta da Foz
13 Quinta da Eira Velha
14 Quinta do Junco
15 Quinta do Cavadinha
16 Quinta das Manuelas
17 Quinta do Fojo
18 Quinta do Noval
19 Quinta do Amarela
20 Quinta do Bomfim
21 Quinta da Carvalhas
22 Quinta do Pedrogão
23 Quinta do Roriz
24 Quinta da Vila Velha
25 Quinta Milieu
26 Quinta dos Malvedos
27 Quinta do Tua
28 Quinta da Alegria
29 Quinta da Ferrandosa
30 Quinta da Vargellas
31 Quinta do Vesuvio

**Key to major German sweet wine areas:**

1 Ahr
2 Mittelrhein
3 Mosel-Saar-Ruwer

4 Nahe
5 Rheingau
6 Pfalz

7 Franken
8 Württemberg
9 Baden

**Key to major Italian fortified and sweet wine areas:**

| | | |
|---|---|---|
| 1 Valle d' Aosta | 6 Friuli Venezia- | 11 Marche |
| 2 Piemonte | Giulia | 12 Latium |
| 3 Liguria | 7 Veneto | 13 Calabria |
| 4 Lombardia | 8 Emilia-Romagna | 14 Marsala |
| 5 Trentino | 9 Toscana | 15 Sardegna |
| | 10 Umbria | |

**Key to major
Austrian sweet
wine areas:**
1 Kremstal
2 Wachau
3 Kamptal
4 Weinviertel
5 Thermenregion
6 Neusiedlersee

Linz

Krems

Wien

Donau

Neusiedler See

Mur

Graz

# Part two: sweet wines

There's a paradox about sweet wine: many fervent wine-lovers consider that sweet wines are somehow vulgar and mediocre; at the same time the most expensive wines in the world are sweet, very sweet. It has always been that way. The royal courts of Europe favoured sweet wines above all others: Yquem, Tokaji and very sweet Cristal Champagne took pride of place in St Petersburg, for example.

Of course, there is a distinction between merely sweet wines and great sweet wines. It's not difficult to make sweet wine: all you need is overripe grapes, and in warm regions such as southern Italy such ripeness levels ate obtained routinely. But it takes more than sugar to produce sweet wine of good quality. Mere sweetness can be cloying and flabby; it must be balanced by acidity, to give the wine vigour and freshness. Mineral extract and alcohol can also add to the wine's complexity. All great sweet wine is a balancing act between various factors, of which sweetness, although crucial, is just one.

## How sweet wine is made

There are four basic methods of production. The first method is simple overripeness, the second is to wait for noble rot to concentrate the sugar and acidity within the grapes, the third is to pick healthy bunches and dry them, and the final method is to freeze them.

### Overripeness

Overripeness can produce sweet wine of high quality only if it is balanced by acidity. There are few regions where overripeness alone is sufficient, but one classic example is Jurançon in southwest France. Here the local grape variety, Petit Manseng, has very high natural acidity, which balances the residual sugar. Extreme overripeness, which results in dehydration, is known in France as *passerillage*.

### Noble rot

Noble rot is also known by its Latin name of *Botrytis cinerea*. It is a parasitical fungus of the Ascomycetes family. Its airborne spores are provoked by humidity to attack the skins of the grapes. Thus, very specific climatic conditions are required for noble rot to do its work: a combination of humidity, often in the form of early-morning fog, followed by sunshine that will dry the grapes and deter more destructive forms of rot.

The botrytis spores perforate the grape skin with tiny filaments, and the fungus then spreads beneath the skin into the flesh. The consequences of this are multiple. The skin becomes permeable and turns an unappetising purple-brown colour, and the grape shrivels. In the course of these transformations a number of chemical actions take place. The shrivelling reduces the grape's water content and concentrates the sugar;

glycerol levels also rise; tannins from the skins enter the interior of the grape; and acidity is also concentrated.

But botrytis strikes sporadically, so the harvesters must select only those bunches of grapes that are clearly botrytised, avoiding bunches suffering from other, less desirable moulds that would taint the wine. The practice of selective and repeated harvesting (*tries successives* in French) is crucial to the production of high-quality sweet wine. There are occasions when botrytis can be uniform and widespread, but they are exceptional. In the Loire there are usually three to five *tries*, in Sauternes up to twelve.

Once the grapes for a dry white wine have been picked, the winemaker can choose from a number of different ways to vinify them. But with botrytised fruit, the winemaker's options will have been confirmed by the time the grapes have been picked. It is the chemical processes sparked off by botrytis that will determine the flavour, structure and sugar and acidity levels of the resulting wine. That is why low yields and *tries successives* are so crucial.

After the grapes have been pressed, vinification takes place in tanks or in barrels. The must, rich in flavour and glycerol, usually benefits from fermentation and ageing in barrels. However, the grape variety plays a part too, and high-acidity grapes such as Chenin Blanc and, especially, Riesling do not require barrel-ageing, although it is being used increasingly for Chenin Blanc. Fermentation is usually arrested by the addition of sulphur dioxide or by chilling, either of which will kill off the remaining yeasts. Sometimes fermentation ends without human intervention, once the alcohol has reached a level at which the yeasts die off. Fermentation rarely continues above an alcohol level of 15 degrees, leaving the remaining grape sugar in the wine to give it its sweetness.

Botrytis wines are inevitably expensive. Yields need to be three or four times lower than for great red wine, harvesting is very expensive, and selection will require the costly elimination of unsatisfactory lots.

## Drying grapes

Drying grapes to concentrate sugar content is a procedure that dates back at least to Roman times. It is widespread in Italy, where the technique is known as *appassimento*, and the wines are known as *passito*. The grapes are picked quite early in the season to ensure that bunches are healthy and free from any taint; botrytis is considered undesirable. The bunches are laid on shallow trays or boxes, or suspended from rafters. Good ventilation is crucial, both to assist the drying process and to prevent rot. In very hot regions, the grapes are simply sun-dried and are usually ready for pressing after a few weeks, whereas attic-drying can take five months. During this time the grapes shrivel, lose a great deal of their moisture and volume, and sugar levels rise.

The same techniques are used in France to produce Vin de Paille, and in Austria the grapes are dried on reeds. The principle and consequences remain the same.

### Freezing

A highly effective method of attaining high sugar levels is by freezing the grapes on the vine. This is most commonly encountered in countries such as Germany and Canada, where severe frosts are likely in October or later. Vines selected as candidates for Icewine, as it is called, are often netted or otherwise protected from birds, as the grapes need to be in healthy condition, with no botrytis or other infection, at the time of harvesting. The frost freezes the water content, which is removed in the form of ice during pressing, leaving the must highly concentrated in sugar and acidity.

In some regions producers have sought to duplicate the effects of botrytis or Icewine by artificial methods, such as placing healthy bunches of grapes in a humidified chamber and infusing it with botrytis spores, or by freezing the bunches in a cold chamber. In general the final result is rarely as impressive as a wine made by natural means.

# Sauternes

## The history

The Sauternes region lies within the southern Graves, bordering the River Garonne to the east. There were probably vineyards here in Roman times, but only in the 17th century did the region become known for its sweet wines. By this time it had become routine to harvest in late October, when the grapes would have been overripe, very sweet and quite probably infected by noble rot.

By the 1780s the reputation of Yquem and other Sauternes was already elevated enough to attract the attentions of Thomas Jefferson, then American envoy in Paris. An even greater boost was given to the reputation of Sauternes when Grand Duke Constantine of Russia, bewitched by a taste of 1847 Yquem, paid a small fortune for a large barrel of the wine in 1859.

By this time Sauternes was being made exactly as it is today. Harvesters made repeated forays into the vineyards (*tries successives*) to seek out nobly rotten berries. It was not unusual for the harvest to be prolonged over a two-month period, since botrytis rarely arrives at one time.

Royal patronage and rarity factors, not to mention the exquisite taste of the wine, ensured Sauternes its renown throughout the 19th century and into the 20th. After The First World War its fortunes ebbed. The Russian court had ceased to exist. Edwardian appetites, which enjoyed sweet wines with fish courses, were reined in by austerity and changing tastes. Diseases such as oïdium and phylloxera had devastated the vineyards, which had to be replanted. Prohibition brought exports to the United States to an end during the interwar period. By the time the Second World War was over the region was in serious decline.

It isn't difficult to see why Sauternes is very costly to make. The maximum authorised yield is a mere 25 hectolitres per hectare, and most good estates harvest considerably less. Yquem famously claims that its average yield is some 9 hl/ha. When one compares such production figures with those of the Médoc, where yields of 60 hl/ha are routine, one can easily see that the basic costs of production are far higher in Sauternes than in red wine districts. Moreover, noble rot does not strike every year, and in some years – 1992 and 1993 are recent examples – virtually no wine could be made.

The costs of harvesting by *tries successives* are also extremely high, since harvesters must be well trained and on call for up to two months. Even when the wine is made, it is likely that certain lots must be weeded out for a variety of reasons: insufficient noble rot character, perhaps, or dilution, or a taint of black rot.

By the 1960s and 1970s, however, Sauternes had lost much of its reputation. Prices were low, so many estates began to cut corners. *Tries successives*, where still practised, were less rigorous than before. Costly oak barrels were abandoned in favour of concrete tanks. Grapes were picked well before they had become nobly rotten and then chaptalised by up to two degrees. (Chaptalisation is the addition of sugar to the must, which boosts alcohol levels but contributes nothing to the flavour of the wine. Although light chaptalisation can sometimes improve the finished wine, routine chaptalisation of weak musts results in poorly balanced wines. Top estates such as Yquem never chaptalise, arguing that to do so is to admit viticultural failure.)

In 1976 one proprietor went so far as to uproot his second-growth vineyards at Château Myrat. Other properties increased their production of dry white or even red grapes. Many estates, including Guiraud and Nairac, were sold. Then came the 1983 vintage. There had been great vintages in the 1970s, but only a few exceptional wines were produced. In 1983 almost everyone made good wine, and some estates made great wine. New investments were beginning to pay off. Estates that had abandoned small oak barrels, such as Lafaurie-Peyraguey, had recognised the errors of their ways. The world of wine began to sit up and take notice of Sauternes once again. By the time the next good vintage came around in 1986, standards had improved radically. Prices rose too, allowing proprietors to make long-overdue investments. The decade ended with a trio of glorious vintages: 1988, 1989 and 1990. At long last the region was once again producing magnificent wines of richness, power and complexity. Yet Sauternes seemed condemned to occupy a niche market, partly because this is a special wine that isn't consumed on an everyday basis, and partly because the Sauternes producers could rarely be bothered to promote their wines.

But at least Sauternes is back on the map. Whereas in the 1970s most classified growths were not producing wine remotely worthy of their status, that is emphatically not the case today. Nor is this success limited to the classified growths, as many excellent Crus Bourgeois regularly attain comparably high standards.

# Grapes for Sauternes

Three grape varieties are encountered in Sauternes: Sémillon, Sauvignon Blanc and Muscadelle. Sémillon dominates, favoured for its susceptibility to noble rot and its capacity to produce long-lived wines. Sauvignon Blanc is less prone to botrytis but has higher acidity than Sémillon, and some growers like the freshness it brings to the wine. Muscadelle, prized for its perfume, is in decline, as it succumbs easily to all manner of diseases.

Severe pruning is necessary to ensure that yields are kept very low so that grapes reach full maturity before noble rot appears. The climatic conditions necessary for botrytis to develop are provided by the confluence of the small River Ciron with the larger Garonne. The Ciron is cold, so when its waters flow into the Garonne, mists are generated that swathe the vineyards and activate the botrytis spores.

# How Sauternes is made

After pressing the grapes, most good estates will ferment the juice in *barriques*. In a good vintage, the botrytised grapes will have a potential alcohol level of 19–21 degrees. Most châteaux like a final alcohol level of about 14 degrees, the remaining potential alcohol expressed as residual sugar. On the other hand, there are vintages where grapes need to be picked at about 15 degrees, which is insufficient to make Sauternes of distinction. The estate can either sell off the wine to wholesalers and cut its losses or it can try to muddle through by chaptalising the wine by up to two degrees. Successive harvesting means that there will be many separate lots, which must gradually be blended, with unsatisfactory barrels eliminated from the blend.

There is considerable controversy over the technology, developed in Bordeaux in the 1980s, known as cryo-extraction. Simply put, cryo-extraction employs a sealed chamber that can be chilled to a very low temperature. It was widely adopted by many estates, including Yquem. Its most obvious use is in rainy vintages, when botrytised grapes become diluted. Chilling freezes the water content, which can be removed easily in the form of ice, thus in effect returning the grapes to their pre-rainfall condition. Cryo-extraction can't turn poor fruit into good; instead, it can save a proportion of the crop that might otherwise prove unusable.

In rainy but otherwise healthy vintages such as 1987, cryo-extraction undoubtedly had its uses. Some critics argue that it can alter the balance of the finished wine. The present consensus appears to be that cryo-extraction is helpful in wet vintages, but must be used with care, and that only a small proportion of the wine should be made from cryo-extracted juice.

# Communes and classifications

Five communes, encompassing 2,100 hectares of vineyards, are entitled to the Sauternes appellation: Sauternes itself, Bommes, Fargues, Preignac and Barsac. Claims are made for distinct difference in character between communes, but in practice only Barsac emerges as truly distinctive. The wines from the commune of

Sauternes are often the richest of the region, sumptuous but some-times lacking finesse. Those from Bommes tend to be a touch fresher than those of Sauternes, although they can be very similar. Fargues is cooler, and the grapes often ripen later. Preignac, which borders Bommes and Sauternes, has extremely varied soils. The wines from Barsac are often marked by a greater freshness and by citrus flavours, possibly derived from the limestone subsoil. Despite its seeming lightness, Barsac can be the most long-lived.

The vineyards, like those of the Médoc, were classified in 1855. There have been minor modifications to this classification, as some properties have been amalgamated or divided. But despite the passage of almost 150 years the classification has remained essentially intact. Château d'Yquem, uniquely, is given its own supreme status as a Premier Grand Cru. The other Premiers Crus, in alphabetical order, are Climens, Clos Haut-Peyraguey, Coutet, Guiraud, Lafaurie-Peyraguey, Rabaud-Promis, Rayne-Vigneau, Rieussec, Sigalas-Rabaud, Suduiraut and La Tour Blanche. The Deuxièmes Crus are d'Arche, Broustet, Caillou, Doisy-Daëne, Doisy-Dubroca, Doisy-Védrines, Filhot, Lamothe, Lamothe-Guignard, de Malle, Myrat, Nairac, Romer du Hayot and Suau.

## Best vintages
The best recent vintages for Sauternes have been 1975, 1976, 1980, 1983, 1986, 1988–90 and 1996–98.

## Principal producers
### Château d'Arche ☆☆
*Sauternes, 33210 Langon*
This ancient property has been leased by Pierre Perromat since the early 1980s. The wine is aged in barriques, of which about 40 per cent are new. His initial vintages were impressive, bold and richly lush but rather high in alcohol. More recent vintages have been better balanced if lacking in complexity.

### Château d'Armajan-des-Ormes ☆
*Preignac, 33210 Langon*
This 15-hectare estate produces a powerful, quite alcoholic wine, which is usually chaptalised - a pity. In top vintages a Crème de Tête is made. The standard bottling is sound and dependable.

### Château Bastor-Lamontagne ☆☆
*Preignac, 33210 Langon*
This ancient property was acquired by the Crédit Foncier bank in 1936, and has been impeccably run. Yields are quite high, but the wine is well made none the less, extremely reliable and relatively inexpensive. It is aged for 18 months in *barriques*, of which 25 per cent are new. The wines of the late 1990s have been exceptional.

### Château Broustet ☆☆
*Barsac, 33720 Podensac*
This estate belonged to the Fournier family of Château Canon in St-Émilion until 1994, when family squabbles forced its sale. The

wine was usually tank-fermented, and Fournier liked a good deal of alcohol in Broustet, maintaining that this was the traditional style in Barsac. Be that as it may, the wine often seemed unbalanced and lacked charm and succulence. The new proprietor is Didier Laulan of neighbouring Château St-Marc. He has given Broustet some additional vigour and spice.

### Château Caillou ☆
*Barsac, 33720 Podensac*

Since 1909 this estate has been owned by the enthusiastic Bravo family, but the wine was often disappointing. The must is fermented in steel tanks and aged in 20 per cent new oak. There are two cuvées. The better of the two, a selection of the most botrytised lots and produced only in top vintages, was known until 1975 as Crème de Tête but is now labelled Private Cuvée, and given longer ageing in oak. The regular bottling is usually quite lean and fresh but lacks richness and complexity.

### Château Cantegril ☆
*Barsac, 33720 Podensac*

A 16-hectare property owned by the Dubourdieus of Doisy-Daëne (*see* entry), its wine is made in the same way as the Deuxième Cru. A good, straightforward, reliable and inexpensive Barsac.

### Château Climens ☆☆☆☆
*Barsac, 33720 Podensac*

There is not much to see at Climens: a long, low, white building with perfunctory towers at either end and a row of shuttered windows occasionally opened to provide ventilation for the *chai* (cellar). However, Climens effortlessly produces one of the great wines of the region. In 1971 the property was bought by Lucien Lurton and is run by his daughter Bérénice. Christian Broustaut has been making the wines since 1969.

The vineyards are mostly in a single parcel and occupy the highest land in Barsac, which is not saying much. But the vines, all Sémillon, are old and the drainage excellent. The wine spends up to two years in *barriques*. Between one-third and two-thirds new oak is used, and youthful Climens can taste quite oaky.

Broustaut has the knack of turning out fine wines even in vintages that other estates find problematic. In 1973 and 1991, for example, Climens excelled. When quality is not up to standard, the wine is bottled under the second label, Les Cyprès de Climens, as in 1984, 1992 and 1993. It takes a few years for Climens to acquire its complexity. When young, it is fresh and appealing but seems to lack richness. But after ten years that richness and structure do emerge, yet the wine retains its elegance and verve. Many consider that, after Yquem, Climens is the finest wine of the region. It is hard to disagree.

### Château Clos Haut-Peyraguey ☆☆☆
*Bommes, 33210 Langon*

This small property once formed part of Château Lafaurie-

Peyraguey (*see* entry) but became detached in 1879 after a family squabble. In 1914 it came into the hands of the Pauly family. Until the late 1980s Clos Haut-Peyraguey was well made but light and relatively one-dimensional. Jacques Pauly realised that changes were needed and since 1989 has employed more barrel-fermentation and more new oak. The improvement has been marked, and the wine has shown greater intensity and elegance while retaining its pineappley freshness and vigour.

## Château Coutet ☆☆☆

*Barsac, 33720 Podensac*

Coutet already existed as an estate in the early 17th century, and Thomas Jefferson declared Coutet to be finest of all Barsacs. In the late 1970s the estate was bought by the industrialist Marcel Baly.

The must is barrel-fermented in new oak, but with each racking the wine is put back into older barrels, until for the final six months of the ageing process it is returned to new oak. Coutet is light in colour when young and doesn't exhibit much force or weight. Yet the wine is elegant and can age for decades. Until the late 1980s Coutet could be disappointing, but since 1989 it has been showing more verve and complexity.

In good vintages Coutet releases a luxury *cuvée* called Cuvée Madame. A particular parcel is set aside each year in the hope that it will succumb fully to botrytis. A mere 1,600 bottles are produced. Not surprisingly, the wine is very expensive, but it can rival Yquem in certain vintages.

## Cru Barréjats ☆☆☆

*Mareuil, 33210 Pujols*

Only three hectares are planted here, close to Château Climens (*see* entry), and the first vintage was in 1990, but it was a sensational debut. Dr Mireille Daret and Philippe Anduran spared no effort or cost, fermenting their wine entirely in new oak. The resulting wine is intense and very oaky but of very high quality.

## Château Doisy-Daëne ☆☆☆

*Barsac, 33720 Podensac*

Owned by the Dubourdieu family since 1924, Doisy-Daëne is made by a man who admits he doesn't much like Sauternes. Pierre Dubourdieu, one of nature's iconoclasts, is a wizard at dry white winemaking and relishes elegance and vivacity above all else. So although he practises selective harvesting, his vinification is aimed at preserving the wine's vigour. He detests chaptalisation and high alcohol and prefers cryo-extraction as a means of concentrating the fruit.

The outcome is always a wine of remarkable finesse and longevity, a pure Sémillon that is racy, charming and exceptionally pure in flavour. Pierre Dubourdieu likes to experiment, and he once produced a Vin de Noël from grapes harvested during Christmas 1978, and in 1990, 1996 and 1997 made "L'Extravagance" from grapes picked at a must weight of 42 degrees rather than the usual 20 or 21!

### Château Doisy-Dubroca ☆☆
*Barsac, 33720 Podensac*

This tiny four-hectare property has been run since 1997 by Louis Lurton. Before then the wine was made by Christian Broustaut of Climens (*see* entry). With a minute production of only 9,000 bottles, the wine is rarely encountered. Less powerful or complex than Climens, it is a true Barsac none the less, lean and elegant.

### Château Doisy-Védrines ☆☆☆
*Barsac, 33720 Podensac*

The Castéjas are a celebrated Bordeaux négociant family, and Pierre Castéja has lived at this fine 27-hectare property since 1947. Thanks to old vines, scrupulously selective harvesting and a very high proportion of new oak, Doisy-Védrines is the most opulent of the three Doisy wines. It is now one of the most reliable, if least typical, of all Barsacs.

### Château de Fargues ☆☆☆☆
*Fargues, 33210 Langon*

The gaunt ruins of this castle, gutted in 1687, are the ancestral home of the Lur-Saluces family (*see* Château d'Yquem). The harvesting and winemaking follow the strict guidelines established by Yquem. Yields are exceedingly low, averaging 7.5 hl/ha. However the *terroir* is not exceptional, which is why the Yquem team always insist that, however attractive Fargues may be in its youth, Yquem will eventually emerge as the greater wine. The major difference between the two wines is that Fargues is aged in one-year-old *barriques*. It's a great wine in its own right: extremely concentrated, tightly structured, quite oaky and long-lived.

### Château Filhot ☆
*Sauternes, 33210 Langon*

No proprietor knows more about the history of Sauternes than Henri de Vaucelles, who has lived at this splendid château since 1974. So it always seems odd that the wine is usually mediocre. Thomas Jefferson thought highly of the wine in 1787, but the estate had become very run down by the time the Vaucelles, descendants of the Lur-Saluces clan (*see* Château d'Yquem), arrived. Henri de Vaucelles is no fan of barrel-ageing, so Filhot usually lacks richness and complexity. It is not a bad wine; it just could be so much better, as occasional successful vintages confirm.

### Château Gilette ☆☆☆
*Preignac, 33210 Langon*

This is the most eccentric of all Sauternes estates. Its five hectares have been owned by the Médéville family of Château Les Justices (see entry) for over two centuries. The wine is fermented in tanks, then left in epoxy resin-lined concrete vats for 15 to 20 years. Any wine not considered up to the Gilette standards is either sold off or blended with Les Justices.

Christian Médéville claims this strange production method gives him a large stock of mature wines to offer his clients. This is true, but since the wine is very expensive, it is clear that Médéville, quite justifiably, charges for his ageing policy. And might the wine not be even better if it were oak-aged and bottled after a few years? Be that as it may, Gilette can be a most impressive wine, quite alcoholic and high-powered but with opulent marmalade and peach flavours.

## Château Guiraud ☆☆☆
*Sauternes, 33210 Langon*

Scandalously neglected during the 1940s and 1950s, Guiraud was bought by the Canadian ship-owner Frank Narby in 1981. He made huge investments in the 85-hectare property, which has long been directed by Xavier Planty. Guiraud has a much higher proportion of Sauvignon Blanc than most other Sauternes châteaux, and this, says Planty, gives the wine a subtle smokiness. By the early 1990s all the wine was being barrel-fermented, and in top vintages it is aged in 50 per cent new oak.

Guiraud is a super-rich wine with almost tarry botrytis tones that can come perilously close to oxidation. The best, however, is yet to come, as many vines are still young. Guiraud can lack elegance but certainly offers a rich mouthful of wine.

## Château Haut-Bergeron ☆☆☆
*Preignac, 33210 Langon*

The Lamothe family own 22 hectares in various communes, with vines of an average age of over 50 years. They are strong believers in late harvesting, so the wine is deep-coloured, rich and luscious. Sold mostly to private clients, it is less well-known than its outstanding quality deserves.

## Château Les Justices ☆☆
*Preignac, 33210 Langon*

The Médévilles of Château Gilette (*see* entry) make a reliable Sauternes from this property close to the River Garonne. Since 1985 the wine has been aged in *barriques*, of which one-third are new. Yields are quite high, so the wine can lack intensity, but at its best it is stylish and balanced.

## Château Lafaurie-Peyraguey ☆☆☆☆
*Bommes, 32210 Langon*

In 1917 this charming medieval property was acquired by the well-known Bordeaux firm of Cordier. Standards had slipped by the 1970s, but Cordier realised the error of their ways, and since the early 1980s the wines have once again been excellent.

Michel Laporte, the resident winemaker since 1981, is fanatical about selective harvesting and often succeeds in producing wines with a clear botrytis character in the most troublesome vintages, such as 1984, 1987 and 1991. Since 1985 Laporte has aged the wine is 50 per cent new oak for up to 22 months. The second wine is La Chapelle de Lafaurie.

The Lafaurie style blends richness with finesse, and the oakiness is quite marked but always integrated. The result is extremely stylish, enjoyable relatively young but capable of being bottle-aged for many years.

### Château Lamothe ☆
*Sauternes, 33210 Langon*

The Lamothe estate was divided in the late-19th century, and since 1961 the Despujols family have owned this portion. Yields are quite high, and the wines are fermented and aged in large vats as well as mostly older *barriques*. Until 1990 the wine was mediocre, but the installation of Guy Despujols as winemaker saw a slight improvement in quality.

### Château Lamothe-Guignard ☆☆
*Sauternes, 33210 Langon*

After the disposal of Château Lamothe (*see* entry) to the Despujols family, the remaining section was sold to the Guignard brothers, Philippe and Jacques, in 1981. The brothers renovated the property, and initial vintages were promising. The wine is aged in oak for up to 15 months, the proportion of new wood varying according to the vintage. This is rarely a luscious wine, but in good years it shows delicious fruit and fine concentration.

### Château de Malle ☆☆☆
*Preignac, 33210 Langon*

The Comtesse de Bournazel and her children inhabit this loveli-est of Sauternes châteaux. Her late husband, who was related to the Lur-Saluces family (*see* Château d'Yquem), inherited the estate in the 1950s. After his death in 1985, his widow and son have run the property with energy and panache. Not until 1988 did the wine begin to improve in quality. Previously dilute and heavily sulphured, de Malle is now a rich, lively and often very exciting Sauternes.

### Château de Myrat ☆☆
*Barsac, 33720 Podensac*

The ancestors of the owners of Myrat, the de Pontac family, once owned Haut-Brion and were major players in Bordeaux. In 1976 Comte Maximilien de Pontac, fed up with low prices for his wines, uprooted his vineyards. After Maximilien's death in 1988, his heirs took the brave decision to replant. Their timing, alas, was dreadful, as the initial vintages were plagued by frost and black rot. Winemaking is classic, with fermentation in barrels, of which half are new. It is too early to see the true potential of Myrat, but recent vintages have shown promise.

### Château Nairac ☆☆☆☆
*Barsac, 33720 Podensac*

Nairac has been in existence since the 17th century, but the wine, rarely bottled under the château name, remained little known until 1971, when the estate was bought by Nicole Tari and her

American husband Tom Heeter. Heeter soon revived Nairac's reputation, producing a series of splendid, if rather oaky, wines, even from mediocre vintages. An acrimonious divorce sent the estate through a bad patch in the late 1980s. In 1993 the Heeters' son Nicolas took over as winemaker, proving himself every bit as dedicated as his father, with scrupulous selective harvesting and a ruthless selection process. Nairac, like Climens (*see* entry), continues to excel in tricky vintages, such as 1994, and the wines of the late 1990s have been of the highest quality.

## Château Piada ☆☆
*Barsac, 33720 Podensac*
This nine-hectare estate, long underrated, lies close to Coutet (*see* entry). Yields are fairly low, chaptalisation is rare, and the wine has long been fermented and aged in *barriques*, of which about 25 per cent are new. This is a classic Barsac, with freshness, vigour and a refreshing citrus edge.

## Château Rabaud-Promis ☆☆
*Bommes, 33210 Langon*
Once the single estate known as Château Rabaud, it was divided in 1903, briefly reunited from 1929 to 1952, then divided again, the other section being Château Sigalas-Rabaud (*see* entry). Philippe Dejean owns the property and has radically improved the quality of the wine, which was dire in the 1970s. Since 1989 the entire production is barrel-fermented in about one-third new oak. After a year in wood, the wine completes its maturation in steel tanks, as Dejean is keen to retain the freshness of the wine, which often has a flavour of dried apricots.

## Château Raymond-Lafon ☆☆☆☆
*Sauternes, 33210 Langon*
In 1972 this property, close to Yquem and Sigalas-Rabaud (*see* entries), was bought by Yquem's long-time winemaker, Pierre Meslier. He always claimed that Raymond-Lafon was produced in the same way as Yquem, and in general that was true: very low yields and lengthy ageing in mostly new oak. The style is powerful and oaky, and it takes a few years for the solid rich fruit to emerge from its coating of oak and tannin. But patience will be rewarded, and, as at so many other leading Sauternes estates, the Mesliers have also produced superb wines in mediocre vintages. The 1983 has not, however, aged well.

## Château Rayne-Vigneau ☆☆☆
*Bommes, 33210 Langon*
Rayne-Vigneau is one of the largest Sauternes properties. In 1971 the estate was acquired by the *négociant* house of Mestrezat, which invested heavily in both the vineyards and the winery. The vines are planted on a hill, and many consider the estate's soil and exposition to be the finest after Yquem (*see* entry)itself. If Rayne-Vigneau has yet to reach the top level, it may be because the vines are still relatively young. Patrick Eymery, the genial

director, separates the youngest vines and those planted at the base of the hill and relegates them to the second wine, Clos l'Abeilley. Only part of the must is fermented in barrels, although the entire wine is barrel-aged in fifty per cent new oak for up to two years.

The style is fresh and graceful rather than rich and heavy. The wine, poor throughout the 1960s and 1970s, made a fine recovery in 1983. But it was in 1988 that a real leap in quality was made, and since then Rayne-Vigneau has been exemplary, showing tremendous vigour, integrated oak and dazzling fruit.

### Château Rieussec ☆☆☆☆
*Fargues, 33210 Langon*

Since 1984 Rieussec has been one of the properties owned by the Lafite-Rothschild group, under the overall direction of Charles Chevallier. Previously Rieussec was run by Albert Vuillier, and production was patchy, although he made some splendid wines in 1971 and 1983. Since 1988 Chevallier has been ageing the wine for up to two years in oak, and there has been a stricter selection of grapes.

Under Vuillier Rieussec gained an image as a fat, dark, raisiny, voluptuous wine, but under the Lafite team the style has become more slender and elegant, which, they assert, is a return to the authentic Rieussec style. With its generosity of fruit and immediate appeal, Rieussec is deservedly popular, and in recent vintages has usually been in the very top league.

### Château Rolland ☆
*Barsac, 33720 Podensac*

Owned by the Guignard family since 1971, this 13-hectare estate has more potential than the wines show at present. Grown on well-drained soil on the Barsac plateau, the grapes are fermented in tanks but aged in *barriques*. In top vintages Rolland can show a surprising degree of peachy richness and unctuosity.

### Château Romer du Hayot, Château Guiteronde ☆
*Barsac, 33720 Podensac*

The château was demolished years ago, so this wine is produced at another of André du Hayot's properties, Château Guiteronde. The vineyards are close to Suduiraut (*see* entry). M du Hayot takes an unashamedly commercial approach, so this is not a Sauternes of great distinction. Yields are quite high and only part of the production is oak-aged. Although the wine lacks concentration, it is soundly made and relatively inexpensive.

### Château St-Amand ☆☆
*Preignac, 33210 Langon*

For decades this charming property was run by Louis Ricard, and after his retirement in the early 1990s his daughter took over. Ricard never wanted an over-botrytised wine, so yields were quite high and *triage* limited. The wine spent only six months in *barriques*, being aged mostly in tanks. St-Amand has always been attractive none the less, a light fruity wine of considerable elegance. In some markets the wine is labelled Château de la Chartreuse.

### Château Sigalas-Rabaud ☆☆☆☆
*Bommes, 32210 Langon*

At 14 hectares, this is the smallest of the Premiers Crus. In 1982 Comte Emanuel de Lambert des Granges took over running the estate, and despite a very laid-back approach produced many fresh and delicious wines, ageing them in tanks as well as in barrels. Even in lesser vintages, such as 1991, Comte Emanuel managed to produce an exquisite wine. But in 1995 he gave up the struggle and leased the estate to the Cordier company, which already owned Lafaurie-Peyraguey (*see* entry). Cordier immediately applied the same techniques and resources that had made such a success of Lafaurie. Under Michel Laporte's direction the vintages of the late 1990s have been dazzling.

### Château Simon ☆☆
*Barsac, 33720 Podensac*

For five generations the Dufour family have run this well-managed estate. The wine is aged in *barriques*, of which a small proportion are new, except in the richest vintages such as 1989 and 1990, when more new oak was used. Those great vintages also persuaded M. Dufour to produce special *cuvées* aged entirely in new oak. Given the fairly high yields and limited oak-ageing, quality is quite high.

### Château Suau ☆
*Illats, 33720 Podensac*

The vineyards of this most obscure of classed-growth Barsacs lie just south of the village. Only in the 1990s was oak-ageing introduced, and there has been a slight improvement in the quality of what used to be a very dull wine. Suau remains relatively simple and grapey but can be enjoyable.

### Château Suduiraut ☆☆☆
*Preignac, 33210 Langon*

The stately château is surrounded by gardens designed by Le Nôtre, who laid out the park at Versailles. The absentee Fonquernie family sold the property in 1992 to the insurance company AXA, which already owned great properties elsewhere in Bordeaux.

Suduiraut acquired an elevated reputation for its rich, boldly flavoured wines. In the 1980s harvesting tended to be earlier than it should have been, resulting in some disappointing wines. In addition, there was frequent chaptalisation and little barrel-fermentation. All that has now changed, and the winemaking is of a high order.

At its best, as in 1989 and 1990, Suduiraut is lustrous gold and rich in botrytis. In some exceptional years, such as 1989, Suduiraut gilds the lily by releasing a Crème de Tête, a lot selection aged in new oak. Here indeed is a wine that can rival Yquem itself. Since 1993 there has been a second wine, Castelnau de Suduiraut. The vintages of the late 1990s have been sound rather than exceptional.

## Château La Tour Blanche ☆☆☆☆
*Bommes, 32210 Langon*

In 1855 La Tour Blanche was given pride of place after Yquem in the famous classification. Yet the wine was mediocre until the arrival in 1983 of Jean-Pierre Jausserand as the estate's dynamic director. He discontinued chaptalisation, so only fully ripe and botrytised grapes are selected. He is also keen on new oak, and in the 1989 vintage the entire crop was aged in new wood. More recently this enthusiasm for wood has been slightly moderated. Jausserand has raised the quality of the wine to a very high level. At its splendid best, La Tour Blanche is powerful and richly flavoured, clearly marked by oak, with striking nuances of pineapple and apricots.

## Château d'Yquem ☆☆☆☆
*Sauternes, 32210 Langon*

The pre-eminence of Yquem, recognised long before the 1855 classification, is not mere hype. This is the supreme Sauternes. The fortified château lords it over the landscape, and its location is directly related to the quality of its wines. The château came into the hands of the Sauvage d'Eyquem family in 1593, and in 1785 its heiress married the Comte de Lur-Saluces, proprietor of Château de Fargues (*see* entry). The marriage of the young Marquis de Lur-Saluces in 1807 brought a number of other properties, notably Filhot and Coutet (*see* entries), into the family fold. In 1968 Alexandre de Lur-Saluces took over the reins and maintained the very highest standards. In 1996 the luxury goods group LVMH made its bid to add Yquem to its portfolio of properties. After a prolonged battle, LVMH secured Yquem but agreed that Comte Alexandre should remain in place as Yquem's director. So it seems unlikely that Yquem's admirers need fear any diminution of quality under the new regime.

Yquem is rightly famous for the rigour of its harvesting, employing up to 130 pickers. But that alone does not explain Yquem's supremacy, which stems from its 111 hectares of vineyards. These are planted on all sides of the hillock crowned by the fortress, and these varied exposures and soil types give the winemakers at Yquem a large palette from which to compose their final blend.

All the wine is fermented and aged in new *barriques* for three and a half years. As there is no second wine at Yquem, any unsatisfactory lots are sold off to wholesalers. In difficult vintages such as 1973 and 1978 Yquem sold off 85 per cent of the crop; in 1992 no wine was bottled at all.

Since the 1970s everything bottled under the Yquem label has been excellent, even in lesser vintages such as 1984. Time and again Yquem emerges in blind tastings as the finest Sauternes of all, although nowadays a few other estates can rival its sublime quality. Yquem can sometimes taste very oaky in its youth, but the wood is thoroughly integrated into the wine, and as it ages it loses its overt oaky tones. Although rich, Yquem is rarely heavy, thanks to its fine acidity; none the less it is the wine's sumptuousness and unctuosity that make the initial impression on the palate, but it is its elegance and length of flavour that mark it out as altogether exceptional.

If, from time to time, other châteaux perform almost as well as Yquem, it is because their standards have improved, not because Yquem's have declined.

# Other sweet wines of Bordeaux

In addition to Sauternes and Barsac, the other appellations dedicated to sweet-wine production in Bordeaux are Cérons, just north of Barsac, and, on the other side of the River Garonne, Cadillac, the Premières Côtes de Bordeaux and Cadillac, Ste-Croix-du-Mont and Loupiac. The best vintages are similar to those in Sauternes.

## Cérons

Cérons is in effect a northerly extension of Barsac. Yields for Cérons are higher: 40hl/ha. The other difference is that any Sauternes vinified dry is entitled only to the lowly Bordeaux appellation, whereas Cérons vinified dry may be sold as Graves. Since Graves fetches a decent price nowadays, and since yields for a dry white are generous, this regulation acts as a powerful disincentive to produce Cérons. But the potential for high-quality sweet wine is beyond question. A century ago a good Cérons was regarded as equivalent in quality to a second-growth Sauternes. But production is feeble, at about 300,000 bottles.

A major debate is going on between two leading producers. Jean Perromat, owner of the Château de Cérons, favours lowering the yields to 25 hl/ha. Olivier Lataste of the Grand Enclos au Château de Cérons agrees with this but has also resumed labelling his dry white as Cérons, claiming that he is merely reviving an old tradition. To Perromat this is the desecration of a famous name that should be reserved for sweet wines only; to Lataste this is the only way to salvage the reputation of a wine that, if present trends continue, may soon be extinct. Who is right? Only time will tell.

### PRINCIPAL PRODUCERS
#### Château de Cérons ☆☆☆
*33720 Cérons*
The imposing white-haired Jean Perromat has been making wine here for well over 50 years, and crusades ardently for the merits of Cérons. As a major producer of Graves, Perromat bottles only a small quantity of his crop as Cérons, usually about 16,000 bottles. It's a rich yellow-gold wine, lush and creamy, aged in *barriques* of varying ages. Yields never exceed 25 hectolitres, so the wine always has good concentration and a rich palette of flavours.

### Château Chantegrive ☆☆
*33720 Podensac*

Best known as a Graves producer, Chantegrive also releases in exceptional years an elegant and distinctly oaky Cérons.

### Clos Bourgelat ☆
*33720 Cérons*

The genial Dominique Lafosse takes a hard-headed attitude towards Cérons. In years when botrytis arrives early, he produces a sweet wine. If noble rot is tardy, he doesn't wait, preferring to make the entire crop as a dry wine. None was released in 1997, but both 1996 and 1998 are of good quality. Mostly vinified in tanks, the wines are simple, fresh and stylish, and best drunk young.

### Château des Deux Moulins ☆☆
*33720 Illats*

The modest M Pastol uses only his oldest vines for Cérons and does not produce the wine every year. When he does the result is a sweet, succulent unoaked wine with a suggestion of boiled sweets.

### Château de l'Emigré ☆
*33720 Cérons*

The Despujols family produce a wide range of wines and inaugurated a Cérons only in 1997. Most of it is sold to supermarkets under the label of Château de Valdor, but the small quantity bottled as l'Emigré is aged in *barriques* and of higher quality, being lush and fruity if not enormously concentrated.

### Grand Enclos au Château de Cérons ☆☆☆
*33720 Cérons*

Olivier Lataste is best known for his elegant dry wines, but his Cérons can be excellent. Since 1988 he has been barrel-fermenting the wine, with varying proportions of new oak. These are the most sophisticated wines of Cérons, spicy, elegant and discreetly oaky. Lataste waited too long in 1997 and 1998 and lost his crop, but the 1995 and 1996 are fine, as are the quartet from 1988 to 1991.

### Château Haura ☆
*33720 Illats*

A change of generations here meant that hardly any wine was made here between 1990 and 1996. In 1997 Bernard Leppert resumed production. At present the wine is unoaked and unremarkable, but in 1999 he hopes to initiate some barrel-ageing. In exceptional vintages Haura produces a Cuvée Madame, from its most botrytised fruit.

### Château Huradin ☆☆
*33720 Cérons*

Approximately 6,000 bottles of Cérons are produced here. The wine is unoaked and can lack concentration, but the fruit quality is fine, and in years such as 1996 the botrytis is clearly detectable.

# Ste-Croix du Mont

Probably the most important of the Bordeaux sweet-wine appellations after Sauternes and Barsac, its 450 hectares lie on a plateau above the cliffs that rise from the banks of the Garonne. Close up, one can see how the subsoil is composed of fossil deposits, which line the walls of the grottoes and cellars dug into the cliff.

Not surprisingly, there is a high limestone content underlying the mostly clay topsoil. But the soil structure is very varied, with parts of the plateau being stony, while other sectors are less rich in limestone and heavier in clay. Noble rot is less frequent here than in Sauternes, but it does arrive with reasonable frequency. Frost is rarely severe, and a fresh wind often dries the grapes after unwelcome rain showers in the autumn. Harvesting is manual.

Until a decade ago most growers, discouraged by low prices, could scarcely afford to practise the kind of viticulture that was necessary to ensure high-quality botrytised grapes. In the absence of good grapes it was hardly worth bothering with good-quality oak barrels either. Fortunately a few determined estates, aware that in the past Ste-Croix had made great wines, opted for quality and have succeeded in producing some striking wines, especially since 1990.

The maximum yield here is a generous 40 hl/ha, but the more conscientious growers voluntarily impose a self-discipline almost as rigorous as that found in Sauternes. However, wholesale prices for the wine are just over half those of Sauternes, so this emphasis on quality can be costly.

The top estates know that unless their wine is first-rate, the appellation will fade away. There is little market, internationally, for the feeble, sulphury sweet wines once ubiquitous here. It will no longer do to pick slightly overripe grapes with little serious selection, chaptalise to the maximum and hope for the best. The top estates here, whatever their winemaking choices, have demonstrated how good the wines of Ste-Croix can be, and theirs is the path that the others must surely follow.

## PRINCIPAL PRODUCERS

### Château des Coulinats ☆
*33410 Cadillac*

Camille Brun's principal estates are in the Premières Côtes. In Ste-Croix he has four hectares, from which he produces a rich, fruity unoaked wine. M. Brun favours a full-throttle style, with high alcohol and marmalade flavours, which can add up to an overpowering mouthful.

### Château Crabitan-Bellevue ☆☆
*33410 Cadillac*

The Solane family cultivates 33 hectares of vines, of which 20 are in Ste-Croix. The regular Ste-Croix is unoaked and unexceptional, but in good vintages Solane produces a Cuvée Spéciale aged in *barriques*, with a sizeable proportion of new oak. These special bottlings can be excellent, rich and smoky.

## Château Grand Peyrot
*See* Château La Grave

## Château La Grave ☆☆☆
*33410 Cadillac*

The Tinon family own La Grave and lease Château Grand Peyrot. The two estates, and wines, are markedly different. La Grave is planted on clay and gravel, while Grand Peyrot is on a limestone subsoil and has older vines. Both wines are aged in tank, although there is also a barrique-aged bottling from La Grave in outstanding vintages. M. Tinon is keen on cryo-extraction, which he regards as a preferable alternative to chaptalisation. It took him a few years to master barrique-ageing, but from 1988 the oaked bottling has been very fine.

## Château Loubens ☆☆☆
*33410 Cadillac*

This fine property, with its outstanding vineyards, is perched on the cliff-top overlooking the Garonne. Galleries punched into the cliff face used to contain the estate's store of barrels, but Arnaud de Sèze gave up oak-ageing his wines years ago. Given the excellence of his sumptuous, orangey, long-lived wine, one can only regret that he doesn't give them the further accolade of serious oak-ageing. The second wine is Château des Tours.

## Château des Mailles ☆
*33410 Cadillac*

The Larrieu family cultivates 12.5 hectares of vines, including some parcels over a century old. But yields are high, and the wine ages in a rotation of tanks and barrels. In top vintages Larrieu produces a Réserve Personelle, which shows the power and richness of which these vineyards are capable.

## Château Les Marcottes ☆
*33410 Cadillac*

Gérard Cigana's large estate includes 20 hectares within Ste-Croix. Yields are high and the wine is not especially distinguished, although the Prestige bottling, made in top vintages, is aged in older barrels from Yquem and shows more finesse.

## Château du Pavillon ☆☆
*33410 Cadillac*

This well-located property, with an abundance of very old vines, was bought in 1994 by physicist Alain Fertal. Great importance is attached to the harvesting, with Fertal's team going through the vineyards as often as six times. The winemaking is non-interventionist, and the wine is aged in tanks for up to 22 months. The result is a rich, powerful style with considerable finesse.

## Château La Rame ☆☆☆
*33410 Cadillac*

For some years this estate has been the appellation's most serious producer. Yves Armand is an enthusiast for cryo-extraction, although its use entails a loss of volume. His best lots of wine are aged for a year in *barriques*, of which one-third are new, but they are made only in top years. This oaked *cuvée*, the Réserve du Château, is often the finest wine of the appellation, oaky, stylish and sleekly structured.

# Loupiac

Loupiac borders the River Garonne and lies northwest of Ste-Croix-du-Mont. As in Ste-Croix, the maximum yield is 40 hl/ha, and grapes must be harvested manually. The soil is equally varied, with clay and limestone soils to the east, and a subsoil of clay and gravel on the plateau; closer to the river the soil is predictably alluvial. About 410 hectares are dedicated to sweet-wine production, and some 50 properties bottle their own wine.

Loupiac has been beset by the same problems as Ste-Croix, with a vicious circle of lack of demand leading to low prices, and low prices leading to falling standards of wine production. Fortunately, some producers are seeking to halt this trend. In terms of quality-conscious producers, Ste-Croix seems to have the edge, although wholesale prices in Loupiac are slightly higher. There is no unanimity about the authentic style of Loupiac, although Patrick Dejean of Domaine du Noble (see entry) says it has a slightly leaner, more vigorous structure than Ste-Croix. Other growers assert that Loupiac is a light wine, but this is often an excuse for picking fruit that is not nobly rotten. There is little bad wine produced in Loupiac, but a good deal is mediocre. The leading growers, spearheaded by Patrick Dejean, want to change this, principally by lowering the maximum yield to about 32 hl/ha.

## PRINCIPAL PRODUCERS

### Château du Cros ☆☆
*33410 Cadillac*

Michel Boyer is an enthusiastic producer of Loupiac from this large estate. The wines are fermented in tanks, but a proportion is aged in *barriques*. The amount of new oak varies according to the vintage. Not surprisingly, the top vintages such as 1989, 1990 and 1996 are the best, with a rich smokiness and ample elegance. Lesser years can be somewhat one-dimensional. The second wine is Fleur du Cros.

### Château La Gravette ☆
*33410 Cadillac*

Didier Lejeune produces about 2,000 cases of Loupiac from 5 hectares of fairly old vines. The wines are unoaked but are fresh, lean and stylish.

### Clos Jean ☆
*33410 Cadillac*

Lionel Bord runs this attractive property, with its 11 hectares of white grapes. He also produces Loupiac from the smaller Château Rondillon, which is on clay soil (Clos Jean is more gravelly).

Yields are high, and Bord has little patience with those arguing for higher must weights and greater richness, which he feels are opposed to the light Loupiac style he favours. The wines age well but rarely develop much complexity.

### Château Loupiac-Gaudiet ☆☆
*33410 Cadillac*

Courteous Marc Ducau, now assisted by his nephew Daniel Sanfourche, has run this estate, together with its neighbour Château Pontac, for many decades. The properties vary in that Pontac lies on more gravelly soil, but both wines are vinified identically. They are unoaked, as M. Ducau seeks freshness and elegance in his wines. Given the fruit quality, I have always suspected that the wines would be even better with a touch of oak, and in 1998 tentative moves in this direction were made.

### Domaine du Noble ☆☆☆
*33410 Cadillac*

Patrick Dejean, president of the Syndicat Viticole, has been leading the drive to higher quality, advocating lower yields and selective harvesting. Since 1988 part of the crop has been barrel-fermented, and in 1990 he began producing two bottlings, one oaked, the other not. The wines are consistent and balanced, with lush apricot fruitiness.

### Château de Ricaud ☆☆
*33410 Cadillac*

This neo-Gothic pile and its vineyards are owned by Champagne producer Alain Thiénot. The Loupiac is made mostly from Sémillon grapes. The wine is tank-fermented but aged in *barriques*, with a considerable proportion of new oak in good vintages. Over the past decade quality has greatly improved. Never a blockbuster, Ricaud puts the emphasis on elegance and a gentle oakiness.

## Cadillac and the Premières Côtes

The Premières Côtes de Bordeaux stretch along the banks of the River Garonne, opposite the vineyards of the Graves, for some 60 kilometres and stretching back into the hills. Thirty-seven communes are entitled to the Premières Côtes appellation, and within that area the 22 communes best suited to sweet-wine production are entitled to the Cadillac appellation. Although some 1,200 hectares theoretically qualify to be Cadillac, a much smaller (but growing) area is dedicated to producing the wine.

A century ago Cadillac's wines had a fine reputation, but during the 1950s and 1960s the market was dominated by whole-salers primarily interested in sweetness levels. So growers abandoned selective harvesting and began routinely to chaptalise the wines. Quality – and thus image and price – plummeted. Now there is growing pressure to increase quality, although the use of the Alsatian term "Grains Nobles" on the label may be premature. The regulations resemble those that apply to Loupiac and Ste-Croix- du-Mont. A further requirement stipulates that Cadillac may be sold only in bottle; thus, bulk sales to wholesalers are forbidden. In 1998 the production of Cadillac amounted to 800,000 bottles.

Premières Côtes is a fairly dismal appellation, since its rules permit machine-harvesting – a far cry from selective picking – and maximum yields are a generous 50 hl/ha. Not surprisingly, a typical Premières Côtes lacks noble rot character, and sometimes any character at all, other than a light insipid sweetness. The handful of good Premières Côtes are made from hand-picked grapes; in effect, they conform to the Cadillac rules but are produced outside the somewhat haphazardly defined Cadillac region. In the late 1990s Cadillac, alone among the right-bank sweet-wine appellations, has made a major effort to promote its wines, opening a Maison du Vin where wines may be tasted and bought. Whereas ten years ago the average quality was dire, there is now a growing choice of well-made, increasingly sumptuous wines.

## PRINCIPAL PRODUCERS

### Château Berbec☆ (made at Château des Coulinats)
*33410 Cadillac*
Camille Brun makes a soft, fruity Premières Côtes from hand-picked grapes. The wine is sound and inexpensive.

### Château Carsin ☆☆
*33410 Rions*
This estate, better known for its excellent dry white wines, also makes a small quantity (about 9,000 bottles) of barrique-fermented Cadillac. The style is fresh and lively but tightly structured.

### Château Cayla ☆☆☆
*33410 Rions*
Made from 50-year-old vines, the best *cuvée* from this estate is vinified in new oak but has excellent fruit and fresh racy acidity.

### Château Chasse-Pierre ☆
*33410 Cadillac*
A reliable source of Premières Côtes, made from hand-picked grapes. This unoaked wine is straightforward but fresh and fruity.

### Château Fayau ☆
*33410 Cadillac*
For many years this was the best-known estate in Cadillac, but the wine was rarely distinguished, although vintages from the 1920s and 1930s are still going strong, suggesting that standards were once very high. In recent years the Médéville family have made efforts to improve quality and have introduced a barrique-aged bottling, which is rich but rather heavy.

### Château Manos ☆☆☆
*33550 Haux*
The best wine here is the Réserve, made only in 1990, 1995 and

1997, from very old vines thoroughly attacked by noble rot. Yields are very low, and the must is fermented in new oak. The wine is intense, powerful and oaky, and fetches a very high price.

### Château Mémoires ☆☆
*33490 St-Maixant*

The ambitious Menard family acquired vineyards in various appellations here and made some fine Loupiac in 1990, but they are now focusing their efforts on Cadillac, where their vineyards include some centenarian vines. The wine is floral and citrussy and consistently well made.

### Château Poncet ☆
*33410 Omet*

Although inland, these vineyards are touched by botrytis and are planted with very old vines. The wine is aged in tanks or *barriques* according to the quality of the vintage.

### Château Renon ☆☆
*33550 Tabanac*

Jacques Boucherie makes some 9,000 bottles of unwooded Cadillac from three hectares of vineyards. In good vintages the wine is sleek and stylish.

### Château Reynon ☆☆☆
*Béguey, 33410 Cadillac*

Reynon, owned by the distinguished oenologist Denis Dubourdieu, is best known for its dry wines, but the Cadillac is excellent too: rich, tight and oaky, with ample concentration and power.

### Domaine du Roc ☆
*33410 Rions*

A simple but well-made wine, unoaked, creamily textured, but lively and citric. Sensibly priced too.

### Château La Tour Faugas ☆☆
*33410 Gabarnac*

André Massieu is an enthusiastic promoter of Cadillac and makes a rich, full-bodied version without any oak influence.

# Alsace

The Alsatians have adopted a Germanic approach to sweet wine production, specifying not only acceptable grape varieties but also minimum degrees of potential alcohol. Despite its easterly location close to the Rhine, Alsace has a dry, sunny climate. Vines planted on the best slopes in Alsace – usually Grand Cru sites – can ripen effortlessly in good vintages and, if yields are kept low, late-harvested grapes can attain very high degrees of potential alcohol.

# Grapes and alcohol levels for Alsace

Only four grape varieties can be labelled as either Vendange Tardive (VT) or Sélection de Grains Nobles (SGN), the two categories of sweet wines from Alsace: Riesling, Gewurztraminer, Pinot Gris (sometimes known as Tokay d'Alsace) and Muscat. Chaptalisation is not allowed. With VT levels for Riesling set at a potential alcohol level of 13 per cent, and for Gewurztraminer and Pinot Gris at 14.3 per cent, it is perfectly possible to ferment these wines to dryness. Thus, VT wines will be excluded from this section; some do indeed have discernible residual sugar, but others are dry or close to dry. In vintages such as 1997, many Rieslings, for example, were harvested at well above VT minimum levels in Grand Cru sites, so that it became difficult for winemakers and consumers alike to differentiate between a Grand Cru and a VT.

For SGN, the potential alcohol levels are set at 15.2 per cent for Riesling and Muscat; for the other two varieties at 16.5 per cent. Riesling and Muscat are rarely encountered at this level. In practice, the most conscientious estates will use these regulations only as guidelines, and will require higher must weights before the wine is marketed as SGN. As in Germany, there is frequent declassification, and many estates prefer to sell a superlative VT than a lightweight SGN from the same grapes. But there is nothing to prevent the lazy or cynical from offering SGNs that are simply inadequate.

Most SGN grapes are harvested, as in Sauternes, by *tries successives*, although some good producers of the style prefer to wait until an entire parcel of vines is botrytised, and then to pick the lot. For conscientious growers, it is important to distinguish stylistically between VT and SGN by selecting only fruit that is fully botrytised or raisined for the latter category.

## Quantities produced

These wines – especially SGN – used to be rarities but are no longer. In a vintage such as 1983, which was of fine quality though not ideal for sweet wines, the total production of SGN was 791 hectolitres. By 1988, an exceptional year, the figure had risen to 3,443 hectolitres. In 1989, a year of widespread botrytis, an astonishing 12,276 hectolitres of SGN were declared. This has not been matched since, but in 1994 6,372 hectolitres were produced, and in 1997 almost 11,000. These wines are hardly thin on the ground. Vast quantities of undistinguished but legally valid (according to appellation rules) SGNs are produced in propitious years. Unfortunately, several producers find it difficult to sell these wines, which are costly to produce and for which the market is keen but limited. This may explain why certain top Alsace growers, such as André Kientzler, have not produced SGN since 1989.

Muscat is mostly consumed as an apéritif wine, so Muscat SGN is rare, although it does exist. Pinot Gris and Gewurztraminer can show great opulence, power and aromatic richness at this level, with nuances of tropical fruits, honey, pineapple and peach being particularly prominent. It is widely accepted that

Riesling can produce the greatest SGNs of all thanks to its steely acidity and capacity to evolve over years or decades, developing ever greater complexity. Tiny quantities of Vin de Paille ("straw wine") have been produced in Alsace, ever since André Ostertag revived the tradition in 1987. Other estates that have occasionally made Vins de Paille are Hugel, Zind-Humbrecht and Deiss. As far as I know they are not commercially available.

# Best vintages
The best recent vintages for SGN have been 1976, 1983, 1988–90, 1994, 1995, 1997 and 1998.

# Principal producers
### Léon Beyer ☆☆☆
*68420 Eguisheim*
As winemaker since 1983, Eric Schueller has made some sensational wines, such as the exotic and unctuous 1989 Gewurztraminer SGN and the intensely sweet and creamy SGNs from Gewurztraminer and Pinot Gris in 1998.

### Paul Blanck ☆☆☆
*68240 Kientzheim*
Philippe Blanck is passionate about the *terroirs* in this 25-hectare estate. Gewurztraminer from Grand Cru Furstentum is often the source of some delicious and intense SGN, as in 1994.

### Bott-Geyl ☆☆
*68980 Beblenheim*
Jean-Christophe Bott doesn't like very high alcohol in his wines, so in ripe years such as 1997 even the lesser bottlings can be quite sweet. But his SGN, as in the 1997 Pinot Gris Sonnenglanz, is distinguished by its fresh persistent acidity.

### Ernest Burn ☆☆
*68420 Gueberschwihr*
Burn's finest wines come from Clos St-Imer, a parcel at the top of Grand Cru Goldert. Gewurztraminer SGN from the site can be smoky and powerful, as in 1994.

### Marcel Deiss ☆☆☆☆
*68750 Bergheim*
Indisputably one of Alsace's finest, and most obsessive, wine-makers, Jean-Michel Deiss practises biodynamic viticulture. He produces both a "regular" SGN and, in certain vintages, a super-SGN called Quintessence. This translates into a must weight of over 19 per cent for Riesling and about 24 per cent for Gewurztraminer. It's hard enough to make a Riesling SGN in the first place, but in 1989 Deiss made a now-legendary Quintessence from the variety. The 1989 Gewurztraminer Altenberg was splendid, but far surpassed by the 1995, with its marvellously racy acidity. Altenberg is also the source of some Riesling SGNs, and the 1989 was uncharacteristically opulent and exotic.

### Hugel ☆☆☆☆
*68340 Riquewihr*

The Hugel family were among the pioneers of the VT and SGN styles in the late-19th century. But it was the 1976 vintage that made the wider world realise what marvellous wines these could be. The grapes usually come from Grand Cru Schoenenbourg. The Hugels set high standards for themselves, requiring a potential alcohol of 18 per cent rather than the legally acceptable 16.6 before they will even think of bottling a wine as SGN. The 1976s were deservedly celebrated but were overshadowed by the superlative 1989s.

In 1989 there were two Gewurztraminer SGNs, the Cuvée "S" being all honey, peaches and velvet, while the Crème de Tête was more lychees and pineapple. The 1989 Pinot Gris was slightly exotic, with lush orangey overtones; and there was a Pinot Gris super-SGN that year that surpassed all records for potential alcohol at harvest.

### Marc Kreydenweiss ☆☆☆☆
*Andlau, 6719 Barr*

Andlau lies in northern Alsace, and a certain austerity in the Kreydenweiss wines may reflect the harsher climate here – or they may be a reflection of Marc Kreydenweiss's personality. A fanatic about terroir and yields, and Alsace's leading biodynamic producer, Marc relishes the opportunity to produce SGNs.

Even in an unpromising vintage such as 1987, Marc managed to make a sound, if slightly underpowered, Gewurztraminer SGN. A Riesling SGN followed the next year, but Marc's most astonishing wine in this style is surely the sublime 1989 Pinot Gris Moenchberg (picked at 26 per cent), with its aromas of oranges and barley sugar and with a quite amazing concentration of flavour. The 1990 Pinot Gris is a lovely wine too, delicately mandarin-tinged and very elegant, but it can't match the power of the 1989. Kreydenweiss often vinifies his sweet wines in older *barriques*, but there is no overt oak flavour in the wines.

### Kuentz-Bas ☆☆☆
*68420 Husseren-le-Château*

This highly dependable grower and *négociant* house believes in harvesting its VT and SGN grapes at one fell swoop. Thus, in 1983 the Gewurztraminer was picked on 18 November. Kuentz-Bas were relative latecomers to the style, producing their first sweet wines in the early 1980s, naming their VT Cuvée Caroline and their SGN Cuvée Jeremy.

Kuentz-Bas produce these wines infrequently – none in 1985, 1986 or 1988 – as they believe the grapes must come from old vines planted in top sites, otherwise the end result will simply be sweet without complexity. In 1989 they made SGN from Pinot Gris (an elegant pineappley wine) and Gewurztraminer, and in 1997 and 1998 made the style from these varieties plus Riesling.

### Seppi Landmann ☆☆
*68570 Soultzmatt*

Seppi Landmann will try anything. He delights in such mysterious *cuvées* as Sylvaner VT, Sylvaner not being one of the recognised varieties for sweet wines. And very good it is too. Landmann's vineyards, mostly in Grand Cru Zinnkoepflé, are exceptionally warm and sunny, so ripeness is never a problem. Indeed, he has produced SGN in every vintage since 1988. In his opinion, the 1994s are his finest, and I have tasted wonderful Gewurztraminer SGNs from 1988 and 1997, and delicious Pinot Gris from 1997 and 1998.

### Albert Mann ☆☆☆
*68920 Wettolsheim*

Winemaker Maurice Barthelmé runs the estate on close to organic lines. By depriving certain parcels of vines of anti-botrytis treatments, he can be fairly sure of attracting botrytis relatively early in the autumn. Indeed, in 1995 Barthelmé was able to produce an intense raisiny Riesling SGN so early in the autumn that he was denied the right to label the wine Sélection de Grains Nobles, so instead it appeared under the label Cuvée Antoine. 1994 was a great vintage at this property, with a succulent Gewurztraminer Furstentum, yet surpassed by a Pinot Gris from the same site.

### Muré ☆☆☆☆
*68250 Rouffach*

The heart of this domaine is Clos St-Landelin, which is enclosed within Grand Cru Vorbourg. René Muré believes the SGNs of the mid- and late 1990s are superior to those produced in 1989 and 1990, which he finds too overpowering and insufficiently elegant. The estate made great wines in 1994, 1996 and 1997, few better than the 1996 Pinot Gris, which was lush and very powerful, but at the same time graced with a thread of fresh acidity. From time to time Muré produce a rarity: delicious sweet Muscat VT.

### Domaines Schlumberger ☆☆☆
*68500 Guebwiller*

The Schlumbergers own a huge estate, much of it Grand Cru, in southern Alsace, and make their wines in a plump, rounded style that keeps surprisingly well. Their sweet wines are given *cuvée* names: Cuvée Christine is a Gewurztraminer VT and their Gewurztraminer SGN is called Cuvée Anne. Pinot Gris at SGN level is rare – after 1964 there was a gap of 25 years until it was produced again in 1989 (the wine is known as Cuvée Clarice). For all their sweet wines the Schlumbergers require higher potential alcohol than the regulations stipulate. Another Schlumberger policy is not to produce a VT and an SGN from the same variety in the same vintage. Quality can be exceptional. The 1976 and 1989 Cuvée Anne were stupendous, sweet but beautifully balanced and enhanced by a ravishing silky texture. The 1989 Cuvée Clarice didn't quite match this quality, being smoky and complex but lacking some elegance.

### Domaine Schoffit ☆☆☆☆
*68000 Colmar*

The heartbeat of this impressive estate lies in the Clos St-Théobald within one of Alsace's most spectacular Grands Crus, Rangen. In 1998 the vineyard produced a glorious sweet Muscat, but quantities were minuscule. In 1990 delicious and powerful SGNs were made from Pinot Gris and Gewurztraminer, both from Rangen.

SGNs were made in 1995 and 1996 from Pinot Gris, and the former is a great wine, suffused with botrytis and intensely concentrated and long.

### Bruno Sorg ☆☆☆
*68420 Eguisheim*

With low yields, old vines and some outstanding vineyards, it's not surprising that Sorg makes excellent wines. Often wines that could be labelled as SGN are declassified to VT, so that only the richest and most concentrated wines are offered as SGN. Of some superb examples: 1988 Pinot Gris and 1994 Gewurztraminer stand out.

### Trimbach ☆☆☆
*68150 Ribeauvillé*

This famous *négociant* house, best known for its classic dry wines, also produces some terrific sweet wines, always from its own vineyards. A 1989 Gewurztraminer SGN was particularly memorable, reeking of tropical fruits. The 1986 Pinot Gris SGN was outshone by the same wine in 1989, which managed to be peachy and racy at the same time. The 1990 was far more lean, with less botrytis influence, but very elegant. In outstanding years they produce a kind of super-SGN that they label Hors Choix.

### Domaine Weinbach ☆☆☆☆
*68240 Kaysersberg*

Colette Faller and her two daughters — one of whom, Laurence, is the winemaker – run this impressive estate. Riesling is the dominant variety, but some wonderful SGNs have been made from Gewurztraminer and Pinot Gris. Botrytis can easily overwhelm varietal character, but not here: the 1983 and 1988 Gewurztraminers were remarkable for their typicity. Pinot Gris SGN fared better in 1989 than 1990, although both are excellent wines. The 1989 is racier, with a bracing flavour of candied oranges. In 1983 and 1989 Colette Faller created a kind of super-SGN called Quintessence, which was aged in new oak.

### Zind-Humbrecht ☆☆☆☆
*68230 Turckheim*

First Léonard Humbrecht and now his son Olivier have brought this domaine well-deserved fame. There are no secrets to their success: low yields, late harvesting, scrupulous vinification and ageing on the fine lees. The drawback, though not everyone considers this disadvantageous, is that even in modest vintages such as 1991 almost the entire crop of Pinot Gris was officially at VT level (plus two SGNs). In great years the grapes are so ripe that even modest quality levels have ample residual sugar. At the top level these are sweet, rich and concentrated wines, usually with enough acidity and extract to prevent cloying sugariness.

Since Zind-Humbrecht have produced so many outstanding VTs and SGNs over the years, it is impossible to single out individual wines. Their top sites include Clos Jebsal, Clos St-Urbain in Grand Cru Rangen, and Clos Windsbuhl.

Since so many estates in Alsace produce SGN wines when conditions are right, it has been impossible to cite more than a handful of leading producers. Others worth looking out for include Albert Boxler (Niedermorschwihr), Théo Cattin (Voegtlinshoffen), Lorentz (Bergheim), Meyer-Fonné (Katzenthal), Rieflé (Pfaffenheim), Rolly Gassmann (Rohrschwihr), Pierre Sparr (Sigolsheim), Stentz Buecher (Wettolsheim) and Willm (Barr).

# The Loire Valley

With rare exceptions the sole grape used for sweet wine production in the Loire Valley is Chenin Blanc. There are two principal regions where such wines are made: Vouvray and Montlouis, near Tours; and the Coteaux du Layon, south of Angers. Attached to the Coteaux du Layon are other appellations that have slightly different traditions and regulations attached to them.

## Anjou

Briefly stated, the Coteaux du Layon is a region of 1,700 hectares and includes 27 different communes. The soil is pebbly, with topsoils of schist, chalk or clay. The maximum yield is 35 hectolitres per hectare. However, six communes – Beaulieu, Faye, Rablay, Rochefort, St-Aubin and St-Lambert – are entitled to attach their name to the words Coteaux du Layon on the label, and for these wines the yield is reduced to 30hl/ha. One further village, Chaume, can also append its name, and its maximum yield is only 25hl/ha.

To the east of Coteaux du Layon, the Coteaux de l'Aubance produces wines in a similar style, though they are usually less rich. Here about 100 hectares are dedicated to sweet-wine production, the rest being vinified dry and sold as Anjou – and the maximum yield is 30hl/ha.

In addition, there are two appellations that are the most highly prized of all: Bonnezeaux and Quarts de Chaume. Bonnezeaux, an AC since 1951, encompasses 110 hectares, all located on south- and southwest-facing slopes near Thouarcé on varied soils, predominantly schist. Yields are 25 hectolitres per hectare. The Quarts de Chaume appellation consists of a mere 45 hectares. Yields are a mere 23 hl/ha, so production is very limited. The vines swathe four hillocks close to the River Layon; the soil is very thin, and in many places the schist is exposed.

Proximity to the river and the sheltered position give Quarts de Chaume a very special microclimate, and botrytis is more widespread here than elsewhere in the Coteaux du Layon. If Bonnezeaux at its best is rich and luscious, Quarts de Chaume is marked by its elegance, raciness and mineral qualities.

The sweet wines are made either from overripe *passerillé* grapes or from fruit botrytised after fogs rise from the Layon and provoke noble rot. Thus, 1989, a great vintage, was a year of *passerillage*, whereas in 1990 botrytis was widespread.

Until recently the wine was vinified in tanks, but today many producers ferment and age the wine in *barriques*. Growers who use barrels often say they like oak as the best medium in which to allow the wine to aerate gently and achieve the greatest harmony and balance. But very fine wines can be made by both methods.

Until the mid-1980s the market for sweet Anjou, with a few notable exceptions, was moribund, and selective harvesting was rare. Mechanical harvesting and chaptalisation were routine. The results were predictably dire: lightly sweet wines with a hefty dose of alcohol and headache-inducing sulphur dioxide. Such wines are mercifully rare today, and since 1989 there has been a huge improvement in overall quality, and harvesting by *tries successives* has become routine at good estates.

A succession of fine vintages has tempted some growers to produce ultra-concentrated *cuvées*, often labelled as Grains Nobles or Sélection de Grains Nobles (SGN). Parcels of vines most susceptible to botrytis will be picked at optimal ripeness at must weights comparable to a German Trockenbeerenauslese. The result is usually a wine of modest alcohol – about 10 – and very high residual sugar of between 200 and 300 grammes per litre, as opposed to the 80 or so that is more usual in a Coteaux du Layon. Traditionalists decry such wines as atypical; their advocates favour pushing sweet-wine production to its furthest limits. These wines are difficult to produce, as there must be a high level of acidity to keep the wine fresh and vigorous and to balance the very high sugar content. Fortunately, Chenin Blanc is a high-acidity grape, so this is rarely problematic.

It has led to some legal difficulties, however. To counter winemakers' tendency to pick insufficiently ripe grapes, the minimum alcohol level for Coteaux du Layon was increased in 1998 from 11.5 to 12 degrees. This is an admirable move to ensure higher quality, but grapes destined for SGN and picked with must weights of between 25 and 30 degrees rarely attain such levels of alcohol, as the surfeit of sugar inhibits the yeasts from fermenting beyond about 10 degrees. Thus, many SGN wines are technically deficient in alcohol. Philippe Delesvaux of St-Aubin, a specialist in this style, has to bottle his wines as simple Coteaux du Layon, as they rarely reach the alcohol levels required for a Coteaux du Layon Villages. But this relatively technical matter need not deter the consumer from trying these exceptional wines. (The rules established by INAO for SGN wines, incidentally, require a minimum must weight of 17.5 per cent, and the harvesting and vinification are subject to inspection by INAO officials.)

## PRINCIPAL PRODUCERS

### Domaine Mark Angeli (Domaine de la Sansonnière) ☆☆☆
*49380 Thouarcé*

The only biodynamic producer in Bonnezeaux, Mark Angeli produces small quantities of very fine, very expensive wine. The emphasis is on a Grains Nobles style with low alcohol and very high residual sugar.

### Domaine de Bablut ☆☆☆
*49320 Brissac*

This large domaine in the Coteaux de l'Aubance is run by Christophe Daviau, who trained in Bordeaux and Australia. His best *cuvées*, Grandpierre and Vin Noble, are both fermented and aged in *barriques*. Vin Noble is very rich, being picked with a potential alcohol of at least 20 per cent. The lesser bottlings are more routine.

### Domaine des Baumard ☆☆☆
*49190 Rochefort*

Jean Baumard has ceded the direction of this famous estate to his son Florent, who is maintaining his father's high standards. The standard Coteaux du Layon Le Paon is not especially concentrated, but their flag-bearing Clos Ste-Catherine is very stylish indeed. The Quarts de Chaume is no blockbuster but places the emphasis on finesse and balance.

### Château de Bellerive ☆☆☆
*49190 Rochefort*

In 1993 the largest producer of Quarts de Chaume, Jacques Lalanne of Bellerive, sold the estate to the Malinge brothers from Normandy, although Lalanne stayed on as winemaker. The richest *cuvée*, produced only in exceptional years, is called Quintessence. However, the overall style of the wines is one of balance rather than super-concentration.

### Château de Breuil ☆☆
*49750 Beaulieu*

Marc Morgat's estate produces three different *cuvées* of Coteaux du Layon Beaulieu. The Vieilles Vignes comes from vines at least 85 years old. Even older vines are used for the Vendange Tardive de Vignes Centenaires; Cuvée Orantium is oak-aged for at least 18 months and is slightly richer than the Vieilles Vignes. The wines overall are sound and reliable but lack a little elegance and freshness.

### Domaine Philippe Cady ☆☆☆
*49190 St-Aubin*

Although Cady makes a small quantity of Chaume, he is best known for his St-Aubins. Les Varennes comes from a single parcel, but the most impressive bottlings are often the Cuvée Eléonore and the Cuvée Volupté, made in an SGN style with high residual sugar. The 1997 is exceptional.

## Domaine Philippe Delesvaux ☆☆☆☆
*49190 St-Aubin*

A Parisian who came to Anjou in the 1980s, Delesvaux claims to have pioneered the barrel-fermented Grains Nobles style here. He keeps his yields low so as to ensure that the grapes are fully ripe when botrytis attacks. The regular St-Aubin is usually made from *passerillé* grapes, as is the old-vine bottling known as Clos de la Guiberderie. But it's the SGNs that are his most celebrated wines.

Delesvaux is a non-interventionist winemaker, eschewing both chaptalisation and cultivated yeasts. Although the wines are very sweet, they are always balanced by tangy acidity. There are two super-concentrated wines even more extreme than the SGNs. Cuvée Carbonifera, made from a specific terroir, was picked at 27 per cent, and the Parker-acclaimed Anthologie was, in 1997, picked at 31.5 per cent.

Many producers and wine writers decry the Delesvaux wines as atypical. He would no doubt argue that he is merely showing the full potential of a long-neglected terroir. Were it not for their sensational acidity and concentration, the wines would be sticky and cloying; instead they are magnificent.

## Château de Fesles ☆☆☆
*49380 Thouarcé*

Once the most celebrated sweet wine domaine in Anjou, Fesles has been through troubled times. For many years home to the Boivin family, it was bought in 1990 by the *pâtissier* Gaston Lenôtre. He invested heavily but knew more about desserts than wines and ran into a string of bad vintages. In 1996 he sold the estate, together with his other domaines of La Roulerie and La Guimonière (*see* entry), to Bernard Germain of Bordeaux. Germain soon turned things around, and the 1997 vintage was exceptionally sumptuous. With 14 hectares within Bonnezeaux, Fesles is once again the appellation's leading domaine. The wines are fermented and aged in barrels, and it seems safe to predict that they will soon recover the fame they enjoyed under Jacques Boivin. The 1997 is excellent.

## Domaine des Forges ☆☆☆☆
*49190 St-Aubin*

This is quite a large property, and its 20 hectares within Coteaux du Layon include four and a half hectares in Chaume and one hectare, acquired in 1997, in Quarts de Chaume. The most concentrated wines are the delicious, *barrique*-aged SGNs (from both appellations), but there are also lovely, fruity, vivacious bottlings such as the Chaume Les Onnis.

## Château de la Genaiserie ☆☆☆
*49190 St-Aubin*

Yves Soulez produces three wines: two from St-Aubin (La Roche and Les Simonnelles) and one from Chaume (Tetuères). La Roche tends to be the firmer and richer of the St-Aubins, with Les Simonnelles showing greater finesse.

### Château de la Guimonière ☆☆
*49190 Chaume*

This old property was acquired in 1996 by Bernard Germain, who introduced the ageing of the wines in 400-litre casks. The wine is good but lacks zest, but these are early days for the new owners.

### Domaine de Montgilet ☆☆☆
*49610 Juigné-sur-Loire*

In top years this Coteaux de l'Aubance estate, owned by Vincent and Victor Lebreton, produces three bottlings of sweet wine. The best are Le Tertereaux and Les Trois Schistes. Le Tertereaux is exceptionally rich, honeyed and peachy. The wines are partially fermented and aged in *barriques*.

### Domaine Ogereau ☆☆☆
*49750 St-Lambert*

Vincent Ogereau produces three *cuvées* from St-Lambert. The Cuvée Prestige is partly fermented and aged in new oak and shows more botrytis character and concentration than the regular bottling. Top of the range is Clos des Bonnes Blanches, with its silky texture, delicious fruit and clean finish.

### Domaine du Petit Val ☆☆
*49380 Chavagnes*

The diffident Denis Goizil owns 2.5 hectares in Bonnezeaux, which is his most celebrated wine. It is made entirely in tanks. In top vintages he produces a single-vineyard wine from La Montagne and a rich Grains Nobles marked by dried-fruits aromas and flavours. However, some of these *cuvées* are marred by high alcohol and a lack of elegance.

### Domaine des Petits Quarts ☆☆☆☆
*49380 Faye*

With 12 hectares in Bonnezeaux, Jean-Pascal Godineau is, with Château de Fesles (*see* entry), the leading player in the appellation. Back in the 1970s, these were the only estates in Bonnezeaux to persist with selective harvesting.

Today the estate produces three single-vineyard wines – Malabé, Melleresses, Beauregard – and in fine vintages a succulent Premier Tri version from each. There is also an oaked Bonnezeaux, for which even Godineau works up little enthusiasm. Connoisseurs of extreme wines will relish the 1997 Quintessence, which has 300 grammes of residual sugar, wonderfully balanced by exquisite acidity.

### Château Pierre Bise ☆☆☆☆
*49750 Beaulieu*

Claude Papin makes a wide range of wines from Coteaux du Layon, including Beaulieu, Rochefort, Chaume and Quarts de Chaume. The wines are unoaked, but often made in an SGN style with great intensity of fruit and racy acidity. The 1997s are simply brilliant.

## Domaine Jo Pithon ✩✩✩
*49750 St-Lambert*

Jo Pithon is fanatical about harvesting only the richest and most concentrated grapes, so his wines are intense, luminous and high in residual sugar. His bottlings include wines from a number of single vineyards in St-Aubin, St-Lambert and Beaulieu.

## Domaine René Renou ✩✩
*49380 Thouarcé*

René Renou produces only Bonnezeaux from his ten hectares of vineyards. The regular bottling is called Tri de Vendanges; then there are single-vineyard wines from Beauregard, Melleresses and La Montagne. Cuvée Anne is made from grapes picked with a potential alcohol of 18-20 per cent; the very costly Cuvée Zenith is made from fruit picked at over 20 per cent. The wines are fermented in tanks and aged in older barrels, but from 1999 Renou will begin fermenting part of the crop in *barriques*. The style stresses elegance rather than excessive richness, yet despite Renou's devotion to Bonnezeaux the wines, other than Zenith, lack some vigour and concentration.

## Domaine Richou ✩✩
*49190 Mozé-sur-Louet*

The Richou brothers produce three *cuvées* of Coteaux de l'Aubance. Sélection is the basic bottling, mostly vinified in tanks. Les 3 Demoiselles is vinified in older barrels, and Pavillon is made from a single parcel of old vines, also fermented and aged in barrels. Only in 1995 did the Richous produce all three in the same vintage. The aim here is to provide well-balanced succulent wines without exceptionally high levels of residual sugar.

## Domaine de Sauveroy ✩✩
*49750 St-Lambert*

Pascal Cailleau's best wines are the barrique-aged Cuvée Nectar and the even richer Cuvée des Anges, which in 1997 was picked at almost 26 degrees.

## Château Soucherie ✩✩✩
*49750 Beaulieu*

The Tijou family preside over a large 35-hectare estate, from which they produce a fresh, fairly simple Coteaux du Layon, an elegant creamy Chaume, the Beaulieu Cuvée S (half aged in older *barriques*), and the acclaimed Beaulieu Cuvée de la Tour, the last usually vinified in new oak – a delicious wine, not excessively marked by the wood.

## Château de Suronde ✩✩✩✩
*49190 Rochefort*

François Poirel is a newcomer, having acquired the property from Pascal Laffourcade in 1995. Poirel rapidly established a claim to be the finest producer of Quarts de Chaume. Fanatical about quality, he has reduced yields to between 12 and 16 hl/ha. Poirel ferments the wines in *barriques* without chaptalisation or added yeasts. The regular Quarts de Chaume is picked with a potential alcohol of 20-21 per cent, but in exceptional vintages such as 1996 and 1997 he has also produced a Trie Victor et Joseph, for which the grapes are picked berry by berry. These are wines in an SGN style with, in the case of the 1997, residual sugar of an astonishing 330 grammes. But even the regular bottling is sensational.

Other fine domaines in Coteaux du Layon include Domaine de la Poterie (Quarts de Chaume), Domaine des Sablonettes (Rablay), Château La Varière and Domaine Rochais (Rochefort).

# Touraine

The Coteaux du Layon and its satellites aim to produce mostly sweet wines, but in Vouvray and Montlouis growers make wines in a predominantly dry or off-dry style. Sweet wines (*moelleux*) account on average for no more than four per cent of production. As in Germany, sweet-wine production is seen as a bonus in exceptional vintages. The run of fine vintages from 1989 to 1990, and then from 1995 to 1997 have been very much the exception to the rule. Foreau (*see* entry below), for example, produced no sweet wine between 1976 and 1983.

Vouvray encompasses 2,000 hectares spread over eight communes. Maximum yields are 55 hl/ha, but in practice they are considerably lower for sweet wines. Montlouis has slightly lower yields (45 hl/ha), and the region is smaller, some 350 hectares spread over three communes.

It is often the earlier *tries* that deliver the grapes most suitable for *moelleux*. Labels sometimes specify that the wine comes from the first *trie*, the implication being that this will be the best of the crop. This is because the bunches that flower earliest will be the ripest by the time botrytis or *passerillage* occurs.

The soils are very varied, with chalky subsoil dominant in some parts of Vouvray, and flint more pronounced away from the river. The nuances of terroir are significant but more easily discernible in dry and off-dry wines than in the sweet ones. One major difference is that the wines from the commune of Rochecorbon tend to be slightly lower in acidity.

For some years the growers have been petitioning the INAO for the creation of a Sélection de Grains Nobles category similar to that which exists in Anjou. Were it to come into being, the rules would stipulate a potential alcohol at harvesting of at least 17 per cent, no adjustments of sugar (ie chaptalisation) or acidity, and certification by a tasting panel.

Although there have been legendary vintages in Vouvray, such as 1947 and 1976, it was the 1989 that initiated the revival of *moelleux* wines. This was a year of *passerillage*, and in the views of many growers 1990, which was heavily botrytis-infected, was an even greater vintage. Another factor that must have come into play was experience. Whereas celebrated domaines such as Huet and Foreau (*see* entries below) had always made *moelleux* wines when climatic conditions obliged, other domaines had almost lost the habit. The 1989 vintage gave them the opportunity to vinify very rich, sweet wines, but the 1990 vintage enabled them to produce some truly great wines.

The growers of Montlouis declare that their wines are less powerful than Vouvray but have a subtlety and finesse that are revealed only after some years of bottle-ageing. In blind-tasting Montlouis alongside Vouvray, I have found the wines indistinguishable.

Sweet Vouvray and Montlouis are usually marked by a sharper, fresher acidity than their counterparts from Anjou. They are rarely as lush and creamy as the top wines of the Coteaux du Layon, but they are often more racy and elegant, and their acidic backbone allows them to age for decades. Their flavour profile is complex. Their relatively high acidity brings out hints of apple, lemon and quince as well as, from some producers in some vintages, mango, banana, apricot, peach and pineapple.

## PRINCIPAL PRODUCERS
### Domaine des Aubuisières ☆☆☆
*37210 Vouvray*
Bernard Fouquet made great wines in 1989 and 1990, putting his domaine on the map. His many *cuvées* from the late 1990s are no less impressive. His style is fruity and forward, although there is no reason to think the wines will not age superbly.

### Clos Baudoin ☆☆
*37210 Vouvray*
This 22-hectare estate was purchased just before the First World War by the grandfather of the present owner, Prince Philippe Poniatowski. The vines are mostly old, the yields modest, and fermentation takes place in 600-litre barrels without cultivated yeasts. The wines are often quite austere, and Clos Baudoin appears to have been overtaken in quality and dynamism by some younger producers.

### Domaine Bourillon d'Orléans ☆☆
*37210 Rochecorbin*
The opinionated Frédéric Bourillon runs his 19-hectare estate on lines that are close to organic. His *moelleux* wines can lack concentration but are fresh and lively.

### Domaine Brisebarre ☆☆
*37210 Vouvray*
The dynamic Philippe Brisebarre produces two *cuvées* of *moelleux*, the quince-scented Grand Réserve and the richer, sweeter Réserve Personelle.

### Domaine Le Capitaine ☆☆
*37210 Rochecorbon*
Brothers Alain and Christophe Le Capitaine are among Vouvray's rising stars. The standard *cuvée* is crisp and appley but not especially concentrated. Far better is the Réserve, which is more racy

and elegant and can have minerally overtones. In top vintages such as 1997 they produce an SGN-style Cuvée Marie Geoffrey, which is intense, sweet and honeyed without showing any heaviness.

## Domaine Champalou ☆☆☆
*37210 Vouvray*

Didier Champalou is a rarity in Vouvray, an outsider, although his offence is mitigated by his being married to Catherine, a local girl. In 15 years they have built up an impressive property. Their basic *moelleux* is known as Cuvée Moelleuse. More impressive is their *cuvée* called Trie de Vendange, which with residual sugar levels of 160–180 grammes is close to an SGN style. The 1990 was brilliant, and the 1997 rivals it in intensity and lushness.

## Domaine François Chidaine ☆☆☆
*Husseau, 37270 Montlouis*

François Chidaine uses large two-year-old barrels to age his sweet wines, of which the finest is Les Lys, picked grape by grape from a single parcel of very old vines to give a lean assertive wine with delicious peachy fruit. But the standard *moelleux* is very good too.

## Cave Coopérative: Producteurs de la Vallée Coquette ☆☆
*37210 Vouvray*

This co-op handles up to 15 per cent of Vouvray's total production each year, but the quality of its sweet wines is surprisingly high. The basic *moelleux* is outflanked by the Réserve des Producteurs, which is tightly structured and tastes of peaches and quince.

## Domaine de la Fontainerie ☆
*37210 Vouvray*

Catherine Dhoye-Deruet, who took over her family's five-hectare estate in 1990, is one of the few winemakers to use new oak. She admits that those who taste the wines either adore them or detest them. I am in the latter camp and greatly prefer the soft, gently acidic Les Brûlées to the wildly over-oaked Coteaux La Fontainerie.

## Domaine Foreau (Clos Naudin) ☆☆☆☆
*37210 Vouvray*

There is no one more passionate, or knowledgeable, about Vouvray than Philippe Foreau, who has been making the wines here since 1983. He cultivates his 12 hectares of vineyards without herbicides, and there is no chaptalisation or addition of cultivated yeasts. Thus, the winemaking is as natural as possible. The *moelleux* is fermented in older 300-litre oak casks.

In most good vintages, Foreau produces both a *moelleux* and *moelleux réserve*, the latter produced only from nobly rotten grapes. In the greatest years, such as 1990, there may be additional *cuvées* produced from individual *tries*. These wines, marked not only by fine concentration of fruit but by tangy and palate-cleansing acidity and exceptional length, are among the most complex and intellectually enthralling wines of the Loire.

# Château Gaudrelle ☆☆☆☆

*37210 Vouvray*

Alexandre Monmousseau tends 14 hectares of vines, many of them very old. His Réserve Spéciale has charm rather than power and concentration, and his best fruit goes into the Réserve Personelle, which is racy, citrussy and beautifully structured, ensuring a very long life. Only the 1996 is disappointing.

# Domaine Huet ☆☆☆☆

*37210 Vouvray*

Sipping Vouvrays from 1937 and 1947 with Gaston Huet, the man who made these wines, was a memorable, indeed moving, experience. M Huet, who is now well into his eighties, has passed the reins to his son-in-law Noel Pinguet, who has transformed the domaine into a biodynamic estate. In other respects the wines are unchanged. They come from three sites – Le Mont, Haut-Lieu and Clos de Bourg – and are vinified in large casks with minimal intervention.

These wines are invariably among the most elegant of all Vouvrays. They can seem underpowered in their youth but gain in majesty with age. There is, in addition to the regular moelleux, an occasional Premier Trie bottling, and in top years (1989, 1995, 1997) the celebrated Cuvée Constance, a blend of the best wines from the various sites.

# Domaine Laisement ☆

*37210 Vouvray*

The genial, welcoming Jean-Pierre Laisement has conserved his galleries filled with 600-litre chestnut and oak casks in which his wines are aged. The wines are light and somewhat inexpressive in their youth, but they can age well.

# Domaine Levasseur ☆☆

*37270 Montlouis*

Claude Levasseur produces two fine *moelleux*. The more impressive is the Tri de Vieilles Vignes, which in 1997 offered a rich mouthful of delicious appley fruit.

# Château Moncontour ☆☆

*37210 Vouvray*

This very large estate near Rochecorbon has under-performed for years, but since its purchase in 1994 by M Feray the quality has improved. The *moelleux*, aged in older *barriques*, has been good if not exceptional since 1995. In 1997 an intense and deliciously fruity *cuvée* called Nectar de Moncontour was produced.

# Domaine Moyer ☆

*37270 Montlouis*

For many years this domaine failed to impress, but there are clear signs of improvement in the late 1990s, and the 1997 *moelleux* is a lively, tangy, assertive wine of great character.

### Domaine François Pinon ☆☆☆
*37210 Vernou*

The unassuming M Pinon, based in the lovely Vallée de Cousse, produces a bewildering variety of wines. Depending on the vintage, there can be different bottlings according to whether the grapes were *passerillé* or botrytised, as well as individual *tri* bottlings. Yet there were no serious disappointments at a tasting of vintages from 1964 to 1997.

### Domaine de la Taille aux Loups ☆☆☆
*Husseau, 37270 Montlouis*

Jacky Blot founded this eight-hectare estate as recently as 1988, and it is run on near-organic lines. Blot is keen on new oak, but wood tones do not seem to dominate his sweet wines. His standard *moelleux*, aged in older *barriques*, is good, and the richer, more honeyed Cuvée Romulus is delicious and marked by a long spicy finish.

### Domaine Vigneau-Chevreau ☆☆☆
*37210 Chancay*

This estate is run on biodynamic lines. In outstanding vintages such as 1997, Jean-Michel Vigneau produces as many as three *cuvées*, of which the finest are Clos Baglin and Château Gaillard. These are stylish, assertive wines with lovely racy acidity, delicious young but surely capable of a long life in bottle.

Other excellent Vouvray *moelleux* come from Champion, Pichot, Benoit Gauthier (Cuvée Théo) and Gauthier-L'homme; and fine Montlouis from Deletang. In addition to very infrequent sweet wines produced from Sauvignon Blanc in Pouilly-Fumé and Sancerre, there are other pockets of sweet-wine production based on the Chenin grape: Azay-le-Rideau (where Pavy is the principal producer) and Savennières, where there has been a return to *demi-sec* and, less frequently, *moelleux* styles. Domaine Pierre Soulez is a leading producer of sweet Savennières.

# Monbazillac
## The history

Today Monbazillac, which lies east of Bordeaux and just south of Bergerac, finds itself re-emerging after a period of crisis. The same economic difficulties that afflicted sweet Bordeaux were mirrored in Monbazillac, and standards of production plummeted. I have tasted 1929 Monbazillacs comparable to the finest Sauternes, providing evidence of the region's potential. Indeed, according to Bruno Bilancini, a leading producer, prices for Monbazillac before the First World War were higher than those for Sauternes.

By the 1960s and 1970s Monbazillac had become banal. The Comte de Bosredon recalls that when he took over his estate in the early 1980s not a single vineyard worker was familiar with *tries successives*. Grapes were usually picked by machine, any deficiencies in the grapes were "corrected" by routine chaptalisation, and excessive sulphur dioxide disfigured the final wines. Some growers, it was rumoured, souped up their wines with honey and caramel. Labour-intensive practices, such as selective harvesting and barrel-fermentation, were dispensed with. The cheapness of Monbazillac may have appealed to bargain-hunters, but it spelled doom for the renown of the region.

By the early 1990s Monbazillac was in a state of civil war, with two Syndicats representing diverse interests. The best growers wanted regulations to eliminate the worst abuses; others defended the status quo. Fortunately, the modernisers won. The minimum degree of potential alcohol at harvest was raised to 15 per cent, harvesting machines were phased out, and yields were lowered from 40 hectolitres per hectare to 27. (Machines were retained for the lesser appellation of Bergerac Moelleux, which is hardly ever worth drinking in the first place.)

Monbazillac is not out of the woods yet. There are still too many mediocre wines, and over half the production is sold to wholesalers for undistinguished supermarket and export blends. But there is also a growing band of conscientious producers releasing small quantities of first-rate wine. There is much discussion between those who feel Monbazillac should, whenever possible, be made in the richest imaginable style, and those who prefer leaner wines with more finesse.

## Grapes for Monbazillac

Monbazillac's grape varieties, Sémillon, Sauvignon Blanc and Muscadelle, are identical to those found in Sauternes, and the methods of harvesting and vinification are very similar. Morning fogs roll up from the River Dordogne, providing botrytis in most vintages.

There are some differences between Monbazillac as a region and Bordeaux. There is more Muscadelle, though in recent years it has been giving ground to the more dependable Sémillon. However, Château Belingard and Domaine de l'Ancienne Cure (*see* entries below) have planted more Muscadelle. Whereas the vineyards of Sauternes are mostly on flat ground, here the vines are planted on slopes, the climate is more continental, and the harvest is usually later. Vines not suited to sweet-wine production can be vinified dry and sold as Bergerac Sec.

## Saussignac and Haut-Montravel

Precisely the same revival as Monbazillac's is taking place in two neighbouring appellations, Saussignac and Haut-Montravel, which by the mid-1980s were almost extinct. The best domaines from these appellations are presented below with those of Monbazillac, which they greatly resemble. Like Monbazillac, Saussignac is spread over five communes and is in effect its westward extension. Montravel lies north of the River Dordogne (unlike Saussignac and Monbazillac), midway between Bergerac and Libourne.

In Saussignac only about 50 hectares are devoted to sweetwine production. According to INAO regulations, the Saussignac appellation is *moelleux* rather than *liquoreux*, but the serious growers are almost all interested exclusively in the latter. The obvious solution is to amend the rules so that Saussignac becomes a *liquoreux*, with *moelleux* sold as Bergerac Moelleux; but this leaves the producers of the latter unhappy. Alternatively, a new AC, Saussignac Noble, may be created for the *liquoreux*.

Montravel AC is a dry white appellation, from 240 hectares in 14 communes. Haut-Montravel is a *moelleux* from higher land, encompassing about 50 hectares in five communes. Côtes de Montravel is also often *moelleux* and derives from nine communes over 60 hectares; it is usually lighter than Haut-Montravel. (Red wines are sold as Bergerac.) As in Saussignac, the best growers are keen to separate *moelleux* from *liquoreux*.

## Best vintages

1990 is the greatest vintage in recent times (preceded by 1989, 1976, 1967, 1947, 1929 and 1928). The next decent year was 1994, followed by an excellent trio from 1995 to 1997. The 1995 is richer than 1996 but often less elegant; 1997 is reckoned to be slightly lighter. 1998 is likely to be quite good, but a small crop.

## Principal producers

### Domaine de l'Ancienne Cure ☆☆

*24560 Colombier, Monbazillac*

Christian Roche began bottling his wines in 1989 and has made great progress. The regular bottling is vinified in tanks and of modest quality. The better *cuvée* is Cuvée Abbaye, fermented in new oak and produced only in good vintages. The 1990 was over-alcoholic, but in recent years the wine has been well-balanced, with more elegance.

### Château Belingard ☆☆

*24240 Pomport, Monbazillac*

It took some years for the Bosredon family to focus on high quality here, but today standards are high. The standard *cuvée* is vinified in tank and aged in older barrels, a relatively simple wine with an appealing freshness. Blanche de Bosredon is picked more selectively and aged for two years in barrels. This wine is lush and creamy but has good acidity. The 1995 is exceptional.

### Château La Borderie ☆☆

*24240 Sigoules, Monbazillac*

Armand Vidal can take much of the credit for salvaging the reputation of Monbazillac, and he is one of the few producers who made good wines throughout the region's dark ages. His best wine, Cuvée Prestige, has been aged in *barriques* since 1989. The wines are very good, especially the 1995, but quantities have diminished. Vidal's son has set up his own domaine, and the charming but ageing Armand Vidal no longer markets his wines worldwide. The Vidals also produce very good Monbazillac from Mme Vidal's domaine, Château Treuil de Nailhac.

### Château Caillavel ☆
*24240 Pomport, Monbazillac*

M Lacoste runs a large efficient domaine, introducing selective harvesting in the 1990s and buying second-hand barrels from Yquem, although he also uses new oak for his Cuvée Prestige. The wines are sound but one-dimensional and lack concentration. However, prices are low.

### Cave Coopérative de Monbazillac ☆
*24240 Sigoules, Monbazillac*

This large cooperative specialises in wines from the many châteaux it owns or leases. The best known is the show-piece Renaissance Château de Monbazillac, but others include Septy, La Brie, Le Touron and La Croix Poulvère. Quality has been mediocre, but a new director seems determined to improve quality. There remains plenty of room for improvement.

### Château Dauzan La Vergne ☆
*Ponchapt, 33220 Porte-Ste-Foy*

These Montravels are, somewhat confusingly, produced at Château Pique-Segue. The Côtes de Montravel has a dash of Muscadelle and is unwooded. The Haut-Montravel, a honeyed, well-balanced and spicy wine, comes from the oldest parcels and is barrel-fermented.

### Clos Fontindoule ☆☆
*24240 Monbazillac*

There is no more traditional grower than the octogenarian Gilles Cros, who claims to have changed nothing since his grandfather's day. He says he always picked by hand, kept his yields low, and picks as late as possible.

The wines are vinified in tanks and then stored, sometimes for a decade or more, in old casks. There are usually two vintages on offer at any one time, and the older may well be 15 years old. The style is somewhat rustic and alcoholic, but the wines are golden, rich, satisfying and inexpensive.

### Château Haut-Bernasse ☆
*24240 Monbazillac*

Jacques Blais is both a cellist and a self-taught winemaker. His yields are very low, and the wines are aged in older *barriques*. The Haut-Bernasse wines are attractive and tangerine-tinged with considerable charm.

### Château La Maurigne ☆☆
*24240 Razac-de-Saussignac*

Patrick and Chantal Gérardin acquired this small property in 1996, so these are early days. The *liquoreux* Saussignac is made from 70-year-old Sémillon vines that yield about 12 hl/ha. The wine is very rich and is aged in new oak. It has attractive flavours of apricot and pineapple and a distinctive streak of refreshing acidity.

### Château Le Payral ☆☆☆
*24240 Razac-le-Saussignac*

Thierry Daulhiac produces an exceptionally lush, peachy Cuvée
Marie Jeanne here in Saussignac. The wine is undoubtedly voluptuous and creamy but lacks a little acidity.

### Château Puy Servain ☆
*33220 Porte-Ste-Foy*

Daniel Hecquet is passionate about Montravel and has been
encouraging the revival of the *liquoreux* style since 1989. Despite
his enthusiasm the wines lack some richness and botrytis character. The best vintage has been 1995.

### Château Richard ☆☆
*24240 Monestier*

Richard Doughty cultivates his vineyards organically, producing a
rich, creamy Saussignac with powerful peachy fruit.

### Château Theulet ☆
*24240 Monbazillac*

This large estate produces two *cuvées*. The simpler is made from
*passerillé* grapes. It's a good fresh wine but surpassed by the much
richer Cuvée Prestige.

### Château Tirecul La Gravière ☆☆☆☆
*24240 Monbazillac*

The oenologist Bruno Bilancini leased this estate in 1992
and eventually bought it in 1997. He was determined from the
start not only to produce the finest possible wine but also to focus
exclusively on sweet wine. Average yields are a pitiful 11 hl/ha
and there are between four and ten *tries*, all in search of the
most botrytised fruit. Unusually, Muscadelle dominates the
vineyard. Today these wines are rightly acclaimed as the finest
in the region.

There are two *cuvées*, the more concentrated being the
ultra-expensive Cuvée Madame. In fine years such as 1995 the
majority of the crop was released as Cuvée Madame, so the idea
is not simply to cream off the best in any vintage. The wine
is aged for about two years in about fifty per cent new oak, and
the Cuvée Madame may receive a greater proportion of new
wood. In 1997 the grapes for Cuvée Madame were picked at a
potential alcohol of 24.5 per cent, a richness rarely encountered
in the past in Monbazillac.

### Clos d'Yvigne ☆☆☆
*24240 Gageac et Rouillac*

An Englishwoman, Patricia Atkinson, runs this 15-hectare
Saussignac estate. After five to seven *tries*, the must is fermented
in new oak and aged for two years. The style is lush, powerful,
with rich flavours of apricot and quince.

# Other French sweet wines

## Gaillac

In 1988 Robert and Bernard Plageoles in Cahuzac launched a crusade to rescue the traditional varieties and styles of this rural region in southwest France. The main variety for sweet wine is Ondenc, which had virtually disappeared but was revived from vine selections within the Plageoles' vineyards. Their range of sweet wines includes an oaked Muscadelle and Vin d'Autan, made from very low yields of Ondenc grapes concentrated by *passerillage*, and the occasional Grain d'Autan made from botrytised grapes. The result is wonderfully intense and honeyed, with aromas of peach and a hint of bitter almonds. The 1997 Vin d'Autan is spectacularly rich.

A few other Gaillac growers have followed the lead set by Plageoles: Domaine Cosse Marine, Domaine de Ginestre and Domaine Rotier.

## Jurançon

France offers few more entrancing sights than the snow-capped Pyrenees glimpsed from the Jurançon vineyards just south of Pau. Jurançon has two major areas of production: around Monein, and just south of the town of Jurançon along the ridges close to the hamlet of La Chapelle-de-Rousse. Jurançon is never a botrytised wine. Its sweetness comes from late-picked *passerillé* grapes. The region's long, sunny and dry autumns make possible the production of sweet wine almost every year.

Three local grape varieties flourish here: Gros Manseng, Petit Manseng and Petit Courbu. Courbu is in decline, while Petit Manseng is on the increase. As the name suggests, the Gros Manseng berries are larger, while the Petit berries are not only smaller but more widely spaced. Thus, Gros is more prone to rot, whereas the dispersed berry-set of Petit Manseng allows for good aeration and thus better resistance to rot. Some inexpensive sweet wines are made from Gros Manseng, but the variety is mostly used for Jurançon Sec, while all the best sweet Jurançons are made solely from Petit Manseng. Yields vary too: the maximum for Gros Manseng is 60 hl/ha, while those for Petit Manseng are only 40.

Although Jurançon gained its AC status in 1936, by the 1960s and 1970s the wine was in danger of extinction. Many of the vineyards were planted with nondescript varieties that yielded mediocre wine for rapid consumption in local bars. It took the determined efforts of a few true believers – notably Robert Latrille and Henri Ramonteu – to encourage the replanting of Petit Manseng in the 1980s. Over the past 15 years the area under vine has doubled to just over 800 hectares. Today about 65 per cent of production is of sweet wine, and quality is far higher than it was 20 years ago.

Petit Manseng has naturally high acidity, and so does the finished wine. The absence of botrytis means that rich aromas and flavours of honey and peach are rarely encountered. Instead, floral aromas and flavours of dried lemons and apricots dominate. A good Jurançon should be fruity, fresh and lively, with refreshing acidity. In some years the vineyards around La Chapelle-de-Rousse give grapes with rather fierce acidity levels, but in very ripe years that high natural acidity can give more vigorous wines than the vineyards of Monein.

There are varying views about barrique-ageing. If the wine is sufficiently concentrated, it can support an oaky underpinning without picking up woody flavours. However, some outstanding unoaked Jurançons are also made. Some prestige *cuvées* are barrique-aged wines; others are related to the date of harvesting, and thus the richness and intensity of the grapes. One or two growers have adopted the term Vendange Tardive, which requires minimum potential alcohol levels, cannot be picked until six weeks after the start of the harvest, and is monitored at harvesting by officials from Institut National des Appellations d'Origine (INAO).

The 1985 was a good year, and 1988 great. The 1989 and 1990 were also excellent, but 1991 and 1992 were poor and 1993 was only slightly superior. The 1994 was an average year, but 1995 was very hot, giving rich, powerful wines. The 1996 was excellent, and superior to 1997. In 1998 there was some rot in late September, but growers who eliminated rotten bunches and waited for fine weather to return, as it did, made excellent wines.

# PRINCIPAL PRODUCERS

## Domaine Bellegarde ☆☆

*64360 Monein*

Pascal Labasse's basic *moelleux* blends 70 per cent Gros Manseng with 30 per cent Petit Manseng. Cuvée Thibault is pure Petit Manseng, fermented and aged in *barriques*. His finest wine, Sélection DB, comes from two old parcels of Petit Manseng picked in late November and aged in new oak. It is only made when climatic conditions permit, as in 1989, 1993, 1995 and 1998.

## Domaine Bordenave ☆☆

*64360 Monein*

Only when Gisèle Bordenave returned from studies in Bordeaux did this ancient property begin to bottle its own wines. In addition to the regular *moelleux*, there is a Cuvée des Dames (Petit Manseng) and the excellent Cuvée Savin, made from the final *tries* and aged in one-third new oak. Cuvée Savin is marked by smoky aromas and ripe apricot flavours.

## Domaine Bru-Baché ☆☆☆

*64360 Monein*

Claude Loustalot has been running this well-known estate since 1991. There are four different *cuvées*. The basic bottling is unexciting, but the Cuvée des Casterrasses (75 per cent Petit Manseng, and aged in older *barriques*) has more vigour and dash. Quintessence is pure Petit Manseng that sees a good deal of new

oak and is marked by powerful flavours of lemon and quince. The
top wine is the stunning L'Eminence, from Petit Manseng picked
in mid-December and vinified entirely in new oak.

## Domaine Castéra ☆☆
*64360 Monein*

Christian Lihour claims to have been one of the first growers, in
1985, to produce pure Petit Manseng, a wine that is still youthful.
He produces two *cuvées*, both unwooded. The lesser is mostly Gros
Manseng and somewhat characterless. The Cuvée Privilège (Petit
Manseng) is richer and more elegant, though it lacks complexity.

## Domaine Cauhapé ☆☆☆☆
*64360 Monein*

Henri Ramonteu, in the early 1980s, picked up Jurançon by the
scruff of its viticultural neck and gave it a good shaking. He
insisted on selective harvesting and sang the praises of Petit
Manseng. He was one of the first to use *barriques*, and his highly
successful self-promotion helped raise the public's general aware-
ness of the merits of Jurançon.

The names of his *cuvées* change from time to time, but their
intensity (and price) are directly related to their dates of harvesting. Ballet d'Octobre is from Gros Manseng picked in late October
and intended for relatively early consumption. Symphonie de
Novembre is a first *trie* of Petit Manseng, fermented in new oak.
Noblesse du Temps is Petit Manseng picked in late November and
aged in new oak for up to 18 months.

Top of the range is the fabled Quintessence, produced from
two parcels of vines picked in late December or early January;
often the grapes have been frost-affected, adding to their complexity of flavour. This is an amazingly complex wine: my notes
on the 1994 detect dried peaches, mango, coffee and wood smoke
on the nose, and an equally complex palate. Quintessence is
extremely costly to produce, but even so the price tag of £60–£70
seems a trifle steep.

## Clos Thou ☆☆☆
*La Chapelle-de-Rousse, 64110 Jurançon*

A rising star, this estate's best wine is the grandly named Suprême
de Thou: a racy, pineappley Petit Manseng with bracing acidity.

## Clos Oroulat ☆☆☆
*64360 Monein*

Charles Hours was a pioneer of *barrique*-fermentation for
Jurançon in 1985 and continues to produce a single bottling of the
wine, using one-third new oak. Pure Petit Manseng, it is made in
an elegant, well-balanced style.

## Domaine Gaillot ☆☆☆
*64360 Monein*

François Gaillot has been running this ancient family property
since 1990. Less renowned than some other domaines in the

region, it produces a superb Petit Manseng called Sélection, a wine of great intensity and high acidity which needs bottle-age to show its full rich apricot complexity.

### Château Jolys ☆☆
*94290 Gan*

Robert Latrille is Jurançon's greatest booster and owns one of its largest estates and best-equipped wineries. His regular *moelleux* lacks excitement, but Cuvée Jean, from late-picked Petit Manseng and given some barrel-ageing, is plump and full-bodied. Jolys produce a Vendange Tardive, picked in December and oak-aged for 28 months. The result is a tight, citrussy wine of great finesse.

### Domaine Larredya ☆☆☆
*La Chapelle-de-Rousse, 64110 Jurançon*

The voluble, welcoming Jean-Marc Grussaute has adopted barrique-ageing with enthusiasm. The regular *moelleux*, dominated by Gros Manseng, is sound and well balanced, but the Sélection, made from Petit Manseng aged in 50 per cent new oak, has far greater lemony intensity. In top years, such as 1995 and 1998, Grussaute makes the superbly structured Cuvée François from part of the final *trie*, and this is aged for two years in *barriques*.

### Domaine de Souch ☆☆☆
*Laroin, 64110 Jurançon*

This stunningly beautiful estate is the only one in the region run biodynamically. Widowed in 1985, Yvonne Hégoboru decided to plant a vineyard at this property in 1987 when she was 60 years old. Guided by her long-time cellarmaster Abel Pires, she has elevated the domaine into the top ranks. The best wine, Marie-Kattalin, has an abundance of peach and apricot fruit and considerable elegance.

Other domaines worth looking out for include Domaine de Cabbarouy (Cuvée Ste-Catherine), Domaine Cancaillaù (Cuvée Gourmandise), Clos Guirouilh, Cru Lamouroux, Clos Lapeyre, Domaine de Malarrode (Cuvée Préstige) and Domaine Nigri.

## Jura

The Jura is the principal source within France of Vin de Paille ("straw wine"). The style came close to extinction about 20 years ago, as the wine is costly to produce and demand was limited.

The Jura has a bizarre mix of grape varieties, mostly Poulsard and Trousseau for reds, and Savagnin and Chardonnay for whites. Any of these may be used for Vin de Paille. Poulsard is often considered the most suitable, as it gives the greatest sugar levels and richness, but its drawback is that it dries slowly. Nowadays many producers use mostly Chardonnay, but this can lack the raisiny overtones of Poulsard. Savagnin gives body, power and acidity, and Trousseau is considered as not really suitable for Vin de Paille.

The grapes are picked relatively early and dried for at least two months. A hundred kilogrammes of grapes will yield anywhere between 15 and 25 litres of must. After pressing, the must is fermented, which can take up to two years. The wine used to be aged for about ten years in sealed casks, but that is no longer practised, and the minimum ageing period today is three years.

Now that Vin de Paille is back in fashion, some growers cut corners in order to generate sufficient quantities to meet the demand. Jean-François Bourdy of Jean Bourdy (*see* entry below) argues that although the regulations require a minimal sugar content at pressing of 306 grammes per litre (18 per cent potential alcohol), in practice you need at least 320 or 350. The reason for this is that fairly high alcohol levels – from 14.5 to 16 per cent – are favoured so as to avoid any risk of secondary fermentation. With such high alcohol, the level of residual sugar is rather low if the sugar content at pressing is on the low side. Bourdy recalls that the grapes used to be aged for four months to ensure the optimal concentration of sugars, but that entailed a volume of no more than 15 litres per 100 kilogrammes, whereas most producers find that making the wine is economical only if they can retain 20 to 30 litres.

So although the revival of "straw wine" is most welcome, quality is variable, and it is only worth buying the best. Like any great sweet wine, the lusciousness of a fine Vin de Paille needs to be balanced by extract and acidity.

There are four appellations in the Jura: the large Côtes du Jura, and the smaller Arbois, L'Etoile and Château-Chalon. Vin de Paille may be produced within any of them, but the Château-Chalon appellation is reserved for dry Vin Jaune, so its Vin de Paille carries the Côtes du Jura appellation.

## PRINCIPAL PRODUCERS

### Jean Bourdy ☆☆☆
39140 Arlay

This conservative estate still offers older vintages, such as 1921 Vin de Paille, for sale. Jean-François Bourdy has little time for those who produce a fairly commercial version. His is made, usually from Poulsard and Savagnin, in minute quantities and is at least four years old on release.

### Richard Delay ☆☆☆
*39570 Gevingey*

Delay's Vin de Paille is mostly Chardonnay, a lovely honeyed wine, sweet, intense and bracing.

### Fruitière Vinicole d'Arbois ☆☆
*39600 Arbois*

This high-quality cooperative revived its production of Vin de Paille in 1989, using a blend of Poulsard (for fruit), Chardonnay (for elegance), and Savagnin (for structure). Cultivated yeasts are added to ensure an alcohol level of at least 15.5 per cent. The 1994 has a rich caramel nose and strong tones of honey and dried fruits.

### Henri Maire ☆☆
*39600 Arbois*

This very large company produces two bottlings of Vin de Paille. La Vignière from the Côtes du Jura (Poulsard, Chardonnay and Savagnin) has overtones of caramel and toffee; the Vin de Cour from Arbois is more racy and delicate. The quality of recent vintages, such as 1995 and 1996, has increased considerably.

### François Mossu ☆☆☆
*39210 Voiteur*

This Château-Chalon grower has a special enthusiasm for Vin de Paille, which he makes from one-third each of Chardonnay, Poulsard and Savagnin. The musts far exceed the minimum sugar content, and in 1997 reached 420 grammes. The wines are aged in very small barrels. Some vintages show excessive alcohol, but these are complex, concentrated wines of high quality.

### Domaine de la Pinte ☆☆☆☆
*39600 Arbois*

This large domaine produces a very serious Vin de Paille. Savagnin is the dominant variety, plus a little Poulsard. The grapes are dried for up to five months. The result is a must rich in sugar – often about 400 grammes. Fermentation takes place in barrique and can last two to three years. The wine has aromas of preserved fruits and is raisiny on the palate with intense caramel flavours.

### Xavier Reverchon ☆☆☆
*59800 Poligny*

Reverchon make an intense, quince-flavoured Vin de Paille from Poulsard, Chardonnay and Savagnin.

### Rolet ☆☆☆
*39600 Arbois*

This excellent sophisticated producer favours Chardonnay for half the blend, the rest being Savagnin and Poulsard with a dash of Trousseau. The 1994 is rich, extracted and powerful.

### André Tissot ☆☆☆☆
*39600 Montigny-les-Arsures*

Stéphane Tissot uses all four permitted varieties, and the grapes are dried until February. No added yeasts are used, and fermentation can be prolonged. The 1994 had splendid aromas of apricot and honey and is a sumptuous, concentrated wine with fine acidity.

## Pacherenc du Vic-Bilh

Madiran lies north of Jurançon and shares some of its white wine varieties, in particular Gros and Petit Manseng. These, together with Arrufiac and Petit Courbu, form the basis of Madiran's white wine, which has the cumbersome name of Pacherenc du Vic-Bilh. This is made in dry and sweet styles, and the latter, made mostly from Petit Manseng, does bear a family likeness to Jurançon. The maximum yield is 40 hectolitres per hectare. Many of the more serious examples are aged in *barriques*. The wine is usually less intense than a fine Jurançon, and good examples are marked by vigour and freshness as well as sweet apricot-tinged fruit. Good examples are made by Châteaux d'Aydie, Barréjat, Crampilh and Montus and by the cooperative, Les Producteurs Plaimont.

# Burgundy

## PRINCIPAL PROPERTY

### Domaine de la Bongran ☆☆☆☆

*71260 Clessé*

Jean Thevenet, almost alone in Burgundy, produces sweet wine, usually botrytised, from Chardonnay. He claims that 50 years ago, in the Mâconnais, grapes were routinely harvested with some botrytis, and his Cuvée Levrouté, from lightly botrytised ultra-ripe grapes, pays tribute to this style. He also makes his celebrated Cuvée Botrytis in suitable years such as 1983, 1989, 1994 and 1995, about 3,000 bottles of sumptuous and utterly delicious wine. Since 1992 a few other Mâconnais domaines, such as Gaillerot and Laferrère at Lugny, have dabbled in botrytis wines.

# Rhône Valley

Vin de Paille used to be traditionally produced in the Rhône Valley, but in the mid-1980s it proved impossible to track down a single example. I have since encountered a 1944 example from Chapoutier (gently maderised by 1992), produced from Marsanne; and, also from Chapoutier, a 1982 Marsanne Passerillé, assertive and over-alcoholic at 15.5 per cent. Chapoutier revived Vin de Paille from Hermitage in 1990, and it proved a stupendous wine, honeyed, creamy, very concentrated and enlivened by racy acidity. The price, however, was exorbitant. Gérard Chave's powerful 1989 and 1990 Vins de Paille, with 16 per cent, are of similar quality and equally expensive.

There is also a small quantity of expensive late-harvest wine produced in Condrieu. Cuilleron's Les Ayguets Récoltes Tardives is the best known example, a lightly sweet, intense, elegant wine.

# Vin Cuit

A Provençal tradition, Vin Cuit ("cooked wine") has been revived in recent years. At the biodynamic Château Romanin near St-Rémy, young vines of Cabernet Sauvignon, Grenache and Syrah are pressed, and then the must is heated to 40°C for up to seven days. This reduces the volume by at least 30 per cent. The must is then fermented for a few months. The result is a delicate wine tasting of caramelised oranges.

A similar wine is produced by Château Les Bastides at Le-Puy-Ste-Réparade, giving a wine with pronounced flavours of caramel and coffee. In the same commune, Château La Coste produces a marmaladey Vin Cuit from Muscat of Alexandria and Clairette.

# Germany

## The history

That Germany should be the source of some of the world's greatest and most imperishable sweet wines is, at first glance, something of a paradox. The Riesling grape, from which its finest wines are made, must struggle to reach ripeness, and an alcoholic degree of between seven and ten is considered good going. And yet in certain sites, in certain years, Riesling, especially when attacked by botrytis, can achieve astonishing sugar levels. Not that Riesling needs to be picked at an extreme of ripeness to produce a stylish sweet wine. A simply overripe vine can result in an elegant Auslese. The extremes come with Beerenauslese (BA) and especially Trockenbeerenauslese (TBA), which are made from raisined grapes that are often picked individually. With Riesling everything is a question of balance, and the variety assists the winemaker by retaining abundant acidity, which keeps the wine fresh and helps it to age. It is by no means unusual for a TBA to evolve over a century or more.

The 1971 German wine laws have defined quality levels solely on the basis of must weights (ie grape sugar content) at harvesting, as expressed in the system of measurement known as Oechsle. In most German wine regions grapes must attain 85 Oechsle to qualify as Spätlese; bring them in at 83 and the wine must be sold as Kabinett. This has led to all kinds of dodgy practices, such as blending grapes from different vineyards to nudge the overall Oechsle level up a notch, so the wine could be sold at a higher price.

Worse, some growers, especially in warmer areas, planted early-ripening varieties which attracted botrytis. These easily qualified as BAs, and even TBAs, in certain vintages. The fact that the wine was sickly and cloying didn't matter: the must weight entitled it to be sold as a wine allegedly of the highest quality.

Of course, the best growers resisted this temptation. Declassification is common, and many a fine Auslese is in reality a modest BA. Moreover, top growers have introduced their own internal classifications. Thus, in the Mosel a producer may market three Auslesen, one regular, one Goldkapsel ("gold capsule"), one Lange Goldkapsel ("ong gold capsule"), each richer and probably sweeter than the preceding wine, so preserving the nuances that make fine Riesling so fascinating.

The more northerly the wine region, the more acidic the grapes and the harder it becomes to ripen them. Thus, in the Saar or Ruwer, tributaries of the Mosel, the general chilliness of the climate can pose great problems. But in warm years terminated by an outbreak of noble rot, the growers can make sweet wines of unrivalled intensity. They are rare, costly, indestructible. As one moves southwards into the Rhine regions it becomes slightly easier to achieve the requisite ripeness, but the acidity is lower too, and the wines are softer than those from the Mosel. That's not to say they can't be delicious and long-lived; it's simply that the structure is different. And in southerly Baden, where it can be as warm as in Alsace, it's not that hard, in certain vintages, to make very rich, opulent wines diametrically opposed in style to the lean, racy wines of the north.

Eiswein (Icewine) has become popular since the 1970s and is a different creature altogether. The temperature must drop to -8 °C and remain at that level for at least eight hours. Thus, picking can start only at dawn. The absence of botrytis can give the wines great purity of flavour, but they can suffer from excessive acidity levels.

Although Riesling is the supreme grape of Germany, there are other varieties suited to sweet-wine production. Scheurebe is a cross between Riesling and Silvaner; grapefruity when harvested for dry wine, it can have an attractive tanginess when sweet. Pinot Gris, when sweet, is called Ruländer in Germany. In the south it can produce very rich wines, low in acidity but sumptuous and mouth-filling. Gewürztraminer also makes sweet wines in southern Germany, but rarely reaches great heights.

There was a vogue for planting crossings such as Kerner and Ehrenfelser, but they lack distinction and appear to be in decline. The one truly successful crossing is Rieslaner, another match between Riesling and Silvaner. With its intense acidity, it can produce superb wines. As for the early-ripening cross-breeds such as Optima, Bacchus and Ortega, they are best avoided; such wines may be superficially attractive in their youth but do not age well and invariably lack elegance.

The secret of great German wine lies entirely in the vineyard. Vinification takes place either in steel tanks or in traditional oak ovals or other casks; dabblings in *barrique*-fermentation have been mercifully scarce. Riesling and oak just don't go together. German winemaking still favours a level of intervention that might find favour in Australia but would be frowned on in France. But the dependence on hi-tech gadgetry is less fervent than it used to be. So is the reliance on Süssreserve (unfermented grape juice) to give the wines their sweetness; the best estates seek a natural balance between alcohol and sugar.

It has not been easy to select the "best producers" of German sweet wines. Because sweet-wine production is the icing on the cake, such wine is produced only when conditions are appropriate. And when the climate is favourable, almost every serious estate will make some sweet wine, even if in minute quantities. Thus, in top years great wines can be encountered from dozens, if not hundreds, of estates.

# Baden

Germany's most southerly wine region is vast: 16,000 hectares stretching south from Mannheim to Basel. In the north there is good Riesling, but for the most part this is home to Burgundian varieties, and sweet wines are infrequent, although there are some exceptional Ruländers and even unpromising varieties such as Müller-Thurgau can occasionally be coaxed into delivering a TBA.

Baden is dominated by cooperatives (*Winzergenossenschaften*, often abbreviated to WG), but many are of high quality. The best recent vintages include 1988–1990, 1993 and 1996–1998. However, sweet-wine production in this immense region is dependent on microclimates, so vintage charts are unreliable.

## PRINCIPAL PRODUCERS
### WG Bischoffingen ☆☆
*79235 Bischoffingen*

With well-located sites in Baden's warmest sub-region, the Kaiserstuhl, this cooperative makes some rich and satisfying Eisweins and intensely sweet TBAs from the Burgundian varieties.

### WG Durbach ☆☆
*77770 Durbach*

A northerly village within Baden, Durbach is renowned for its Rieslings as well as for the Burgundian varieties. These, as well as Gewürztraminer, often form the basis for some excellent sweet wines.

### Weingut Dr Heger ☆☆☆☆
*79241 Ihringen*

Joachim Heger produces superlative dry white and red wines from the Kaiserstuhl, but his sweet wines are equally fine: sumptuous BAs and TBAs from a range of varieties including Gewürztraminer, Muskateller, Scheurebe and even Riesling.

### WG Königschaffhausen ☆☆☆
*79346 Königschaffhausen*

This cooperative's long-time director, Willi Merkle, recently retired, produced very high-quality sweet wines when conditions allowed. Gewürztraminer and Pinot Gris are the most common varieties for BA and TBA, but there are also intense sweet wines from Pinot Noir.

### Andreas Laible ☆☆
*77770 Durbach*

Sweet wines are not that common here, but when Laible produces them they are first-rate, being made from Scheurebe and Riesling.

### WG Sasbach ☆☆☆
*79361 Sasbach*

This small Kaiserstuhl cooperative sometimes produces delicious BAs and Eisweins from Ruländer, Gewürztraminer and even Pinot Noir.

Other fine producers of sweet wine include Blankenhorn, Johner, Männle, Schloss Ortenberg, WG Achkarren and WG Ehrenstetten.

# Franken

Franconia lies to the east of Germany's principal wine regions, so the climate is more continental, favouring dry wines over sweet. But the 6,000-hectare region's chief varieties – Riesling, Silvaner and Rieslaner – can, in exceptional vintages, produce excellent sweet wines. But they are rarities and highly priced. The best vintages of the past decade include 1990, 1992, 1993, 1994 and 1997.

## PRINCIPAL PRODUCERS
### Bürgerspital zum Heiligen Geist ✩✩
*97070 Würzburg*

Quality has declined at this vast charitable estate, but from time to time, as in 1997 and 1990, there are some exceptional BAs and TBAs. Auslesen tend to be quite high in alcohol and thus not especially sweet.

### Fürst ✩✩
*63927 Bürgstadt*

Paul Fürst is a specialist in dry wines, but his sweet wines from Rieslaner can be excellent too.

### Fürstlich Castell-sches Domäneamt ✩✩✩
*97335 Castell*

Life is still feudal at Castell, where the local princes still own the village, the bank and the organic wine estate, just as they did in the 12th century. Riesling is rare as a sweet wine, but there is very good Rieslaner and Müller-Thurgau and excellent Silvaner. Standards are high, with minimal Oechsle levels well above the legal requirements.

### Juliusspital ✩✩
*97070 Würzburg*

This large charitable institution produces succulent Riesling and Silvaner from the region's best-known site, Würzburger Stein.

### Staatlicher Hofkeller ✩✩✩
*97070 Würzburg*

This stunning cellar, based in the centre of town, produces classic wines from Riesling and Rieslaner from the town's best vineyards, notably Stein. Quality is now exceptional.

Other estates that do not specialise in sweet wines but produce excellent examples from time to time include "Am Lump", Horst Sauer, Schmitt's Kinder and Schloss Sommerhausen.

# Mittelrhein

This 600-hectare region follows the Rhine to the northwest of the Rheingau. It's Riesling territory, and the best recent vintages have been 1994, 1995 and 1996.

## PRINCIPAL PRODUCER
### Toni Jost ✩✩✩
*55422 Bacharach*

Quantities are tiny, but in appropriate vintages such as 1996 Peter Jost produces wonderfully racy sweet Rieslings up to TBA level. Other good-quality sweet Rieslings are produced by Lanius-Knab and Ratzenberger.

# Mosel-Saar-Ruwer

The renowned steeliness of Mosel wines is no myth. The steep slaty hillsides, bathed by prolonged pallid sunshine reinforced by reflected sunlight from the river below, deliver wines with a pronounced mineral character. In the sweet wines, this mineral complexity is at first masked by the residual sugar, but with time it re-emerges, blending marvellously with the exquisite fruit.

The Mosel region has been blessed with an extraordinary succession of vintages ever since 1988. Only the 1991 vintage is mediocre. The 1996, with its high acidity, may ultimately prove better for its superlative off-dry wines than for its intensely sweet ones, but vintages such as 1989, 1990, 1994, 1995 and 1997 are of the highest quality. All the wines mentioned below are Rieslings.

## PRINCIPAL PRODUCERS

### Bischöfliche Weingüter ☆☆
*54290 Trier*

The vineyards of this large ecclesiastical estate are scattered about the region. Its Auslesen and Eisweins from the Ruwer, especially from Kaseler Nies'chen, can be excellent, and it is also a major proprietor of the great Scharzhofberg vineyard in the Saar.

### Weingut Joh. Jos. Christoffel Erben ☆☆☆☆
*54539 Urzig*

Steep slaty vineyards in the Urziger Würzgarten yield marvellously rich and spicy sweet wines of great character and consistency.

### Robert Eymael (Mönchhof) ☆☆
*54539 Urzig*

After a bad patch with family problems causing some lack of direction, this fine estate is definitely back on form, its top wines emanating from the Erdener Prälat and Urziger Würzgarten vineyards.

### Weingut Le Gallais ☆☆☆
*544459 Wiltingen*

The Egon Müller family of Scharzhof (*see* entry) lease this small estate in the Saar and produce lovely wines from the Braune Kupp vineyards which tend to be a touch fleshier than those from Scharzhofberg.

### Grans-Fassian ☆☆☆
*5430 Leiwen*

Although situated in Leiwen, this estate's best wines come from the Trittenheimer Apotheke and Piesporter Goldtröpfchen vineyards. Often underrated in the past, the Grans-Fassian estate is now producing Auslesen, BAs and occasional Eiswein of very high quality.

### Fritz Haag ☆☆☆☆
*54472 Brauneberg*

The ebullient Wilhelm Haag is arguably the best winemaker in the Middle Mosel, somehow managing to combine richness of fruit and extract with vibrant acidity and ineffable elegance. His best wines always come from the Brauneberger Juffer-Sonnenuhr site. In a fine year such as 1997 he may produce three or four different Auslesen, differentiated by their capsules or AP (official certification) numbers. The wines have become very expensive, but they are as fine as anything in Germany.

### Reinhold Haart ☆☆☆☆
*54498 Piesport*

The great name of Piesport has been dragged through the mud by the German wine laws, which allow it to be used as a catchall for mass-production wines. Theo Haart has restored its reputation, producing rich but elegant wines with a pronounced mineral flavour from the great Goldtröpfchen vineyard.

### Weingut von Hövel ☆☆☆
*54329 Kunz-Oberemmel*

The joviality of Eberhard von Kunow should not disguise the fact that in recent years he has been producing a series of delicious and elegant Auslesen, BAs and Eiswein from his top site, the Oberemmeler Hütte.

### Karthäuserhof ☆☆☆☆
*54292 Eitelsbach*

When Christoph Tyrell isn't out shooting wild boar, he produces some extremely intense wines, finely honed and very long-lived. All the wines come from the Karthäuserhofberg vineyard, a monopoly of the estate.

### Reichsgraf von Kesselstatt ☆☆☆
*54290 Trier*

When the Reh family acquired this magnificent but dispersed estate, Annegret Reh-Gartner focused her efforts on the finest sites, which include the Josephshof (a monopoly in Graach), Scharzhof in the Saar, Kaseler Nies'chen in the Ruwer, and the world-famous Bernkasteler Doctor.

### Schloss Lieser ☆☆☆
*54470 Lieser*

The once-famous Schorlemer estate was allowed to fade into mediocrity, but new owners in the early 1990s restored it to life, and in the late 1990s the property was bought by its winemaker, Thomas Haag, the son of Wilhelm Haag of Fritz Haag (see entry). Under his direction quality has improved beyond recognition.

### Weingut Dr Loosen ☆☆☆☆
*54470 Bernkastel*

Ernie Loosen's vigour, flair and outspoken opinions have made him one of the most controversial figures along the Middle Mosel. But he owns wonderful sites – Erdener Prälat, Urziger Würzgarten and Wehlener Sonnenuhr – and a combination of very low yields, very late harvesting and great ambition have pushed the estate into the very top level. These sweet wines are ravishing in their purity of fruit, richness of extract and racy concentration. Enjoyable young, they seem fashioned to last for ever.

### Maximin Grünhaus ☆☆☆☆
*54318 Grünhaus-Mertesdorf*
The vineyards from the top estate in the Ruwer are of monastic origin: the Abtsberg was attached to the abbot, the Brudersberg to the monks and the Herrenberg to the local seigneurs. The Abtsberg still delivers the finest wines, but the other sites often rival it. These wines are very lean and closed in their youth, and their style is one of delicacy, nuance and exquisite fruit. They are consistently among the very top wines of the region.

### Egon Müller (Scharzhof) ☆☆☆☆
*54459 Wiltingen*
The Scharzhof manor house stands at the foot of the mighty Scharzhofberg. Despite the harshness of the Saar climate, the Müllers often manage to coax BAs, Eisweins and TBAs from this marvellous site. Such is their density of extract and tightness of acidity that they often need ten years in bottle to demonstrate their superlative finesse. Prices are frighteningly high, but the Müllers have no difficulty in selling their wines.

### Dr Pauly-Bergweiler ☆☆☆
*54470 Bernkastel*
Dr Peter Pauly is something of a loner in the Mosel, despite innumerable family connections along the valley. He and his wife (proprietor of the affiliated Peter Nicolay estate) own some outstanding sites: Urziger Würzgarten, Bernkasteler Alte Badstube, Erdener Prälat and Graacher Himmelreich. Dr Pauly likes to dabble in some eccentricities such as red wine, but when he puts his mind to it he can produce Eisweins and TBAs of the highest quality.

### Weingut Joh. Jos. Prüm ☆☆☆☆
*54470 Wehlen*
Dr Manfred Prüm, probably the most highly esteemed of the celebrated Prüm family which dominates Wehlen, delights in bringing visitors unidentified bottles from his capacious cellars. His delight is even greater when even experienced palates gravely underestimate the age of the wine. These are among the most long-lived of German wines, delicate, refined but somewhat inexpressive in their youth, but opening slowly to reveal a wealth of complexity and elegance.

### Weingut Max. Ferd. Richter ☆☆☆
*54486 Mülheim*
Dr Dirk Richter produces excellent wines from the Brauneberger

Juffer-Sonnenuhr, and has specialised for decades in Eiswein from the Mülheimer Helenenkloster. This Eiswein sets a very high standard, being both full of fruit and streaked with racy acidity.

## Schloss Saarstein ☆☆☆
*54455 Serrig*

Christian Ebert has directed this impeccable estate since 1986. The wines are classic Saar: lean, racy and requiring a few years in bottle before the exquisite fruit emerges. The Auslesen and BAs are lovely discreet wines, capable of a very long life.

## Willi Schaefer ☆☆☆☆
*54470 Graach*

Willi Schaefer is the best grower in Graach, but the estate is small and quantities are limited. But anyone seeing these wines needn't hesitate: they are of the highest quality, with the fruitiness typical of Graach but no lack of structure or length or concentration.

## Selbach-Oster ☆☆☆
*54492 Zeltingen*

Zeltingen is less well-known than its neighbouring vineyards of Wehlen, but Johannes Selbach is convinced that their quality is just as high. The Selbachs also own sites in Graach, Wehlen and Bernkastel, and all their wines are highly reliable.

## Weingut Wwe. Dr H Thanisch Erben ☆☆
*54470 Bernkastel-Kues*

Maddeningly, there are two estates here with identical names. This, the better of the two, belongs to the growers' association known as the VDP and bears its logo. The top wines come from the celebrated Bernkasteler Doctor vineyard, and although very good are highly priced.

## Dr Heinz Wagner ☆☆
*54439 Saarburg*

Heinz Wagner produces fine minerally wines from his slaty vineyards in the Saar. Auslese and Eiswein from the Saarburger Rausch can be excellent.

## Zilliken ☆☆☆☆
*54439 Saarburg*

Zilliken is an unimpeachable source of classic Saar wines: steely, racy and concentrated. Tightly structured, his sweet wines need time to evolve. Saarburger Rausch is his top site. In some vintages the Eiswein can be a touch extreme in its acidity.

Other fine producers of sweet wines include Willie Haag, Heymann-Löwenstein, Immich-Batterieberg, Karslmühle, Karp-Schreiber, Heribert Kerpen, Milz (Laurentiushof), S A Prüm, Studert-Prüm and Weins-Prüm.

# Nahe

This dispersed 4,600-hectare region has had difficulty in establishing its own identity, being dominated by the nearby Mosel and Rheingau. Its soils and expositions are very varied, as are the wines. More full-bodied than those from the Mosel, they share some of its mineral character, while having a broader structure more akin to wines from the Rheingau. The best vintages of the past decade have been 1990 and 1993–1997.

## PRINCIPAL PRODUCERS

### Crusius ☆☆

*55595 Traisen*

This highly traditional estate, run by Dr Peter Crusius, has been inconsistent in the past but now seems back on track. Its finest sites are Traiser Bastei and Traiser Rotenfels, giving powerful, complex, mineral wines.

### Schlossgut Diel ☆☆☆

*55452 Burg Layen*

Armin Diel leads a double life as one of Germany's leading wine writers and director of this excellent estate. After dabbling in very dry wines and *barrique*-fermentation, Diel is now focusing on more traditional styles. His Auslesen and Eisweins, usually from top sites in Dorsheim, can be outstanding.

### Hermann Dönnhoff ☆☆☆☆

*55585 Oberhausen*

For some years this has been the top estate in the Nahe, producing highly concentrated and elegant sweet wines, especially Eiswein, from the Oberhäuser Brücke and Niederhäuser Hermannshöhle vineyards.

### Gutsverwaltung Niederhausen-Schlossböckelheim ☆☆

*55585 Niederhausen*

Once a standard bearer in the region, this former state domaine, now owned by the Maurer family, is trying to recover its former renown. Its vineyards are among the best in the Nahe, and the Eisweins can be exceptional.

Other good Nahe estates include Paul Anheuser, Emrich-Schönleber, Kruger-Rumpf, Lötzbeyer, Schloss Wallhausen and Tesch.

# Pfalz

The old Palatinate region is, by German standards, warm, and its sweet wines have a lusciousness that makes up for their occasional breadth of flavour and lack of acidity. The region stretches for some 80 kilometres from north to south. In the north, Riesling thrives; further south, the Burgundian varieties are more successful. Many growers concentrate exclusively on dry wines, but few of the top estates can resist the challenge of producing a great Eiswein or TBA when conditions permit.

## PRINCIPAL PRODUCERS

### Bassermann-Jordan ☆☆
*67142 Deidesheim*

Of the great private estates that dominate the northern Pfalz, Bassermann-Jordan has often proved a disappointment. Now with a new winemaker, Ulrich Mell, things are looking up, and we can hope for a return to the rich, spicy Auslesen and TBAs that were once among the estate's glories.

### Reichsrat von Buhl ☆☆☆☆
*67146 Deidesheim*

After many lacklustre years, a new winemaker, Frank John, was installed and the improvement was swift. John lowered yields, abolished Süssreserve and practised non-interventionist wine-making. For sweet wines their top sites are usually Forster Ungeheuer and Jesuitengarten. In 1994, a great year here for botrytis wines, they harvested a Scheurebe TBA at 280 Oechsle; it has a tooth-wrecking 500 grammes per litre of sugar and an equally punishing 20 grammes of acidity. The 1996 Eisweins are probably the best ever from von Buhl.

### Dr Bürklin-Wolf ☆☆☆
*67157 Wachenheim*

This large estate focuses on its superb dry Rieslings but also makes delicious and intense Riesling Eiswein when conditions permit. And in 1994 they harvested an astonishing Scheurebe TBA at 254 Oechsle.

### Christmann ☆☆☆
*67435 Gimmeldingen*

A small estate with a fine reputation, Christmann produce lovely Rieslings from Deidesheim and Ruppertsberg. The sweet styles are sumptuous without being heavy or cloying.

### Kurt Darting ☆☆
*67098 Bad Dürkheim*

Darting may not have the finest sites but makes the most of them, offering succulent sweet wines from Riesling, Scheurebe and other varieties; the wines tend to be quite soft and approachable young.

### Weingut Dr Deinhard ☆☆☆
*67146 Deidesheim*

Leased for decades by the Wegeler family, the performance of this fine estate has been uneven, but in recent years there have been some splendid BAs and Eisweins from Deidesheim and Ruppertsberg.

### Koehler-Ruprecht ☆☆☆
*67169 Kallstadt*

Bernd Philippi, one of Germany's most innovative winemakers, has a fondness for attempting botrytis wines from Pinot Noir as well as Riesling. He claims that in 1983 he made the first Pinot Noir Eiswein! The overall results can be a bit hit and miss. One of his more consistent wines is Elysium, a BA blended from different varieties and aged for three years in new oak. His Riesling BA from Kallstadter Saumagen is made in a powerful, high-alcohol style not to everyone's taste.

### Lingenfelder ✩✩✩
*67229 Grosskarlbach*

Best known for his Pinot Noirs, Rainer Lingenfelder also produces fine Rieslings and, from time to time, sensational BA and TBA from Scheurebe.

### Georg Mosbacher ✩✩✩
*67147 Forst*

In a region where the wines, even the Rieslings, tend to be quite broad, Mosbacher opts for elegance. These aren't powerful wines, but they have a lovely purity and stylishness.

### Müller-Catoir ✩✩✩✩
*67433 Haardt*

In Germany the cellarmaster keeps a low profile, but every lover of German wines knows that Herr Catoir owns the estate and Hans-Günter Schwarz makes the wines. Schwarz has taught generations of now prominent winemakers, so his influence has spread through the Pfalz.

From vineyards in Haardt and Gimmeldingen, Schwarz has for years produced the most luminous, dazzling, pure and enchanting sweet wines not only from Riesling but from Scheurebe and Rieslaner. The Rieslaner, with its breathtaking acidity, is unfailingly brilliant.

### Pfeffingen (Fuhrmann-Eymael) ✩✩
*67098 Bad Dürkheim*

Doris Fuhrmann manages this excellent estate, which produces broad, rich, sweet wines from Scheurebe as well as Riesling.

### J L Wolf ✩✩
*67157 Wachenheim*

Ernst Loosen, of the eponymous Mosel estate, and co-investors have taken over this faded property, which owns excellent vineyards none the less. Initial vintages suggest there are splendid things to come.

## Rheingau

This celebrated 3,250-hectare region, flanked along the Rhine with a swath of south-facing vineyards planted almost entirely with Riesling, has not been performing with great consistency over the past decade. There has been a good deal of internal politics, and uncertainties about the best styles for the region. But the Rheingau can produce stunning sweet wines. Outstanding vintages include 1990 and 1993–1996.

## PRINCIPAL PRODUCERS

### Georg Breuer ☆☆☆☆
*65385 Rüdesheim*

Bernhard Breuer has in recent years trimmed his range down to dry wines and very sweet ones, mostly from excellent sites in Rüdesheim. These are succulent, honeyed wines with vivacious fruit structure and excellent length.

### Schloss Johannisberg ☆☆☆
*65366 Johannisberg*

This famous old estate, with its marvellous vineyards sloping down towards the Rhine, has not always lived up to its reputation. In recent years there have been some great BAs and Eisweins, but their colossal prices means that they will inevitably disappear into collectors' cellars.

### Johannishof ☆☆☆
*65366 Johannisberg*

The Eser family produce some lovely Auslesen and even sweeter wines from their sites in Johannisberg and Rüdesheim.

### August Kesseler ☆☆
*65385 Assmannshausen*

In addition to fine rich Rieslings from Rüdesheimer Bischofsberg, Kesseler maintains the local tradition of producing sweet wines from Pinot Noir. They are intensely strawberry-scented but an acquired taste.

### Peter Jakob Kühn ☆☆☆
*65375 Oestrich*

Although a specialist in dry Rieslings, Kühn also makes stunning sweet wines up to TBA level. They are usually marketed without a vineyard designation.

### Franz Künstler ☆☆☆
*65239 Hochheim*

Gunter Künstler was a rising star in the 1980s and has now expanded his estate by buying the nearby Aschrott domaine. He gets good ripeness levels from his Hochheim vineyards, and the sweet wines are rich and intense.

### Josef Leitz ☆☆
*65385 Rüdesheim*

An enthusiast for non-interventionist winemaking, Johannes Leitz makes fine sweet wines from steep vineyards in Rüdesheim.

### Schloss Reinhartshausen ☆☆☆
*65346 Eltville-Erbach*

Owned by the princes of Prussia, this large estate has had its ups and downs over the past 15 years. Considerable investment has led to rising standards, and there have been some spectacular sweet wines in recent vintages.

### Balthasar Ress ☆☆☆
*65347 Hattenheim*

Stefan Ress has genuine enthusiasm for sweet wines and produces them up to TBA level. As well as fruit and intensity, they often have an enticing charm and sprightliness.

### Schloss Schönborn ☆☆
*65347 Hattenheim*

This fine aristocratic estate made some wonderful sweet wines in the late 1980s but has performed with less consistency in recent years. But a TBA from the great Erbacher Marcobrunn vineyard can be a mind-blowing wine.

### Staatsweingüter Kloster Eberbach ☆☆
*65343 Eltville*

This enormous state domaine owns some of the finest vineyards in the Rheingau, and in the 1970s and 1980s it was a pioneer of Eiswein under its former director, Dr Hans Ambrosi. Since then its performance has been patchy, but it is still a source of excellent sweet wines.

### J Wegeler Erben ☆☆☆
*65375 Oestrich-Winkel*

Once associated with the Deinhard family, this estate has witnessed many changes. Today it focuses on dry wines and very sweet wines. The latter, often produced from the Oestricher Lenchen vineyard, are rich and vibrant and capable of very long ageing.

### Robert Weil ☆☆☆☆
*65399 Kiedrich*

It has taken only a decade for this estate to emerge as the finest domaine in the Rheingau, offering a plethora of magnificent sweet wines from various sites in Kiedrich, notably the Gräfenberg. These wines have everything: fruit, concentration, complexity, persistence, freshness. Worldwide acclaim means that prices are exceedingly high.

Other good sources of sweet Rheingau wines include Graf von Kanitz, Knyphausen, Hans Lang, Langwerth von Simmern and Prinz.

# Rheinhessen

If the Rheinhessen has a reputation for sweet wine, it isn't a very good one. This is the home of the cheapest German wines, mass produced from high-yielding Müller-Thurgau and other varieties. Yet there is a substantial amount of Riesling here, and certain areas, especially those close to the Rhine and known as the Rheinfront, can produce very fine wines. They rarely have the same acidic structure as those from the Mosel or Rheingau and do not keep quite as well. The best vintages of the past decade have been 1990, 1992, 1993 and 1996, but other than 1991 all years since 1988 have been above average.

## PRINCIPAL PRODUCERS

### Balbach ☆☆
*55283 Nierstein*

An estate mentioned here for its illustrious past and its promising future. It is currently being leased by Fritz Hasselbach of Gunderloch (*see* entry), and he has been breathing new life into the run-down property.

### Gunderloch ☆☆☆☆
*55299 Nackenheim*

The modest Fritz and Agnes Hasselbach secured their starring role in the Rheinhessen in the late 1980s and haven't put a foot wrong since. The best sweet wines come from the steep red-soiled Rothenberg vineyard and have a strong mineral tone. Tightly structured, they keep very well.

### Keller ☆☆☆
*67592 Flörsheim-Dalsheim*

A new star in the Rheinhessen, Klaus Keller makes superlative Eiswein and TBA from the Dalsheimer Hubacker vineyard, Riesling wines with mouth-watering fruit and remarkable concentration of flavour.

### Kühling-Gillot ☆☆
*55294 Bodenheim*

Roland Gillot produces a wide range of wines, including the occasional TBA from Oppenheimer Sackträger. They are made in a fairly opulent style, with the emphasis on rich fruit rather than a racy elegant structure.

### Schales ☆
*67592 Flörsheim-Dalsheim*

With a wide selection of grape varieties at their disposal, the Schales brothers delight in producing an enormous list of wines each year. Consequently, quality is patchy, and some wines are decidedly odd, none more so than the sparkling Eiswein!

### Wittmann ☆☆
*67593 Westhofen*

Wittmann, like so many estates in the Rheinhessen, have a wide palette of grape varieties from which to create their wines, and varieties as different as Riesling, Albalonga and Chardonnay have been used for their rich TBAs.

# Württemberg

This is generally red-wine country, but from time to time sweet wines do emerge.

## PRINCIPAL PRODUCER

### J F Feindert ☆☆
*74321 Bietigheim-Bissingen*

Joachim Feindert is highly unusual in having the courage to

produce nothing but Eiswein, either from Riesling or from the local red grape, Trollinger. The wines are aged in new oak and are extremely expensive.

# Austria

## The history

Austria has been producing sweet wine since at the least the 17th century. Southeast of Vienna, in the Burgenland province, lies a large shallow lake, the Neusiedlersee. Almost every year, autumnal fogs provoke botrytis, and the vineyards around the lake are awash with noble rot. This is one of the few areas in the world where botrytis wines can be produced in prodigious quantities.

Unfortunately, these ideal circumstances led to a scandal that severely damaged the Austrian wine industry. In Germany, high-quality sweet wines are hard to make and costly, so German importers and tourists delighted in the seemingly inexhaustible sources of cheap botrytis wines in Austria. Demand was strong, and in the 1980s a handful of producers doctored their wines with diethylene glycol. The additive was not toxic, but this kind of adulteration constituted fraud. Although only a few producers were directly involved, these malpractices were well-known to be taking place.

Once the scandal erupted in 1985, wine exports collapsed. The Austrian wine authorities eventually took action, jailing the offenders and introducing the toughest wine laws in Europe. Gradually, the market recovered, and by the mid-1990s Austrian sweet wines had become not only acceptable once more but positively fashionable. In large part this was due to the marketing genius of two leading producers, Alois Kracher and Willi Opitz.

## Burgenland

There are two distinctive styles of sweet wines produced around the Neusiedlersee. On the west, around the town of Rust, wines are made in quite an alcoholic style, with the emphasis on body and power as well as sweetness. On the eastern shore, known as the Seewinkel, botrytis is very common in most years thanks to the presence of numerous stagnant ponds as well as the lake, and the wines are more Germanic in style, if slightly richer. In general, wines from Rust have better acidity and are very long-lived, whereas those from the Seewinkel, produced on sandier soils, have lower acidity and age more rapidly. But this is a tendency rather than a firm rule.

Many different grape varieties are used to produce sweet wines. Welschriesling, which should not be confused with Rhein Riesling, is thin-skinned and attracts botrytis easily. Bouvier, a local variety, also ripens early; it can give concentrated wines but lacks acidity and character. Neuburger is similar in structure and ripening but a touch broader. Rhein Riesling is not frequently encountered here and neither is Austria's most prolific white variety, Grüner

Veltliner, but Scheurebe is more common and gives excellent sweet wines with fine acidity. Just to confuse the world, some growers persist in labelling the wine "Sämling 88", the Austrian name for Scheurebe. In recent years there has been a revival of Furmint; the Burgenland was Hungarian territory until 1921, which explains why this Hungarian variety has a foothold here. Muskat Ottonel can give excellent sweet wines. Gewürztraminer (usually known here simply as Traminer) is also quite common. But many of the finest wines are made either from Pinot Blanc (Weissburgunder) or Chardonnay. Alois Kracher (*see* entry below) likes Welschriesling for its finesse and Chardonnay for its power and concentration.

Sweet wines are classified along German lines, but with significant variations. Austrians have their own system for measuring sugar content in the grapes: Klosterneuburger Mostwaage (KMW). The minimum must weights for Beerenauslese (BA) and Eiswein are 25 KMW (127 Oechsle), and 30 KMW (156 Oechsle) for Trockenbeerenauslese (TBA). In addition there is an intermediate category known as Ausbruch, for which the minimum must weight is 27 KMW (138 Oechsle).

Ausbruch, with its distinctive style, is a speciality of Rust. Often a small proportion of non-botrytised fruit is added before fermentation. The alcohol level is about 14 degrees, and thus the residual sugar levels are not that high; 80–120 grammes would be usual. The wine is often deep-coloured and can have a slight oxidative tone; this would have been universal 30 years ago, but today some growers are looking for a fresher style. There is some consternation among the Rust growers since other wine regions have adopted the term Ausbruch on their labels, which is legal but misleading.

Ausbruch dates back to the 17th century, but Schilfwein is a recent revival, having been pioneered by Willi Opitz and then adopted by some other growers. This is a technique whereby healthy bunches are laid out on reeds to dry, a method akin to Italian *passito* traditions. A plastic tunnel is placed over the bed of reeds, allowing the wind to blow through and dry the grapes and protecting them from rain.

1981 was a great vintage here and 1990 excellent for Eiswein. There was a large crop of botrytis wines in 1991 and 1995, with excellent quality too. In 1996 the autumn was cool, and although this has been a fine year for sweet wines, acidity levels are much higher than usual. Very small quantities of sweet wine were produced in 1997. 1998 could well prove a great vintage.

## PRINCIPAL PRODUCERS
### Altenberg ☆
*7122 Gols*

Roman Leitner is a specialist in high-alcohol Eiswein, adding powerful yeasts to bring alcohol levels up to about 18 degrees. Of course, the residual sugar level is correspondingly low. Although I find these wines undrinkable, there seems to be a clientele for them. The TBA can be excellent.

### Feiler-Artinger ☆☆☆☆
*7071 Rust*

Hans Feiler and his son Kurt are masters of Ausbruch, which they usually produce from Welschriesling and Weissburgunder (Pinot Cuvée), although in some years they make a Traminer Ausbruch. The Pinot Cuvée is now aged in new oak, but the wood is not obtrusive. The Feilers also specialise in Essenz, which they say is also a traditional wine of Rust. In 1997 the must for the Essenz was so rich that the fermentation came to a halt at five per cent.

### Martin Haider ☆☆
*7142 Illmitz*

There are many Haiders in Illmitz: this is one of the best. In 1998 a delicious TBA was made from Muskat Ottonel, and in 1995 an unusual TBA was produced from the red Zweigelt grape, as well as a debut Sauvignon Blanc TBA.

### Juris ☆☆
*7122 Gols*

This winery used to be known as Stiegelmar, and Georg Stiegelmar preserved traditional techniques inherited from the Hungarians. As well as Ausbruch, he made fascinating wines called Masslach and Eszensia. Stiegelmar has retired, and his son Axel has renamed the winery and trimmed the range. In 1982 Georg Stiegelmar revived "straw wine" (Strohwein), which is still produced. The grapes are dried for up to six months; after pressing, the wine is partly aged in *barriques*. Bouvier, Chardonnay and Weissburgunder are the preferred varieties for Strohwein.

TBAs are made in the best vintages and aged in new oak. Imperialis is a top-flight sweet wine that varies from vintage to vintage. In 1995 it was a BA from Chardonnay, Welschriesling, Bouvier and Weissburgunder; in 1996, an Ausbruch.

### Kollwentz ☆☆☆
*7051 Markt Grosshöflein*

Kollwentz is best known for its dry wines, but when it does occasionally produce a sweet wine – such as the 1996 Weissburgunder BA or the fabulous 1995 Chardonnay TBA – it is usually exceptional.

### Alois Kracher ☆☆☆☆
*7142 Illmitz*

The formidable Alois Kracher took over the family estate in 1986 and within a few years was widely regarded as the finest sweet-wine producer in Austria. The wines' greatness lies in their balance: all the wines are rich and concentrated and high in extract, with a fine but not over-assertive acidity and wonderful length of flavour.

There are two styles of wine here. Zwischen den Seen ("between the lakes") is aged in neutral casks. The Nouvelle Vague range is fermented in new *barriques* and aged on the fine lees for at least 12 months. Since 1991 Kracher has singled out what he believes is his best, most harmonious wine and dubbed it Grand Cuvée. It is nearly always from Chardonnay and Welschriesling and is produced only in top vintages.

1991 was Alois Kracher's first outstanding year (although his father had made some wonderful 1981s), and the finest vintage thus far is the spectacular 1995, in which he produced no fewer than 15 TBAs. Kracher learns fast, and in each successive year there seems to be ever greater sophistication and finesse.

### Helmut Lang ☆☆☆☆
*7142 Illmitz*
An increasingly reliable source of botrytis wines, Lang made some spicy TBAs in 1995 and 1996 from Scheurebe. Although Ausbruch is more commonly encountered in Rust, Lang has also made a speciality of the style. What's more, his Eiswein is among the best in Austria.

### Münzenrieder ☆☆
*7143 Apetlon*
The Münzenrieder family run a fairly commercial operation, so quality is variable, but they are capable of producing some fine BAs and TBAs, especially from Bouvier, a wine often marked by distinctive creaminess. The Scheurebe TBA can also be very intense if slightly one-dimensional.

### Nekowitsch ☆☆
*7142 Illmitz*
Gerhard Nekowitsch specialises in Schilfwein, including one from the red grape Zweigelt. I prefer the fine 1995 Scheurebe TBA and 1995 Zweigelt Eiswein.

### Willi Opitz ☆☆☆
*7142 Illmitz*
Opitz is a dazzling manipulator of grapes and pretty skilled at handling the media too. In 1988 he made 27 different wines from his few hectares, but it's his sensational sweet wines that are the most exciting. Opitz is an innovator, and in 1989 he invented the technique for producing Schilfwein. Opitz also uses red grapes such as Blauburger to produce Eiswein and TBA. To the intense annoyance of the California estate Opus One, Opitz named one of his wines Opitz One. The Californians didn't find it funny, but everyone else did and the wine has proved successful. It's usually a Schilfwein, blending Zweigelt and Blaufränkisch. The traditional wines are excellent too, such as the exciting 1995 TBAs.

### Josef Pöckl ☆☆☆
*7123 Mönchhof*
Pöckl is best known for his splendid red wines, but in recent years he has been turning to sweet wines too. In 1995 he made TBAs from Scheurebe and Pinot Noir, the latter too acidic, but the Scheurebes are wonderful.

### Peter Schandl ☆☆☆☆
*7071 Rust*

The jovial and kindly Schandl runs a Heurige (wine bar) near the Wine Academy in Rust, and it's a good place in which to sample his wines. Ausbruch is his speciality, often made from Ruländer or Furmint. Yields are very low — 12 hectolitres per hectare in 1995 — and Schandl is careful not to make wines too high in alcohol. Without displaying the least staleness, they often display a smoky, lightly oxidative tone that is entirely characteristic of authentic Ausbruch.

### Heidi Schröck ☆☆☆
*7071 Rust*

Another specialist in Ausbruch, Heidi Schröck often blends Welschriesling, Weissburgunder and Muskat Ottonel. The wines have an intense fruitiness as well as typical Ausbruch power. Her Chardonnay BA is delicious.

### Ernst Triebaumer ☆☆☆
*7071 Rust*

Triebaumer is celebrated for red wines, but in certain years he also makes outstanding Ausbruch. He is one of the few growers who sometimes produces Ausbruch from Sauvignon Blanc. It's a grape well suited to the purity of flavour that he seeks.

### Paul Triebaumer ☆☆
*7071 Rust*

This innovative, sometimes eccentric winemaker, brother of the more famous Ernst (*see* entry above), makes only Ausbruch in top years such as 1991, 1995, 1996 and 1998. He blends a majority of botrytised grapes with some bunches of healthy overripe grapes that will contribute freshness to the wine. The wine is aged in *barriques* for up to 12 months, and he avoids an oxidative style. In 1995 his Ausbruch from Furmint and Muskateller was sumptuous.

### Velich ☆☆
*7143 Apetlon*

Velich is renowned for his oaky Chardonnay, and he also makes a majestic Chardonnay TBA, fermented and aged in new oak. His TBAs from Muskat Ottonel and Welschriesling are excellent too.

### Wenzel ☆☆
*7071 Rust*

The courteous, conservative Robert Wenzel is a specialist in Ausbruch. Now semi-retired, he is making way for his son Michael. The Ausbruch Cuvée is often a blend of Furmint, Müller-Thurgau and Gelber Muskateller; there are also single-variety Ausbruchs such as the assertive Furmint and the brilliant 1993 Sauvignon Blanc. There have also been some very impressive and intense BAs and TBAs over the years. Quality can be exceptional, but there are occasional disappointments.

Very good wines can also be found at Paul Achs (Gols), Angerhof (Illmitz), Josef Gangl (Illmitz), Grenzhof (Mörbisch), Hafner (Mönchhof), Vinzenz Haider (Illmitz), Hammer (Rust), Kraft (Rust), Leberl (Grosshöflein), Seiler (Rust), Steiner (Podersdorf), Terra Galos (Gols), Tinhof (Eisenstadt), Stefan Tischida (Illmitz) and Ziniel (St Andrä).

# Kamptal-Donauland

The valleys just north of the Danube have much in common with the Wachau, which it neighbours to the southwest, although loess as well as volcanic soils give a different structure to many of the wines. This is not ideal territory for botrytis wines, but there are certain vintages when exceptional wines can be made in this style. There was abundant botrytis in 1995.

## PRINCIPAL PRODUCERS
### Baron Geymüller ☆☆☆
*3506 Krems-Hollenburg*
Superlative TBAs – Riesling in 1995 and Chardonnay in 1996 – show what can be done in the Krems area when conditions are right.

### Jurtschitsch ☆☆
*3550 Langenlois*
Best known as fine producers of Grüner Veltliner, Jurtschitsch have made good Eiswein from the variety, as in 1988, and, more recently, splendid TBA from Chardonnay and Grüner Veltliner.

### Malat ☆☆☆
*3511 Furth bei Göttweig*
Gerald Malat is one of Austria's top winemakers, from time to time releasing an outstanding sweet wine, such as the intense 1995 Sauvignon Blanc TBA and the exquisitely balanced 1998 Riesling TBA.

I have also encountered good sweet wines from Hiedler (Langenlois), Mantlerhof (Brunn), Franz Maurer (Schiltern), Toni Mayr (Dross), Metternich-Sándor (Strass) and Nigl (Senftenberg).

# Styria

This gorgeously verdant region, tucked against the Slovenian border, is best known for its exquisite white wines. It is not known for its sweet wines, but there are exceptions. A good deal of Gewürztraminer is grown, and the village of Klöch lays a (scarcely sustainable) claim to producing the best Traminer in the world. Occasionally some BA or TBA can be made from the grape. A few growers also make Ausbruch, to the intense annoyance of the inhabitants of Rust. Winkler-Hermaden in Kapfenstein sometimes ekes out fine BA and TBA not just from Traminer but from Weissburgunder too. In 1995 the two varieties were blended, and the result was rather raisiny. A 1979 Weissburgunder TBA from Sattler was marred by high alcohol.

# Thermenregion

Just south of Vienna is the famous wine village of Gumpolds-kirchen, renowned for its rich, sometimes sweet white wines. In the 1980s its reputation plummeted, as rumours spread that much of the wine sold under its name was not authentic. Gumpolds-kirchen is remarkable for its local grape varieties: Rotgipfler and Zierfandler, the latter also known, confusingly, as Spätrot. They give juice high in sugar, and thus wines high in alcohol. The two varieties are usually blended. Other parts of the Thermenregion produce dry white wines, but fine sweet wines do crop up.

## PRINCIPAL PRODUCERS
### Alphart ☆☆☆
*2514 Traiskirchen*

Although not based in Gumpoldskirchen, Karl Alphart has a good deal of Spätrot and Rotgipfler in his vineyards, and in vintages such as 1990, 1994 and 1995 made some excellent BAs and TBAs.

### Biegler ☆☆☆
*2352 Gumpoldskirchen*

A leading producer of the region, who on rare occasions, such as 1995, manages to make outstanding Zierfandler TBA.

### Franz Kurz ☆☆
*2352 Gumpoldskirchen*

Kurz is known for some outstanding caramelly TBAs from vintages such as 1981, 1989, 1990 and 1995.

### Schellmann ☆☆☆
*2352 Gumpoldskirchen*

Schellmann is best known for dry wines, but the occasional sweet wines, such as the 1995 Chardonnay TBA, can be first-rate.

# Wachau

Botrytis occurs with surprising frequency in the Wachau. It showed up in 1995 and again in 1998. The outbreak is usually partial and not necessarily unwelcome as it can add rich nuances to a dry wine, but in years such as 1998 it affected a sizable portion of the crop, leaving growers with stocks of atypical Auslese and BA-style wines.

## PRINCIPAL PRODUCERS
### Freie Weingärtner Wachau ☆
*3601 Dürnstein*

In the days before this excellent cooperative adopted its new name, it made a habit of producing the occasional sweet wine, such as a peachy but not very persistent Müller-Thurgau BA in 1979. A similar wine was made in 1996, with a smoky botrytis nose and a silky texture.

### Leo Alzinger ☆☆☆
*3601 Unterloiben*

Alzinger produced a BA from Grüner Veltliner in 1983, and then in 1995 made a fine Riesling BA – but unfortunately, only in tiny quantities.

### Nikolaihof ☆☆
*3512 Mautern*

Nikolaus Saahs has been a fairly regular producer of TBAs, often a blend of Riesling, Neuburger and Grüner Veltliner, having made the wine in 1971, 1975, 1983 and 1986. The 1983 was voluptuous and appley.

### F X Pichler ☆☆☆
*3601 Oberloiben*

Austria's greatest winemaker? Perhaps. The unforthcoming Pichler is certainly the most revered, and his dry wines are magnificent. Just occasionally, as in 1994, he produces sweet wines, such as a Grüner Veltliner Eiswein and a TBA from Sauvignon Blanc.

## Weinviertel

This region to the east, north and northwest of Vienna is enormous, so there is a wide range of wine styles. Botrytis is rare, but fine Eiswein can be made. Some suffer from a baked raisiny quality that is unappealing in Eiswein, which should be pure and clean.

The leading Eiswein producer is Friedrich Rieder of Kleinhadersdorf, who has made examples from varieties as diverse as St Laurent (a red grape), Weissburgunder (outstanding in 1991), Müller-Thurgau and Riesling. Strell in Radlbrunn can also be recommended.

# Hungary: Tokaji

## The history

Tokaji's reputation stretches well back to the 17th century. Its wine, produced from *aszú* (shrivelled and botrytised) berries, was adored by the Russian tsars. Louis XIV of France famously pronounced it the king of wines and the wine of kings – a slogan that those promoting Tokaji wine have never allowed us to forget.

The vineyards – clay on volcanic subsoil – line the slopes behind the village of Tokaji and other villages, covering about 5,500 hectares. Furmint is the principal grape variety, giving a powerful wine rich in acidity. The other important variety, Hárslevelü, now accounts for about one-third of the vineyard area, the rest being planted with Muscat. Hárslevelü contributes a floweriness that balances the steeliness of Furmint. Furmint is attacked by botrytis earlier than Hárslevelü, but the latter is less prone to rot should it rain heavily in the autumn.

During the autumn fogs mount the slopes from the River Bodrog, activating noble rot. Grapes untouched by botrytis are picked and vinified in the normal way, and the resulting base-wine is set aside. In October or early November the botrytised grapes are picked by hand then pulped before being added to the base-wine. This addition of sweet paste provokes a further fermentation, which results in the *aszú* wine.

In pre-industrial times the *aszú* grapes were harvested into a hod known as a putton, each holding about 25 kilogrammes of grapes before the fruit was pulped. Up to six hods or *puttonyos* could be added to a *gönc* (136-litre cask) of base-wine. The final wine was said to have as many *puttonyos* as hods were added. Inevitably the higher the *puttonyos*, the sweeter and richer in extract was the final wine.

Well, that's the theory. Today nobody plays around with *gönc* barrels or *putton* hods. But the basic ratios of pulp to base-wine are preserved. Tokaji is available as a three-, four-, five- or occasionally six-*puttonyos* wine, and there is also an off-the-scale style known as Aszú Eszencia. Moreover, there is the very rare Eszencia (not to be confused with Aszú Eszencia), which is the free-run juice, thick and sticky and very high in sugar. This is fermented separately but is so rich in sugar that it can rarely be induced to ferment beyond about six degrees of alcohol, and often there is as little as three. Eszencia, which no doubt was the ultra-intense wine so admired by royalty, can't really be drunk, except a thimble-full at a time. Nowadays it is customarily used as a highly potent blending wine.

At the other end of the scale is Szamarodni, which is a Polish word meaning "as it comes". When botrytised grapes or bunches are dispersed, they are sometimes picked together with healthy bunches and vinified together. The resulting wine can either be dry or lightly sweet; under collectivisation, sweet Szamarodni was defined as having a residual sugar level of between 10 and 50 grammes, whereas a three-*puttonyos* Tokaji had from 60 to 90.

The renown of the wine led to a classification of the vineyards in the early 18th century, long predating other classifications such as the Bordeaux rankings of 1855. But all these distinctions were lost when in 1948 the vineyards were collectivised. No longer were the wines made by innumerable individual producers, each nurturing them in the maze of moist underground cellars tunnelled into the Tokaji hills; instead, wine production was centralised at immense vinification plants. The wine was still aged for many years in the underground cellars, but it was also fined, severely filtered, and pasteurised, which could only have harmed its overall quality. Different standards of Tokaji were produced for different markets, the best being exported westwards, the worst being watered and shipped to Russia.

The state regulators laid down precise criteria for the production of each *puttonyos* level, specifying minimal levels of residual sugar, acidity and dry extract, and the ageing period required in small barrels. Moreover, those barrels were rarely if ever topped up – the humidity levels in the tunnelled cellars were high enough to inhibit evaporation – and inevitably some oxidative tones crept into the wine, resulting in caramelly flavours.

None the less, "industrial" Tokaji was not at all bad, which is probably a tribute to the intrinsic virtue of the *terroir*. But once the Communist era ended in 1990 and new investment flowed into the region, both growers and newcomers began to consider afresh the style and nature of authentic Tokaji. Among these revisionists were István Szepsy, a grower in the village of Mád, and Peter Vinding-Diers of the Royal Tokaji Wine Company.

They believed that Tokaji, contrary to popular belief reinforced by practices under collectivisation, should not be an oxidative wine. Vinding-Diers campaigned to reduce the barrel-ageing periods, seeking to minimise oxidation in the finished wine. The result was sweeter, fresher and cleaner. At first the authorities disapproved, although subsequently they relented and allowed this "new" style of wine to be sold. The revisionists stirred up a good deal of controversy. Some adherents to the oxidative style, notably the remnants of the gradually privatised former State Farm (now known as the Tokaji Trading Company), believed that Royal Tokaji were simply trying to recoup their investments sooner by bottling the wine after only three years of ageing rather than the traditional five to ten. Moreover, they argue, Tokaji never was a fruity botrytis wine in the manner of Sauternes, and the oxidative character is intrinsic to its authenticity. The revisionists insisted, however, that they were merely returning to the authentic style of pre-war Tokaji. Today, the revisionists have the edge, and most commercially available Tokaji nowadays is made in a fresher, livelier style than the toffee-tinged wines of the 1970s and 1980s.

István Szepsy insists that if you are prepared to wait long enough and be selective enough in the vineyard, it should be possible to make some *aszú* wine each year. The great (or at least abundant) years for *aszú* wines have been 1957, 1959, 1964, 1968, 1972, 1973, 1975, 1979, 1983, 1985, 1988, 1989, 1993, 1995 and 1997.

A few of the Tokaji vineyards lie just across the border in Slovakia, which produces a wine reminiscent of the old State Farm bottlings from Hungary. The Hungarians are furious at what they consider a desecration of a famous name. It is certainly true that the Slovaks bottle a two-puttonyos aszú wine that has no equivalent in Hungary. The samples I have tasted have been unimpressive.

# Principal producers
## Chateau Megyer ☆☆
*3950 Sárospatak*

The largest share of the estate is owned by the French insurance company GAN. The first vintage here was 1992, and the wines are produced by a management team headed by Jean-Michel Arcaute of Château Clinet in Pomerol, with Michel Rolland as consultant. The wines are aged in Hungarian oak barrels. In order to differentiate these wines from those of Pajzos (*see* entry below), with which there are formalised links, the Megyer wines are made in a lighter style and have proved somewhat disappointing, even in the fine 1993 vintage.

## Chateau Pajzos ☆☆☆
*3950 Sárospatak*

The 60-hectare Pajzos domaine, created in 1991, occupies vineyards south of Sárospatak. Owned by the French consortium Compagnie Financière des Grands Vins de Tokaji, Pajzos works closely on the commercial front with Chateau Megyer (*see* entry above). Michel Rolland is the consultant to both. Pajzos concentrates on higher-quality wines than Megyer, and produced very good 1993s, including a superb Eszencia with 500 grammes of residual sugar. In 1997 they produced a curiosity: a very sweet Muscat with a powerful grapefruity flavour.

## Disznókö ☆☆☆☆
*3910 Tokaji*

This first growth property was acquired in 1992 by AXA Insurance, who also owns Château Suduiraut (*see* entry) in Sauternes. After much replanting, some 100 hectares are under vine, 60 per cent planted with Furmint. Disznókö has conducted experiments to work out the best way to vinify Tokaji, and appears to favour adding the *aszú* grapes to fresh must rather than to a fermented base-wine. Although the newcomers have been accused of importing French *barriques* and thus imposing alien flavours on Tokaji, Disznókö uses French-coopered Hungarian oak barrels, none new.

1993 was the first really good vintage here, especially the five- and six-*puttonyos*. They also produced an Aszú Eszencia, aged five years in barrel, with 200 grammes of residual sugar. Their pure Eszencia in 1993 fermented for five years and crept up to three per cent, leaving 700 grammes of residual sugar, and 24 grammes of acidity! The 1997 vintage looks promising here too. The overall style is one of freshness and vigour, with complex flavours of apple, quince and, sometimes, tropical fruit such as pineapple, and there is very little oxidative character, which is the way the winery wants it.

## Hétszölö ☆☆
*3910 Tokaji*

This famous 47-hectare estate apparently dates back to 1502, and was administered by the Habsburg monarchy as part of their imperial domaines for two centuries. The new owners are Grands Millésimes de France and the Japanese firm of Suntory. The vineyard is a south-facing classified growth, but the State Farm could never afford to replant vineyards here, so this major task has been undertaken by the new owners, and it will be some time before the true grandeur of the site will be apparent in the wines. The 1993 vintage was good but produced almost entirely from purchased *aszú* fruit. The wine is aged for three to four years in barrels previously used for Sauternes.

## Oremus ☆☆
*3934 Tolcsva*

Oremus, although acquired by Spain's legendary Vega Sicilia estate, was slow to get off the mark. It began by launching wines blended from former State Farm vintages under its own name. Oremus's first vintage was 1993, but it was produced in rushed conditions. At first they made wines in a somewhat oxidative style, but this has been modified in more recent vintages. All wines are aged in Hungarian oak barrels, coopered locally.

Some styles of sweet wines are produced in addition to *aszú* wines. Forditas is made by taking the cake of pressed *aszú* grapes, then macerating the cake with dry wine, giving a further fermentation that results in a wine that resembles a sweet Szamarodni. It seems a somewhat pointless wine, rather like using a tea bag twice. Oremus also make a wine called Noble Late Harvest, made, like Szamarodni, from whole bunches picked together, but made in a non-oxidative style and bottled young after only eight months in oak.

## Royal Tokaji Wine Company ☆☆☆☆
*3909 Mád*

Royal Tokaji, as its name suggests, has pretensions to grandeur. The brainchild of Peter Vinding-Diers, Hugh Johnson and other investors, it is the only major producer of Tokaji to have revived the old vineyard classification, identifying on its labels vineyards that are either first or second growths. The first growths are Nyulászó, Szt. Tamás and Betsek, and Birsalmás is a second growth. Generic *aszú* is produced with a blue label. What is likely to prove the finest site of all is the first-growth Mézes Maly. The first vintage was 1993, and the wine was released, at a very high price, in 1999.

Although some good wines were made in 1991, 1993 was their first outstanding vintage. The style of the Royal Tokaji wines is very distinctive and not always admired by the other producers. Alcohol levels are relatively low, between 10 and 12 per cent, and residual sugar levels very high, frequently over 200 grammes per litre. The analogy is not, as some critics suggest, with Sauternes but with Beerenauslese or TBA.

## István Szepsy ☆☆☆☆
*3909 Mád*

Szepsy was involved initially in helping to set up the Royal Tokaji Wine Company, but for some years he has run his own company, helped by financial backing from a Chinese-American business-man. Whereas some of the other producers release dry wines to generate some cash flow, Szepsy makes only *aszú* wines. He owns only eight and a half hectares, yields are very low at no more than ten hectolitres per hectare, and as consequence production is tiny and prices high. Quality is sensationally good, and the 1993 Aszú Eszencia bottlings were ravishing.

## Tokaji Trading Company ☆☆
*3981 Sátoraljaúlhely*

Until 1990 the company's precursor, the State Farm, owned the lot: vineyards, wineries, cellars, marketing outlets. After privati-sation began, the company had to shed some of its assets; there were numerous re-structurings until in 1994 the present name was adopted. By 1998 its vineyard holdings had shrunk to a mere 70 hectares, but the company remained the region's largest purchaser of grapes. Although the wines have been criticised for their oxidative style, they are by no means mediocre. They lack brilliance and purity, but they can be rich, full-bodied, quite powerful and backed by a firm acidic structure.

# Italy

No country is more enthralling than Italy for the lover of sweet wines. Nowhere else will one find such variety, such maddening diversity. In Italy, *passito* wines are more common than botrytised wines, although, this being Italy, there are numerous exceptions. Even a single grape variety such as Muscat can surface in utterly different forms: compare the feather-light, frothy Moscato d'Asti with the black, caramelly Muscats from Pantelleria. Where else will one encounter majestic, unfortified, sweet red wines? And Italy is stuffed with local grape varieties such as Picolit or Moscato Rosa that produce unique wines, often in tiny quantities.

# Alto Adige

The Alto Adige is the Italian term for the South Tyrol, a territory that until 1919 was part of the Austro-Hungarian Empire. Its vineyards are planted on mountain slopes, and there is a wide range of grape varieties. Most of its sweet wines are Muscats, either Moscato Giallo (Goldenmuskateller) or Moscato Rosa (Rosenmuskateller), which seems to have been brought north from Sicily in the late 19th century. Yields are extremely low, often no more than ten hectolitres per hectare. In order to make the sweet wine (and some versions are dry), the grapes are late-harvested in October. In some years when bad weather intervenes, no Moscato Rosa can be produced.

It is the bouquet that makes this wine so extraordinary, since it resembles a distillation of rose petals; few wines in the world are so powerfully perfumed. Some versions are lightly fortified.

## PRINCIPAL PRODUCERS
### Franz Haas ☆☆☆☆
*Montagna*

The first vintages of Moscato Rosa were not fully convincing here, but Haas now has the measure of this tricky variety, and the wines have all the perfume and profundity one could wish for, especially the Schweizer bottling.

### Josef Niedermayr ☆☆☆
*Cornaiano*

Niedermayr's Aureus is a blend of partially botrytised Chardonnay, Pinot Blanc and Sauvignon Blanc, given vitality by its high acidity. The 1995 was exceptional.

**Schloss Sallegg** ☆☆
*Caldaro*

In the 1980s this was the leading producer of Moscato Rosa, wines with the most wonderful perfume and texture. Unfortunately, the estate's owner had no interest in wine, and this gorgeous and ultra-rare wine (average production was a mere 700 bottles) was in danger of extinction. There has been a turn-around, and this celebrated wine remains in production.

Other good examples of Moscato Rosa are produced by Lageder and Plattner.

# Calabria

Calabria is known for its rare honeyed *passito* wine called Greco di Bianco, produced from the grape of that name. Ceratti is the best-known producer, and the similar Greco di Gerace is made by Ferdinando Messinò. Muscats are widely produced, sometimes in a *passito* style.

# Emilia-Romagnia

Emilia is the home of multi-faceted Lambrusco, but since sweet-ish frothing red Lambrusco usually lacks distinction, there is no need in this context to do more than note its existence. The best usually comes from Sorbara.

Romagna is the source of a more interesting wine, Albana, which, to the perplexity of many, was one of the first appellations to be awarded the prestigious DOCG in 1987. Albana can trace its origins back to Roman times, so it has antiquity on its side. It comes in many forms, from dry to fizzing to amabile (gently sweet) to *passito*, that last its most admired manifestation. It has quite good acidity and a slightly resinous quality – enjoyable enough but not always as great as the claims made for it would suggest.

Malvasia is often produced in an *amabile* style in the Coilli di Parma, and a richer, sweeter version, called simply Malvasìa Dolce, is released by Monte delle Vigne of Ozzano Taro.

## PRINCIPAL PRODUCERS

**Ferrucci** ☆☆
*Castelbolognese*

Stefano Ferrucci produces good *passito* Albana, rich and honeyed, as well as a *passito* from Malvasìa, which is lighter and fresher.

**La Stoppa** ☆☆
*Rivergaro*

Vigna del Volte is a mouth-filling Malvasìa Passita, orangey and fragrant, with a lean, tight structure that gives considerable elegance to a wine that might otherwise seem a bit soupy.

**Fattoria Zerbina** ☆☆☆
*Marzeno Faenza*

Zerbina is the producer of one of the finest Albana wines in a *passito* version, known here as Scaccomatto. Being aged in new *barriques,* it does have oaky tones but is dominated by its vibrant pineappley fruit and fine acidity.

Other good producers of Albana include Celli, Fattoria Paradiso, Cesari, Conti and Tre Monti.

# Fruili

Friuli's best-known sweet wine, though not necessarily its best, is Picolit, which was already fashionable in the 18th century. This grape, which thrives on volcanic soils, is highly delicate, prone to a malady known as floral abortion, which means that full pollination frequently fails to occur, resulting in very low yields. The wine is rarely lush or unctuous, but fine, elegant and marked by fresh acidity. Because of its very limited production it is extremely expensive. It is produced almost entirely within the DOC zones of Collio and Colli Orientali.

A grape variety of arguably greater interest is Verduzzo Friulano, which is also encountered in the eastern Veneto. It has good acidity and some resemblance to Chenin Blanc, but with that slightly bitter twist on the finish that gives a welcome bite to so many Italian sweet wines. The best Verduzzo comes from the Ramandolo zone, which has its own sub-appellation. A thick-skinned variety, Verduzzo can yield quite tannic wine. It is made either from late-picked grapes or by the *passito* method, and since it has considerably more body and weight than Picolit, the wine is better adapted to *barrique*-fermentation and *barrique*-ageing than Picolit. In some cases, Verduzzo and Picolit are blended.

Moscato Rosa, which is more at home in the Alto Adige than in Friuli, is produced in a lightly sweet style by Marco Felluga and Jermann (Vigna Bellina). A few idiosyncratic sweet wines emerge from Friuli, such as Pittaro's Apicio (Chardonnay x Manzoni 6.0.13).

## PRINCIPAL PRODUCERS

### Abbazia di Rosazzo ☆☆☆
*Rosazzo*

Ronco della Abbazia is a *barrique*-aged blend of Picolit and Verduzzo. There is also a lovely Picolit with a gentle almondy finish, and a richer, more complex Verduzzo.

### Coos ☆☆☆☆
*Nimis*

Dario Coos is now Friuli's leading specialist in Ramandolo. The *cuvée* known as Il Longhino is unoaked, but the more serious Ramandolo is, after partial drying, fermented in oak and acacia barrels. The drying ensures that the wine has a good deal of residual sugar, which is balanced by racy acidity.

### Dorigo ☆☆☆
*Buttrio*

Dorigo is the source of a *passito* Picolit, which is aged in *barriques* and has a delicate dried-fruits flavour. The estate also produces Verduzzo Friulano in a fairly alcoholic style.

### Dri ☆☆☆☆
*Nimis*

Giovanni Dri was one of the pioneers of Ramandolo, usually aged in *barriques*. He also makes a tiny quantity of high-priced flowery Picolit, which, unlike the Ramandolo, should be drunk young while it retains its fresh marzipan-tinged delicacy.

### Livon ☆☆☆
*Dolegnano*

Livon's Verduzzo, called Casali Godia, spends ten months in *barriques*. The style is luscious but clean and brisk on the finish.

### Petrussa ☆☆☆
*Prepotto*

The Petrussa brothers offer their rich, sweet Verduzzo under the name Pensiero.

### Roberto Picech ☆☆☆
*Cormons*

This estate produces a rich, figgy Malvasìa called Passito di Pradis. The vinification is unusual. Fermented on its skins in *barriques*, the wine is then decanted into other *barriques* for further ageing.

### Ronchi di Manzano ☆☆☆
*Manzano*

This rising star produces a fine appley Picolit and a more citrussy Verduzzo known as Ronc di Rosazzo.

### La Viarte ☆☆☆
*Prepotto*

Their blend of Picolit and Verduzzo is a *passito* wine called Sium, which is fermented in *barriques* and remains on the lees for up to 20 months.

Other good producers of Picolit and Verduzzo include Ca' Ronesca, Livio Felluga, Gigante, Meroi, Rodaro, Ronchi di Cialla, Ronco dell Betulle, Ronco del Gnemiz, Russiz Superiore and Specogna.

## Lazio – Latium

Not much sweet wine is produced in this Roman wine region, but Aleatico di Gradoli is a DOC in the north of the zone. At its best it is highly aromatic and can age well. There is also a fortified *liquoroso* version produced by the local cooperative. Castel de Paolis are unusual in using Sémillon for their botrytis wine Muffa Nobile.

## Liguria

The steep slopes northwest of La Spezia, rising high above the rocky Mediterranean shore, produce a rare *passito* wine called Schiacchetrà, made from Vermentino and the local grapes Bosco and Albarola. Schiacchetrà has a long and proud history; once in danger of extinction, the wine has been revived in recent years. Amber-gold in colour and apricot-scented, it can be high in alcohol. Good producers include Walter de Battè and the cooperative at Riomaggiore.

# Lombardia – Lombardy

The Oltrepò Pavese DOC south of Pavia produces much sparkling wine, some of which is quite sweet. There are also some Moscato wines: some are *passito*, others sweet and fizzy, and a few are fortified. The best is probably Moscato di Scanzo, but production is extremely limited. La Brugherate is the leading producer.

Mario Pasolini in Mompiano has made some excellent *passito* wines over the years. His Ronco Passito blended Marzemino and Merlot and delivered a huge mouthful of rich, sweet, tannic fruit and spice. Pasolini is close to retirement, so the future of this wine is uncertain.

# Marche – Marches

Verdicchio is the best-known white wine from this region, and although the vast majority of examples are bone-dry, there is a handful of *passito* versions, such as Le Brume from Garofoli, which is rich and honeyed on the nose but far less impressive on the palate. Others include Rojano from Vallerosa Bonci, and Zaccagnini's Cesolano, which is made from sun-dried grapes. There is also a sweet sparkling red called Vernaccia di Serrapetrona, which is made from Vernaccia Nera. A sweet Sauvignon Blanc called Maximo is produced by Umani Ronchi, but the wine is unexciting.

# Piemonte – Piedmont

Asti may have an image problem, but no one who has tasted a fine Spumante or Moscato can be in any doubt that Piedmont can produce the most delectable Muscat. But this is by no means the only sweet wine produced in Piedmont. In addition to those described below, a little sweet sparkling Malvasìa comes from two small regions north of Asti: Casorzo d'Asti and Castelnuovo Don Bosco. Accornero and Mondalino are the leading producers of Casorzo, while Balbiano, Gilli and Bava are the main producers of the latter. Bava's is delightful: rose-scented and *frizzante* on the palate. Moscato di Strevi is produced either in a sparkling form (as in Banfi's version) or as a *passito* wine, of which Domenico Ivaldi's creamy Casarito is the best example. Other *passito* Muscats are made by Batasiolo and I Vignaioli di San Stefano Belbo.

### Asti

Moscato Bianco grows on the light limestone soils of Alessandria and, even more notably, Asti. Vineyard location can affect the character of the wine, even one with such a powerful primary personality as Moscato. The trick with this relatively late-ripening variety is to retain both the floral, grapey aroma of the variety and its acidity.

What is special about both Spumante and its less fizzy *frizzante* version, Moscato, is that they are low in alcohol, sweet and sparkling. The wine is vinified in a pressurised steel tank, in which the temperature of fermentation can be precisely controlled, so that the must, usually pressed with a potential alcohol of around eleven degrees, can ferment to five or six degrees, with the remainder staying in the form of residual sugar.

Moscato is usually superior to Spumante. The best grapes are invariably used for the former, as it is legal to add sugar to Spumante (but not Moscato) in order to boost the alcohol level, which must be a minimum of seven per cent and can be as high as nine per cent, whereas the level for Moscato is usually around five or six per cent.

Reliable producers of Spumante, mostly large firms, include Fontanafredda, Bonardi, Bera, Gancia, Contratto, Cinzano and Martini & Rossi. In contrast, many smaller estates produce Moscato, including Bera, Ca d'Gal, Ceretto (I Vignaioli di Santo Stefano), Cascina Fonda, Chiarlo, Il Falchetto, Rivetti, Saracco, Scagliola and La Spinetta. Caudrina is probably the most highly regarded private estate specialising in Moscato d'Asti.

## Brachetto

This grape variety, mostly used to produce sweet sparkling wines, does best around Strevi, where it has its own DOC as Brachetto d'Acqui. A sweet sparkling red sounds suspiciously akin to Lambrusco, but good Brachetto is exquisite: wonderfully perfumed with red fruits such as strawberries and, like Moscato, low in alcohol. Producers include Banfi, Contero, Grimaldi and Marenco. There is also a *passito* version, which can be excellent. Good producers include Domenico Ivaldi, Giovanni Ivaldi and Malvirà. Pian dei Sogni from Scaglione (*see* entry below) is outstanding.

## Caluso Passito

The small town of Caluso overlooks the Po valley, and on its slopes the local Erbaluce grape is grown. It is vinified as either dry or *passito*. The zone of production is large, but relatively little of the sweet wine is produced. The leading producer used to be Vittorio Boratto of Piverone, who produced a dark raisiny wine with plenty of alcohol. In recent years the estate has been absorbed into that of Luigi Ferrando of Ivrea, who also produces a Caluso called Solativo. Other producers include Orsolani and Cieck.

## Loazzolo

This sub-DOC is within the Asti zone, and the wines are Moscato in a *passito* style. Although a traditional style, it had fallen into neglect until revived by Giancarlo Scaglione. Other producers include Borgo Maragliano, Borgo Sambui and Bricchi Mej.

## PRINCIPAL PRODUCER
### Giancarlo Scaglione (Forteto della Luja) ☆☆☆☆
*Loazzolo*
With his Piasa Rischei, Scaglione revived the traditional *passito* of

the region, but instead of drying the bunches on trays he preferred to leave the grapes on the vine for as long as possible before picking them. Sometimes they were affected by noble rot. The wine, fermented and aged for up to two years in small barrels, is Muscat at its most exquisite, with a fine texture and flavours of quince and dried apricot. He also makes a delightfully floral barrel-fermented Brachetto called Pian dei Sogni.

## Puglia – Apulia

This hot southern region is the source of good Aleatico, a generous sweet red, which is also available in a fortified _liquoroso_ form. One of the best is made by Francesco Candido in San Donaci. There is also a good rich Muscat with its own DOC: Moscato di Trani. Rivera and Torrevento are the leading producers.

## Sardenga – Sardinia

Sardinia is home to a number of Malvasia and Muscat wines as well as sweet red wines from the Monica grape, notably Monica di Cagliari. Many of these wines are fortified; quite a few are coarse. There are also some sweet wines from the Cannonau grape, which is none other than Grenache in local costume.

### PRINCIPAL PRODUCER
**Sella & Mosca** ☆☆
_Alghero_
This leading Sardinian producer makes an exemplary _passito_ wine from Cannonau grapes. Known as Anghelu Ruju, this is a brick-coloured fortified wine with about 80 grammes of residual sugar. A sort of cross in flavour between red _recioto_ and LBV Port, it ages majestically.

## Sicilia – Sicily

Sicily's best-known wine is the fortified Marsala, although Marco de Bartoli (_see_ entry below) also produce some non-fortified Marsalas by a _solera_ system under the label Vecchio Samperi. These have to be sold as Vino da Tavola since they do not conform to the Marsala regulations.

Muscats make their appearance in Sicily, as elsewhere in Italy. On the island of Pantelleria, between Sicily and Tunisia, the Zibibbo clone of Muscat is vinified in all kinds of ways. The local cooperative abandoned production of Tanit, its lightly fortified Moscato, but the label has been taken over by the MID company; its Tanit has a light orangey nose and considerable freshness and creaminess on the palate. Sun-dried Zibibbo grapes are used to make the remarkable Passito di Pantelleria, of which the finest example is made by Marco de Bartoli. Those from Donnafugata and Rallo are considerably lighter; Florio's well-known Morsi di Luce is a very good fortified example.

Another island, Lipari, is the source of the _passito_ Malvasia delle Lipari. The finest used to be produced by a Swiss expatriate called Carlo Hauner, aromatically complex and exceptionally elegant. After his death the winery went through an uncertain period that now seems to be over. A more dilute Malvasia is produced by Colosi. There is also a fortified version.

Other sweet wines from Sicily include Inzolia di Samperi from Marco de Bartoli and the lightly sweet Moscato di Noto, which can be sparkling and is sometimes fortified.

## PRINCIPAL PRODUCERS
### Marco de Bartoli ☆☆☆☆
*Marsala*

In addition to his impressive Vecchio Samperi Marsalas, de Bartoli makes magnificent Moscato Passito di Pantelleria under the name of Bukkuram. The Muscat grapes are picked early to retain acidity and dried on mesh nets in the fierce sunlight for about three weeks. It is fermented and aged in large casks. Very dark in colour, the aromas are raisiny and figgy, and the wine is spared from cloying sweetness by its excellent acidity.

### Salvatore Murana ☆☆☆☆
*Pantelleria*

Salvatore Murana bravely produces wines solely from Zibibbo. The regular Moscato di Pantelleria is very good, but it's the *passito*, made from the *crus* Martingana and Khamma, that is the sensational wine, with its powerful dried-fruit flavours and exceptional length.

# Toscana – Tuscany

Vin Santo is the great sweet wine from Tuscany. Although essentially a *passito* wine, other factors relating to its vinification and maturation make it difficult to produce. There are many disappointing versions, and even from the same winery there can be significant variations from vintage to vintage.

## Aleatico

No one is certain of the identity of this aromatic grape, the perfume of which has led many experts to link it, plausibly, with Muscat. Although grown in various parts of Italy, it is in decline as a variety, although it is undergoing a revival of sorts in southern Tuscany. The best recent vintages have been 1990 and 1997. Some Aleatico is also found on Elba, produced by La Chiusa.

## PRINCIPAL PRODUCERS
### Antinori ☆☆☆
*Florence*

From Sovana in southern Tuscany, this Aleatico is given a lengthy maceration period before being fermented at a fairly low temperature. Antinori have only been producing the wine since 1995, but it's impressive, with delectable redcurrant and raspberry aromas and fresh spicy flavours. It is best drunk lightly chilled.

### Avignonesi ☆☆☆
*Montepulciano*

Avignonesi have acquired vineyards in the Maremma region west of Montepulciano from which they produce a notable Aleatico called Tenimenti di Sovana. It's more sumptuous and tannic than the Antinori wine and has a distinct portiness.

## Moscadello di Montalcino

It seems odd that Montalcino, the source of one of Italy's most profound and powerful red wines, should also be home to an exquisite Muscat, which fortunately has been undergoing a revival thanks to the efforts of Banfi, Col d'Orcia, Il Poggione and Sassetti. The original strain of Muscat here, Moscadelletto, had virtually disappeared but is making a comeback along with Moscato Bianco.

## Vin Santo

The implication of the name Vin Santo is that the wine was used for sacramental purposes, which may well have been the case, although no one seems completely sure. The grapes – Malvasia, Grechetto and Trebbiano in any combination – are picked quite early and dried: the length of *appassimento* will affect the concentration of sugar in the must. Authentic Vin Santo is sweet, but producers seeking to make a drier version will shorten the *appassimento*.

After pressing, the must is transferred into 50-litre barrels called *caratelli*. From this point on, the wine is in the lap of the gods. The casks are sealed, placed in an attic and left undisturbed for up to six years. Very few producers maintain the ageing for the traditional six years; three years would now be considered usual. The wine has to endure a succession of Tuscan winters and summers, but these strong fluctuations in temperature help determine the character of the finished wine. The long cask-ageing gives the wine a slight oxidative tone, and its final balance may be unpredictable. The winemaker, measuring the must weight after pressing, should have a shrewd idea of how the wine will emerge, but the vigour or lethargy of the yeasts, the level of acidity and the effect of cask-ageing will all affect the final outcome. Larger wineries can blend *caratelli* to even out any irregularities in style. Some consistency is contributed by the *madre*, a small amount of wine left in the cask from the previous vintage.

Vin Santo usually reaches high alcohol levels – 16 per cent is not unusual – and the long cask-ageing gives it great complexity. On the nose there is often a hint of Sherry and dried fruits, but the taste is less predictable, as variations in sweetness, acidity and oxidation would suggest. If the wine is well balanced, it can age superbly.

## PRINCIPAL PRODUCERS
### Avignonesi ☆☆☆☆
*Montepulciano*

In addition to their splendid regular Vin Santo, Avignonesi also make a fabulous, and fabulously expensive, bottling called Occhio di Pernice, which is aged for seven years. This is wine of astonishing concentration and purity of flavour.

### Capezzana ☆☆☆
*Carmignano*
This Vin Santo shows distinct oxidative character on the nose, together with aromas of marmalade and caramelised apples. Medium-sweet, it has bracing acidity, a silky texture and exemplary length.

### Isole e Olena ☆☆☆
*Barberino Val d'Elsa*
There are vintage variations, but this Vin Santo is often nutty and raisiny on the nose, with overtones of smoke and caramel. Supple yet concentrated, this is a very stylish example.

### Selvapiana ☆☆☆☆
*Rufina*
Made solely from Trebbiano, this Vin Santo is aged for five to six years in small barrels, giving a tangy, caramelly wine, immensely concentrated and extracted.

Other good Tuscan producers of sweet wines include Bossi, Brolio, Cacchiano, Ciacci Piccolomini, Contucci, Fontodi, Le Pupille and Rampolla.

# Trentino

Three principal sweet wines are produced in Trentino: Moscato Rosa, Moscato Giallo and Vino Santo. The Moscato Rosa is of course the same grape as that cultivated in the Alto Adige. Good examples are produced by Endrizzi, the Istituto Agrario at San Michele, Gaierhof and Casa Girelli.

The local Nosiola grape is the source for Vino Santo, which is made in a similar way to the more famous Tuscan version (*see* Tuscany above). It is often aged for up to five years in casks. At its best it can be a wonderfully rich and vibrant wine, unashamedly sweet and high in acidity. Good versions are offered by Cavit, Francesco Poli, Giovanni Poli and Pravis.

The renowned Pojer & Sandri estate produce a wine they rather grandly call Essenzia. It's surprisingly austere, with only a touch of sweetness. And there's a late-harvest Chardonnay called Sole d'Autunno from Maso Martis.

## PRINCIPAL PRODUCERS

### Letrari ☆☆☆
*Nogaredo*
This Moscato Rosa is marked by lovely rosehip aromas and is quite delicate on the palate despite a formidable alcohol level of 14.5 per cent. Prices are high.

### Fratelli Pisoni ☆☆☆☆
*Sarche*
Pisoni produce a stunning, copper-brown Vino Santo: caramel and burned orange on the nose and very sweet toffee-apple and raisiny flavours. It ages effortlessly.

**Cantina di Toblino** ☆☆☆☆
*Sarche*

Although a cooperative, the Cantina produce sensational Vino Santo, a complex mouthful of toffee, mango and candied orange peel.

# Umbria

Umbria's proximity to Tuscany means that Vin Santo is also produced here, although not in the same ubiquitous manner. Lungarotti's remains a benchmark example. Orvieto has long had a tradition of producing the local wine in an *abboccato* (off-dry) style, and the estate of Decucgnano dei Barbi (*see* entry below) also make, when conditions permit, an intriguing botrytised version.

## PRINCIPAL PRODUCERS
### Antinori ☆☆☆
*Castello della Sala*

Antinori, best known for their wide range of Tuscan wines, are also producers in Umbria. Muffato della Sala is always made from botrytised grapes (Sauvignon Blanc, Grechetto and Riesling) harvested at their Castello della Sala estate. *Muffa nobile* means noble rot – hence the name of this wine. It has charm rather than power, and a gentle peachiness.

### Decugnano dei Barbi ☆☆
*Orvieto*

Their Pourriture Noble, made only in appropriate years, is quite rich and supple, in a fairly light style, and the botrytis influence is discreet. The wine has a silky texture and ample fresh acidity.

Other botrytised Orvieto is produced by Palazzone (Muffa Nobile) and Barberani (Calcaia).

# Valle d'Aosta

This narrow valley not far from the Swiss border looks too inhospitable to grow grapes, but a handful of determined proprietors continue to cultivate their vines along the precipitous slopes. A very good *passito* from Muscat known as Passito di Chambave is made by just two producers, Ezio Voyat and La Crotta di Vegneron. There is also a minute production of a *passito* wine known as Malvoisie de Nus, Malvoisie being a form of Pinot Gris.

# Veneto

This region, stretching into the hills beyond Venice, Padua and Verona, is home to the famous Recioto, which comes in many forms from many sectors within the Veneto. It can be either red or, less commonly, white. A *passito* wine, Recioto has to be made with exceptional care, and growers often set aside those parcels within the vineyard that they believe have the finest potential to make Recioto. It's a costly wine to make, because of the selection involved in picking only the most suitable bunches, and because the drying process reduces the volume by about one-third.

Other sweet wines, mostly rarities, are encountered in specific localities within the Veneto. From the Colli Euganei comes a sweetish Muscat, usually known as Fior d'Arancio; and a Moscato Giallo comes from Le Vigne di San Pietro in Sommacampagna, close to Lake Garda. In Lugana, Ca' dei Frati's Tre Filer is made from Lugana, Chardonnay and Sauvignon Blanc; the bunches are dried for 90 days and aged for a year in *barriques*. Maculan, the celebrated producers based in Breganze, make a number of sweet wines, of which the best known is Torcolato (*see* below), a style they revived in 1971. Maculan also produce Dindarello, a Fior d'Arancio Muscat, light but almost peppery. Tenuta San Antonio produce a lush Chardonnay-based *passito* called Colori d'Autunno. The Gambellara region produces a Recioto, both still and sparkling, and a Vin Santo from Garganega grapes that have been dried for a longer period. The best-known producers are Zonin and La Biancara. The Recioto Classico and Vin Santo from Iseldo Maule can be outstanding.

## Recioto di Soave

This great white wine was revived by Pieropan and Anselmi, and their efforts were rewarded when this Recioto was given DOCG status. It is made from Garganega grapes.

## Anselmi ☆☆☆☆
*Monteforte*

Roberto Anselmi, who from the time he took over his family estate vowed to treat the despised Soave as seriously as if it were fine white burgundy, produces outstanding Recioto, which he calls I Capitelli. After selecting his grapes carefully, they are dried for up to five months, and the wine is aged in a substantial proportion of new French oak. Some of the early vintages were quite oaky, but Anselmi learned fast, and more recent vintages have been beautifully judged, with ample rich apricotty fruit to balance the vanilla oakiness. It can be drunk young with great pleasure.

## Gini ☆☆☆
*Monteforte*

Claudio and Sandro Gini produce two styles of Recioto, Col Foscarin being a traditional style from dried healthy bunches, while Renobilis is made from botrytised fruit.

## Pieropan ☆☆☆☆
*Soave*

Leonildo Pieropan picks his grapes destined for Recioto quite early, to ensure they are healthy and golden in colour. Pieropan releases three different sweet wines. His regular Recioto, called Le Colombare, is made in a lighter, more elegant style than Anselmi's. The more opulent Passito della Rocca uses a blend of Riesling Italico and Sauvignon Blanc; the *appassimento* is shorter but the wine is aged in *barriques*. The third wine is Santa Lucia, a pure Garganega, late-harvested after the grapes have shrivelled and in some cases attracted noble rot. This is a lush wine tasting of stewed peaches, though it can lack the verve of Pieropan's other bottlings. It is made only in outstanding years such as 1995.

Other good producers of Recioto di Soave include La Cappuccina, Coffele, Inama and Portinari.

## Recioto di Valpolicella

It has been claimed that this wine existed in Roman times, which is entirely possible. Classic Recioto is made from the same grapes used for Valpolicella: Corvina, Rondinella and Molinara. After drying, the bunches are pressed and fermented and aged for months or years in casks. The fermentation stops, or is arrested, at about 14 per cent alcohol, leaving a small amount of residual sugar in the wine. In the popular Recioto Amarone style, the wine is fermented to dryness, resulting in a powerful brew with at least 16 per cent alcohol. Neither wine is easy to make in a way that is balanced as well as powerful. Amarone as a dry wine does not concern us here, but Recioto should show a richness of plummy fruit with a coating of silky but by no means sugary sweetness, and the finish should be clean and almost dry.

There is also a sparkling Recioto or Amarone, which has more than a passing resemblance to Australian sparkling Shiraz. Bertani and San Rustico are among its producers. There is also a white Recioto, usually a blend of Garganega and Trebbiano grapes.

Although most producers make their Recioto traditionally, drying the grapes in a well-ventilated attic, technological innovation has crept in in recent years. Some wineries have installed climatised chambers that allow them to shorten the *appassimento* and minimise the risk of rot.

## Allegrini ☆☆☆☆
*Fumane*

This fine estate is run by the Allegrini siblings: Walter (vineyards), Franco (winery) and Marilisa (everything else). They are a formidable team, and Franco ensured that the quality of the wine went from strength to strength. As well as the regular Recioto, there is a single-vineyard (*cru*) wine called Fieramonte. This magnificent bottle can age 20 years or more without any loss of fruit or vigour. Allegrini also produce a delicious appley white Recioto called Fiorgardane. These are all splendidly spicy wines, with tremendous complexity of fruit and no harsh edges.

## Bussola ☆☆☆☆
*Negrar*

Tommaso Bussola releases two ranges of wine, of which the better is called TB. The TB Recioto is intensely fruity, concentrated and elegant, and there is also an occasional white Recioto he calls Peagnà.

### Dal Forno ☆☆☆
*Illasi*

This estate was founded as recently as the 1980s and has rapidly acquired a fine reputation for its Amarone and its full-powered Recioto Monte Lodoletta.

### Masi ☆☆☆☆
*Sant' Ambrogio di Valpolicella*

Dr Sandro Boscaini has been banging the drum for Recioto and Amarone for decades, presenting the wines and explaining them all over the world. Masi have long specialised in *cru* wines, and their top Recioto Mezzanella is a wine that in its youth has a slight tarriness but with age becomes more mellow; like all fine Recioto, it finishes clean. Masi also produce a rich, rounded white Recioto called Campociesa, lightly sweet with a dry finish.

### Quintarelli ☆☆☆☆
*Negrar*

No one produces Recioto of greater magnificence and splendour than Giuseppe Quintarelli. It is impossible to keep track of the range of wines, as Quintarelli is constantly experimenting, and will, if he feels like it, bottle certain casks separately. A Recioto made, unusually, from Cabernet Franc was experimental 15 years ago but has now earned its place as a mainstay of his range. The wines tend to be aged for many years in casks and demijohns, and are bottled only when Quintarelli thinks the moment is right. The style is bold, concentrated and uncompromising, and after fermentation the wine is simply sealed in its cask for about three years, as though it were a Vin Santo. One of his greatest wines is the voluptuous Recioto Riserva Vignetto di Tre Terre, a wine of stunning elegance. There is also a range of wonderful white Recioto, a confusion of bottlings including Extra Amabile and Bandito Amabile. However, a bottle of these hand-crafted white Reciotos can be a gamble; some have shown premature oxidation.

### Serègo Alighieri ☆☆☆
*Gargagnago di Valpolicella*

These excellent vineyards are owned by a descendant of the writer Dante, Count Pieralvise Serègo Alighieri, but the wines are made and marketed by Masi. The Recioto Casal dei Ronchi is classic: rich in fruit and with lively hints of nutmeg and other spices.

### Speri ☆☆☆
*San Pietro in Cariano*

This long-established house produces a small quantity of Recioto known as La Roggia. After an *appassimento* of 120 days, the must is fermented and aged in *barriques* for 18 months. The resulting wine is not especially oaky, thanks to the abundance of rich, plummy fruit and a lively finish of chocolate and mint. There is also a simpler Recioto called I Comunai.

### Tedeschi ☆☆☆
*San Pietro in Cariano*

Tedeschi's Reciotos may be less demanding than some, but they are among the finest on offer. He likes to age the wine in small casks, and believes Recioto is best drunk fairly young, at about five years. This seems right for the style of his wine, which is never massive but invariably graceful and finely balanced. It is worth looking out for his deep-coloured and impeccably structured *cru* wine from Capitel Monte Fontana. There is also a small quantity of delicious white Recioto Vin de la Fabriseria.

Other good producers of Recioto include Accordini (red and white), Baltieri, Bertani, Brigaldara, Boscaini, Campagnola, Castellani, Degani, Montresor, Le Ragose, Trabucchi, C S Valpolicella, Venturini, Viviani and Zeni.

### Torcolato Maculan ☆☆☆☆
*Breganze*

Using the Vespaiola and Tocai grape varieties, Maculan dry the grapes for some months before ageing the wine in *barriques*. The result is a lush, supple wine with complex fruit, fine acidity and a touch of honey. It's powerful too, with about 15 per cent alcohol. There are quite marked variations between vintages. Even more concentrated is the Acininobili, a wine made from fully botrytised grapes.

# Other sweet wines of Europe

## Romania

In the past Romania was celebrated for its sweet wines, which were said to be on the same quality level as Tokaji and Constantia. The most renowned sweet wine came from Cotnari in Romanian Moldavia, a wine influenced by noble rot and, unlike Tokaji, made in a non-oxidative style. The principal grapes used for these wines are the indigenous Tamiioasa, an aromatic grape with a resemblance to Muscat; Grasa, which can reach astonishingly high must weights and contributes weight to the wine; Feteasca Alba, which also gives the wine body; and Francusa, which gives the wine its acidic backbone. The varieties are vinified separately, then blended and aged in large casks. Before bottling, some young wine is added to the blend to give it greater freshness. Only two or three times in any decade is the wine marked by botrytis flavours, as it is principally Grasa that attracts noble rot, and only in certain years.

After the Second World War Cotnari was dispatched to Russia, where wine-drinkers have long had a sweet tooth, and even today the Russian market is strong, as is the domestic market, which prizes Cotnari. Very little reaches Western Europe.

The major region known for sweet-wine production was Murfatlar near Constanta on the Black Sea coast, where the wines were made from Tamîioasa, Pinot Gris and quite often from Chardonnay, all of which can be botrytis-affected, although noble rot is less common here than in Cotnari, since the climate is dry and hot. Muscat Ottonel is also produced here in a sweet style.

North of Bucharest are the vineyards of Dealul Mare, best known as a source of tannic red wines. But the Tamîioasa grape is also planted here, especially in the sub-region known as Pietroasele, where it is subject to attacks of botrytis and can form the basis of an intensely sweet wine.

## Switzerland

In the canton of Valais in southern Switzerland there has long been a tradition of late-harvested wines. Sometimes the grapes are *passerillé*, occasionally botrytised. In such a condition the grapes are known as *flétri* and the word often appears on Swiss wine labels. The wines are very distinctive because of the grape varieties planted. Malvoisie, which is in fact the Swiss name for Pinot Gris, and Johannisberg (Swiss for Sylvaner) are known internationally, but only in Switzerland is Marsanne (known here as Ermitage) frequently late-harvested, and the Petite Arvine and Amigne are indigenous to the Valais. Most of the wines are gently sweet and rather soft, thanks to low acidity, but a few producers have sought to produce wines with great concentration and richness.

There is a growing trend to produce wines that will have a greater international appeal than the supple, late-harvest Ermitage and Malvoisie. Mitis, the flagship wine of the Germanier firm, is a late-picked Amigne fermented and aged in new oak. The first vintage of the wine was 1992. Other wines in a comparable style are the Primius Classicus from Orsat in Martigny, made from Petite Arvine, Cuvée d'Or from Bonvin and made from Johannisberg and Amigne, and Profil from Provins Valais in Sion. Many of these growers with a keen interest in sweet wines have signed up to a charter called Grain Noble Confidentiel. The rules stipulate that the grapes must come from the best sites and be at least 15 years old; that no chaptalisation or must concentration be employed; that grapes be picked at 130 Oechsle or more; and that the wines should be aged in *barriques* for at least 12 months.

## Ukraine

In the 1890s Prince Lev Golitzin founded a winery at Massandra in the Crimea. Here a succession of long-lived sweet wines, many of them Muscats and almost all fortified, were produced until 1945. Prince Golitzin also founded the Massandra Collection, assembling about 10,000 of the best Crimean wines each year and adding them to the cellars. In 1990 and 1991 many of the finest and oldest wines were auctioned off in London.

# United States of America

One of the most depressing statistics in the modern history of wine is the fact that in 1953 California produced 28 million gallons of white and red table wine, and 82 million gallons of dessert wine. Almost without exception, the dessert wines would have been cheap Muscats and raw, alcoholic imitations of Port and Sherry. Moreover, not until 1968 did dry wines began to outsell sweet.

Today, there are a few botrytis wines of outstanding quality, a style pioneered by Wente's "Chateau Yquem" in the 1930s. Myron Nightingale at Beringer (*see* entry, Napa Valley) experimented with the artificial induction of botrytis and released a number of vintages. From 1973 Jerry Luper of Freemark Abbey (*see* entry, Napa Valley) produced botrytised Riesling, as did Richard Arrowood at Chateau St Jean. Sadly, many wineries that used to produce this style – Mondavi, Jekel, Cakebread – have given up.

A style of sweet wine peculiar to California is late-harvest Zinfandel. This style was invented by mistake, when Bob Travers at Mayacamas lacked tank space during the 1968 harvest and asked his pickers to delay harvesting some Zinfandel. When the grapes finally reached the winery and were fermented, the alcohol level soared to over 17 degrees. The wine, surprisingly, was superb, rather like an unfortified style of Port. In the 1980s these high-alcohol wines fell out of fashion, but in more recent years have been revived, although often they are fermented to dryness. The wines are, however, far more palatable with some residual sugar. But, unfortunately, they will always remain an acquired taste.

Muscats remain popular. Muscat of Alexandria is the most widely planted variety, but the best wines are made from Muscat Canelli. Orange and Black Muscats are also encountered, and can be excellent.

## Central Valley
### PRINCIPAL PRODUCERS
Quady ☆☆☆
*Madera, CA 93639*
Andrew Quady has real flair, both as an inventive winemaker and as a packager. His Electra is a low-alcohol Orange Muscat.

## Mendocino
### PRINCIPAL PROPERTY
Navarro ☆☆☆☆
*Philo, CA 95466*
The temperature can get very cool here in Anderson Valley, so varieties such as Riesling never lack acidity. Noble rot is not uncommon, and winemaker Ted Bennett profits from the fact to make some outstanding botrytised Rieslings in certain vintages.

# Napa Valley

## PRINCIPAL PRODUCERS

### Beringer ☆

*St Helena, CA 94574*

In the 1970s and 1980s Myron Nightingale made some celebrated wines by artificially inducing botrytis in a humidified chamber, but the resulting wines often lacked elegance. Botrytised Sauvignons are still produced here, but the Rieslings are usually fresher and better.

### Far Niente ☆☆☆

*Oakville, CA 94562*

When Far Niente decided to make what they called Dolce, they modelled the wine, mostly Semillon, on Yquem, ageing it in new oak for three years. The result is undoubtedly very good, though lacking the concentration and grandeur of a great Sauternes.

### Freemark Abbey ☆☆☆

*St Helena, CA 94574*

Jerry Luper began producing botrytised Riesling here in 1973, and the tradition continues. The BA-style wines are called Edelwein, and TBA-style bottlings are labelled Edelwein Gold. Quality is high, and vintages are rare. Edelwein Gold was last made in 1989 and 1994.

### Joseph Phelps ☆☆

*St Helena, CA 94574*

Phelps's first winemaker, Walter Schug, was German-born and thus familiar with the idea of botrytis wines. Phelps soon became known for their fine late-harvest Rieslings and Scheurebes, as well as for Délices de Sémillon, which was aged in mostly new oak.

The range was thinned down in the 1990s, but the occasional late-harvest wine is still made, as well as Eisrebe, a wine made from Scheurebe frozen after harvesting. Unfortunately, this wine lacks intensity.

### Pine Ridge ☆☆

*Napa, CA 94558*

One of the few wineries to offer late-harvest Chenin Blanc, Pine Ridge made the wine in 1988, 1989, 1992 and 1994. Quantities are tiny.

### Topaz ☆☆☆

*St Helena, CA 94574*

Jeff Sowells, an enthusiast for Sauternes, buys in botrytised Semillon and Sauvignon Blanc in appropriate vintages and crafts his wines in rented facilities. The results, in 1989, 1991 and 1994, were rich and unctuous, a touch weighty and somewhat sweeter than a typical Sauternes.

### Turley Wine Cellars ☆☆
*St Helena, CA 94574*

Helen Turley, and subsequently Ehren Jordan, made the wines here, specialising in late-harvest Zinfandels. Most of the wines are dry, but occasionally some retain residual sugar and are distinctly better for it. The wines are show-stoppers – very powerful, heady, tannic – but whether they are pleasurable is another matter.

### Other wines

The Grgich Hills estate sometimes produces a decent late-harvest Riesling, and the version from Long tends to resemble an elegant Auslese more than a botrytis wine. Other good botrytised Riesling comes from Newlan. Beaulieu have for many years produced a silky, honeyed Muscat, given extended ageing in small barrels. More attractive is the very delicate Moscato Amabile from Louis Martini, which resembles a Moscato d'Asti in style.

## San Luis Obispo County

John Alban, a specialist in growing and producing Rhine varieties, has made some Vin de Paille ("straw wine") from Roussanne and has plans to cooperate with Alois Kracher of Austria on some sweet wines. But this lies in the future. Some charming Muscat Canelli is made by Arciero and Eberle, both in Paso Robles. Talley in Arroyo Grande is best known for his Chardonnay and Pinot Noir, but the occasional late-harvest Rieslings can be delicious.

## Santa Cruz
### PRINCIPAL PRODUCERS
### Bonny Doon ☆☆
*Bonny Doon, CA 95060*

Randall Grahm, who will try anything, has had considerable success with his Vins de Glacière, made from artificially frozen Muscat grapes that are half-thawed and then pressed. The result is intensely fruity but lacks subtlety.

### Ridge ☆☆
*Cupertino, CA 95015*

Ridge have long produced some of California's loveliest Zinfandels, but in vintages when the conditions are correct Paul Draper has made small quantities of Zinfandel Essence from botrytised grapes.

## Sierra Foothills and Lodi
### PRINCIPAL PRODUCERS
### Karly ☆☆
*Plymouth, CA 95669*

This is Zinfandel country, but Karly also produce a rich and unctuous Orange Muscat.

### Madrona ☆☆
*Camino, CA 95709*
At 900-odd metres, these are some of the highest vineyards in California. In certain years, such as 1993 and 1997, they produce late-harvest wines from Riesling and Chardonnay.

### Renwood ☆☆☆
*Plymouth, CA 95669*
Renwood offer a wide range of skilfully made wines, including an oddity called Amador Ice, a Zinfandel Icewine.

### Sobon ☆☆
*Plymouth, CA 95669*
The Muscat Canelli here is nondescript, but Mission del Sol is a real curiosity, a *passito* wine made from Mission grapes, Mission being the variety planted in California by Spanish missionaries in the 18th century. It's unfortified and has some resemblance to Sherry.

### Story ☆
*Plymouth, CA 95669*
This is the place at which to sample sweet wine made from the Mission grape. Called Mission Gold, it's aged for two years in oak and is surprisingly palatable.

## Sonoma

### PRINCIPAL PRODUCERS

#### Arrowood ☆☆☆☆
*Glen Ellen, CA 95442*
Richard Arrowood made the sensational TBA-style wines at Chateau St Jean in the 1970s and 1980s and transferred his enthusiasm to his own winery in 1986. Superb botrytised Rieslings were made in 1995 and 1997, and in some vintages there are also intriguing late-harvest Viogniers.

#### Chalk Hill ☆☆
*Healdsburg, CA 95448*
This winery has never lived up to high expectations, but there have been occasional late-harvest Sauvignons of very good quality.

#### Ferrari-Carano ☆☆☆
*Healdsburg, CA 95448*
This vulgar Italianate show-case winery does produce outstanding wines, and despite its glitzy name Eldorado Gold can be an excellent botrytised wine from Sauvignon Blanc and Semillon.

## Southern California
In Santa Ynez Valley Zaca Mesa under winemaker Dan Gehrs has made some delicious late-harvest Viognier, but with Gehrs' departure this style may be abandoned. Callaway in Temecula has long produced a late-harvest Chenin Blanc called Sweet Nancy, and the winery also releases some sweet Chardonnay.

# Pacific Northwest

A few excellent sweet wines are made north of California. In Oregon Amity produce superb Select Cluster Rieslings with great intensity of flavour, especially 1992 and 1994. Elk Cove's Ultima is made from artificially frozen Riesling; while it's rich, it's slightly cloying.

In Washington Blackwood Canyon once made superb botrytised Riesling and Semillon but has gone out of business. Chateau Ste Michelle, Stewart, Silvan Ridge and Hogue produce some crisp late-harvest Rieslings. Kiona, Covey Run and Preston have made Riesling Icewines.

# Canada

Canadian wine producers realised some time ago that when it came to sweet wines their forte was likely to be Icewine rather than botrytised wines. Given the severity of most Canadian winters, sustained frost is quite frequent. From the start the Canadian wine authorities imposed conditions that would ensure that the wines would be of good quality.

In Ontario Icewine must be made as a varietal wine, and the grapes must be picked at -8°C or colder; artificial freezing is forbidden. Grapes must be harvested at a Brix level of at least 35, and the residual sugar level must be at least 125 grammes per litre. (Similar conditions prevail in British Columbia, although the producers are less numerous.) The freezing process removes about 80 per cent of the grapes' juice content, so the volumes extracted by pressing are small, which is why the wine is very expensive. For botrytised wines the minimum Brix level for a wine called Botrytis Affected is 26 degrees, and for Totally Botrytis Affected 34 degrees.

The first Canadian Icewine was made by Hainle in 1974, and the first commercial vintage was 1978. Not all the early Icewines were successful; some were made in a high-alcohol style, while others had odd bitter flavours. In general, the finest have been produced from Riesling, but other varieties can also deliver wines of high quality. The hybrid variety Vidal is a popular choice, but the wines often lack the verve that the more acidic Riesling delivers. On the other hand it has rich apricot and tropical fruit flavours that have an immediate appeal.

Other, less successful Icewines are made from Kerner, Ehrenfelser and Gewürztraminer. Among French varieties, Pinot Blanc can produce excellent Icewine. Total production is about 20,000 cases from Ontario (Ont), with a few more thousand cases from other provinces, notably British Columbia (BC).

# Principal producers

**Cedar Creek** ☆☆
*Kelowna, BC*
At their best these Riesling Icewines are lean and racy, but in some vintages they show signs of incomplete ripeness and of tartness.

## Château des Charmes ☆☆☆
*St David's, Ont.*

The 1991 Riesling Icewine and the 1997 Paul Bosc Estate Riesling Icewine are about as good as it gets: intensely sweet and acidic, but finely honed and elegant, with tremendous vigour and length. In some years, such as 1995 and 1996, late-harvest Rieslings are produced. The 1996 was cloying, but the 1995 was utterly delicious.

## D'Angelo ☆☆
*Amherstburg, Ont.*

Barley sugar dominates the nose of the 1996 Vidal Icewine, which is full-bodied and creamy, with a suggestion of boiled sweets on the palate. It is considerably better than the 1997.

## Gehringer Brothers ☆☆☆
*Oliver, BC*

Gehringer have made Icewine from Cabernet and Merlot (untasted), but their Riesling is classic: racy, stylish and understated, needing time to develop complexity.

## Henry of Pelham ☆☆☆
*St Catharines, Ont.*

The 1996 here proved a typically balanced Riesling, with 9.3 per cent alcohol, 210 grammes of residual sugar, and a fierce 13.4 grammes of tartaric acid. The upshot was a harmonious and invigorating wine, citrussy and sherbetty, that should age very well. The 1990 and 1992 were also excellent.

## Inniskillin ☆☆
*Niagara-on-the-Lake, Ont.*

This well-known estate was one of the first (in the 1980s) to take Icewine seriously, using both Vidal and Riesling. While undoubtedly lush, they can lack verve.

## Pillitteri ☆☆
*Niagara-on-the-Lake, Ont.*

The 1997 Riesling Icewine has a classic green-apple nose and a rich, creamy texture, though the wine lacks a touch of vigour and concentration. The 1997 Gewürztraminer Icewine, while exotic, is far less successful. The 1997 Vidal, however, is lush and pineappley.

## Quails' Gate ☆☆
*Kelowna, BC*

Founded in 1989, this winery has rapidly established a fine reputation. The 1998 Riesling Icewine is excellent, with pineappley aromas and ample spicy flavour and length on the palate. The 1993 was rounded but lacked flair.

## Strewn ☆☆
*Niagara-on-the-Lake, Ont.*

The 1997 Vidal Icewine is a good example of the variety, with a boiled-sweets nose and considerable plumpness on the palate.

Other fine Riesling Icewine is made by Jackson Triggs and Southbrook Farms, and rich wines with typical Icewine character made from Pinot Blanc are produced by Hester Creek and Sumac Ridge (BC). An unusual Kerner Icewine comes from Tinhorn Creek (BC), and Vidal from Konzelmann can be very fine. Hainle (BC) have a fondness for wines with 16 per cent alcohol or more, which makes them fiery and unbalanced.

# Australia

The great Australian sweet-wine style, Liqueur Muscat, is covered in the fortified wine section. Botrytis wines, however, are increasingly popular. Some impressive botrytised wines have been made over the past two decades, principally Semillon but frequently Riesling too. There was a trend, pioneered by Joe Grilli of Primo (*see* entry, South Australia), to inoculate botrytis spores on to bunches of grapes laid in a humid chamber, but results have been mixed, and the best growers prefer to cultivate particular parcels of vines which, they hope, will attract botrytis naturally. Another technique, widely practised with Riesling, is to cut the canes on which the bunches have been growing; deprived of nutrition, the grapes shrivel and the sugar levels are increased.

Griffith in New South Wales is widely regarded as the best subregion for botrytised Semillon, but there are also many parts of South Australia – including Barossa, McLaren Vale and Coonawarra – where botrytis occurs naturally from time to time.

## New South Wales
### PRINCIPAL PRODUCERS
#### Cranswick ☆☆☆
*Griffith, NSW 2680*
This large winery has made some very fine botrytis Semillons, notably in 1993 and 1995, when the wine was aged in new oak. The wines are very sweet and apricotty but are saved by their fine acidity and good length.

#### De Bortoli ☆☆☆☆
*Bilbul, NSW 2680*
After some unsuccessful attempts to make botrytis wines in the 1970s, Darren de Bortoli finally made a rich, powerful botrytis Semillon in 1982. Not only did the wine cause a sensation in Australia, but it made a considerable impact in Europe, where the wine sometimes featured as a "ringer" in blind tastings of Sauternes. In general the de Bortoli wine proved softer and richer than most Sauternes, but few could resist it. Since 1982 the wine has been made almost every year, except 1989, and it has been renamed The Noble One. About 35 per cent new oak is used to age the wine. This is one of the most consistent of botrytis Semillons, but exceptional vintages include 1982, 1984, 1987 and 1990–1993.

**McWilliams** ☆☆

*Hanwood, NSW 2680*

McWilliams have offered numerous botrytis Semillons over the decades. Recent releases have been from grapes sourced from Griffith and aged in new oak for about 12 months. These wines are very rich and unctuous but can be rather heavy.

Other producers include Bloodwood (Riesling Icewine in 1994), Cartobe (Riesling), McGuigan (Semillon) and Miranda (Semillon). Lillypilly make an unusual botrytised Muscat of Alexandria and sweet wines from Semillon and Traminer.

# South Australia

## PRINCIPAL PRODUCERS

### D'Arenberg ☆☆☆

*McLaren Vale, SA 5171*

The Noble Riesling, first made in 1985, is a very consistent wine, lean, elegant and tangy with crisp acidity on the finish.

### Henschke ☆☆☆

*Keyneton, SA 5353*

Although one associates Henschke with superlative reds, the Noble Rot Riesling, produced in 1984, 1988, 1992 and 1996, can also be outstanding, with a creamy texture and impeccable elegance.

### Lindemans ☆☆

*Connawarra, SA 5263*

This large company has made some fine botrytis wines over the years, including Riesling from Connawarra and Semillon blended from Padthaway and Griffith fruit.

### Petaluma ☆☆☆☆

*Piccadilly, SA 5151*

When Brian Croser turns his hand to botrytis Riesling, the results are formidable. The wines often resemble TBA, with a viscous texture and power without heaviness.

### Primo ☆☆

*Virginia, SA 5120*

Joe Grilli no longer inoculates his Riesling with botrytis spores, and the excellent wines from 1991, 1993 and 1994 were all naturally infected. The Eden Valley and Clare Valley fruit delivers ample botrytis character, but the wines can be rather weighty and lacking in elegance.

### Yalumba ☆☆☆

*Angaston, SA 5353*

The Heggies Vineyard has long been the source of some luscious barley sugar-tinged botrytis Rieslings from Eden Valley, and there is another bottling from Pewsey Vale also in the Eden Valley. The Semillons, sometimes produced from Griffith fruit, have been less impressive, although there are exceptions, such as the smoky, spicy 1987.

Other good botrytis Rieslings are produced by Brokenwood, Grosset (Clare Valley), Hollick (Coonawarra), Knappstein, Mount Horrocks (Clare Valley), Tollana and Woodstock (McLaren Vale). As for botrytis Semillons, other leading producers include Tim Adams, Fern Hill, Haselgrove and Peter Lehmann (Barossa).

# Victoria
## PRINCIPAL PRODUCERS
### Brown Bros ☆☆☆
*Milawa, Victoria 3678*
Brown Bros have had great commercial success with their light, zesty Orange Muscat and Flora, which has found its place as a fine accompaniment for lighter fruit desserts. The botrytis Riesling is a far more serious wine and is labelled as Noble Riesling when botrytised, as Late Harvest when not. A good wine, it can in some vintages be slightly cloying on the finish.

### Coldstream Hills ☆☆☆
*Coldstream, Victoria 3770*
From time to time James Halliday – lawyer and wine journalist as well as winemaker – turns his hand to botrytis Semillon, usually from Griffith fruit. The many vintages show remarkable consistency of flavour and quality. These are high-acidity wines, so the plump, peachy fruit is never cloying, and the finish is clean.

### Seville ☆☆☆
*Seville, Victoria 3139*
A very small operation that occasionally produces botrytis Rieslings of exceptional quality.

# Western Australia
This is not ideal territory for botrytis wines, and the sweet Riesling of Evans & Tate is produced by cutting the canes to allow the grapes to shrivel; the result is an appealing wine that lacks complexity. Evans & Tate also produce a sweet Semillon. Some well-aged fortified wines are produced by Talijancich at Herne Hill.

## PRINCIPAL PRODUCER
### Vasse Felix ☆☆☆☆
*Cowaramup, WA 6284*
This winery is best known for its Cabernet Sauvignons, but its occasional excursions into Noble Riesling are stunning. The wine is now aged in 50 per cent new oak for about 6 months. These Rieslings have great purity of flavour, lushness without heaviness, and fine intensity and length.

# New Zealand

Given that the climate in much of New Zealand is relatively cool and moist, there is a clear potential, which so far has only been partly realised, for sweet botrytis wines. There have long been fortified wines made here, with the emphasis on alcohol and sweetness more than finesse. "Sauterne" was produced mostly from hybrid varieties and Muscat. There is still a loyal clientele for the old-style fortified wines, some of which are of high quality.

Botrytis wines are a more recent creation, dating from as recently as the early 1980s. Riesling is the most promising variety, especially now that a more susceptible tighter-bunched clone from South Australia is being planted, but good wines have also been made from botrytised Chardonnay and Chenin Blanc.

Although botrytis wines have been produced in a number of regions, the most auspicious would appear to be Marlborough in the South Island and Martinborough in the North Island, where heavy dews rather than morning fogs provoke botrytis into action. Many wineries, such as Villa Maria (*see* entry), helped to induce botrytis by abstaining from anti-botrytis spraying, a risky measure since it can open the door to unwelcome grey rot as well.

Icewines have been produced in New Zealand from time to time, but from grapes that have been artificially frozen rather than left on the vine. Examples include a Gewürztraminer from Hermann Seifried (*see* entry) in Nelson, and one from Mission in Hawkes Bay. Selaks have made a Riesling Icewine from artificially frozen Riesling. The first naturally frozen Icewine was made from Riesling grapes by Chard Farm in Central Otago.

Vintages vary according to locality and microclimate, but some of the best years for botrytis wines have included 1987, 1989, 1991, 1993, 1994 and 1997.

# Principal producers

## Cloudy Bay ☆☆☆
*Marlborough*

In 1989 this celebrated winery made its first late-harvest Riesling, which had an elegant botrytis nose and racy lean fruit – not a particularly complex wine but a very attractive one, as were the 1991 and 1996. This Riesling is fermented in steel but aged in older casks.

## Corban's ☆☆☆
*Marlborough*

Corban's Cottage Block Noble Riesling, from Marlborough grapes, has all the rich botrytis character and citrussy vigour one would expect from that area.

### Dry River ☆☆☆
*Martinborough*

Neil McCallum has tried just about everything here, including a botrytised Gewürztraminer, a Beerenauslese-style wine quite high in alcohol, and botrytised Riesling, which was outstanding in 1997.

### Giesen ☆☆
*Canterbury*

The Giesen brothers, immigrants from Germany, are familiar with late-harvest wines from their native Pfalz. Their Noble School Road is a blend of Riesling and Müller-Thurgau, a sweet, melony, one-dimensional wine with little body or depth. They also make more intense botrytised Riesling, sometimes in a very sweet TBA style.

### Millton ☆☆
*Gisborne*

New Zealand's leading organic winery produces an oak-aged Sauternes-style wine called Tête de Cuvée, using Chenin as well as Semillon grapes, and late-harvest wines from Riesling and from Chardonnay. There is also a very rich Noble Chenin Blanc Individual Berry Selection.

### Ngatarawa ☆☆☆
*Hawke's Bay*

Very fine late-harvest and botrytised Noble Harvest Glazebrook Rieslings have been produced by Alwyn Corban at this 18-hectare estate since 1987. The 1991 was especially lush, with candied fruit flavours.

### Rongopai ☆☆☆
*Waikato*

Tom van Dam began making botrytis wine here in 1987. The proximity of water from the Waikiri Lake and the Waikato River means that morning mists are common, which stimulates botrytis spores. Very high sugar levels, up to 58 Brix, have been recorded. Their Botrytis Reserve is made from a blend of grape varieties – Wurzer (a crossing of Müller-Thurgau and Gewürztraminer), Müller-Thurgau, Scheurebe and Bacchus – which are planted in the Swan Vineyard. Of greater interest, however, are the varietal bottlings: outstanding botrytis wines from Riesling and Chardonnay. The 1993 Chardonnay was a brilliant, vibrant, orangey wine, more successful than the Riesling of the same year. The 1997 Chardonnay was very rich, at over 150 grammes of residual sugar.

### Seifried ☆☆☆
*Nelson*

The Styrian-raised Hermann Seifried, who came to New Zealand in 1971, was a pioneer of botrytised Rieslings. The 1985 BA-style Riesling was marked by high acidity, but subsequent vintages of his late-harvest style, which is not always botrytised, have been better balanced, with sufficient rich, appley, Riesling fruit to balance the invigorating acidity.

## Te Whare Ra ☆☆
*Marlborough*

Allen Hogan has been producing wine here since 1982, making him a veteran by Marlborough standards. In 1985 he produced the first botrytised Riesling, a wine he has made in a number of subsequent vintages such as 1991. There are also some late-harvest Gewürztraminers.

## Vidal ☆☆☆
*Hawke's Bay*

The 1994 and 1996 Reserve Botrytis Semillon are gorgeous wines, honeyed and almost tarry on the nose, with fine apricot fruit and excellent balance.

## Villa Maria ☆☆☆
*Auckland*

Villa Maria's Reserve Noble Riesling was first made in 1991 from Hawke's Bay fruit. The 1993 and 1997 were equally successful, with, in 1997, a slight raisiny tone on the nose, as well as aromas of mandarins and pineapple, and remarkable freshness and zest on the palate.

Other good producers of late-harvest Riesling include Coopers Creek (Auckland), Forrest (Marlborough), Jackson Estate (Marlborough), Martinborough Vineyard, Merlen (Marlborough), Mission (Hawke's Bay), Montana (Marlborough), Selaks (Marlborough) and Shingle Peak (Marlborough).

Those who use the Chenin Blanc grape as the basis for sweet or botrytised wines include Esk Valley, who first made the style in 1992, blending in 25 per cent Chardonnay, and have since produced the wine in a barrel-fermented version. Chris Lintz (Martinborough) has used the early-ripening German grape Optima to make tiny quantities of a TBA-style wine. There are late-harvest Gewürztraminers from Matua Valley (Auckland). Wineries that have used Chardonnay for their late-harvest wines include Morton (Bay of Plenty) and Palliser (Marlborough). Those offering late-harvest Sauvignon Blanc include Sacred Hill (Hawke's Bay).

Although fortified wine production is in decline in New Zealand, a faithful clientele remains for these old-fashioned wines. Some of them, such as those from Mazuran in Auckland, are aged up to 20 years before being offered for sale, so there are Port- and Sherry-style wines of good quality to be found. In addition to Mazuran, other producers include Pleasant Valley (Auckland) and Esk Valley (Hawke's Bay), who still make a Liqueur Muscat.

# South Africa

## The history

South Africa is no newcomer to the world of sweet wines.
The Cape wine region of Constantia was planted in the 17th century, and it was here, in the following century, that the wine that
took its name was evolved. Muscadel (Muscat of Alexandria) –
called Hanepoot in South Africa – had been widely planted and
formed the basis of Governor van der Stel's celebrated wine.
Napoleon was among its most famous admirers and customers,
as was King Louis Philippe. Constantia continued to be produced
until well into the 19th century, but then vanished once phylloxera took hold. The wine became the stuff of legend.
In its heyday it had fetched extremely high prices, yet no one
could say precisely how the wine was produced. It was the Klein
Constantia estate that decided in 1982 to revive the style, or an
approximation of it.

As well as the Muscadel "Hanepoot" wines (which are generally, though not always fortified) South Africa produces excellent
examples of late-harvested wines, as well as wines made
from grapes infected with the mould *Botrytis cinerea* (the "noble
rot" or *pourriture noble* or *Edelfäule*). South Africa's generous
climate and fertile soils are more sympathetic to this kind of
wine than the gravelly soils of Bordeaux or the cold slopes
of Germany, and we all know that wine is at its best when it's
had to struggle for its very existence, but there are producers
who can turn out very good examples around the Cape. The
regulations governing how South African sweet wines may be
labelled are as follows:

Late Harvest (LH): 10–30 grammes per litre (g/l) of unfermented sugar after fermentation has stopped naturally. This is
roughly equivalent to a German Auslese.

Special Late Harvest (SLH): as above, but 20–50 g/l sugar. This
is roughly equivalent to a German Beerenauslese.

Noble Late Harvest (NLH): as above, but over 50 g/l sugar and
the grapes must have been affected by botrytis. This is roughly
equivalent to a German Trockenbeerenauslese.

## Principal producers
### Ashanti, Huguenot ☆☆
This newly established Paarl estate launched a number of
sweet wines in 1998, including an NLH Chenin Blanc, aged in
new oak, and an unusual Vin de Paille ("straw wine") from
Colombard grapes.

### Bon Courage, Robertson ☆☆
*PO Box 589, Robertson 6705*
Established in 1984, this firm belongs to the Brouwer
family and has a good track record, with a clutch of winemaking
awards under its corporate belt. Best sweet wine: SLH
Gewürztraminer.

## Boschendal, Groot-Drakenstein, Franschhoek ☆☆☆

Vin d'Or produced here at Boschendal is pure Semillon, rich, with tropical fruit flavours, but saved from heaviness by vigorous acidity.

## Delaire, Stellenbosch ☆☆

*PO Box 3058, Stellenbosch 7602*

Established in 1984, this smallish company was established by the Platters, a winemaking and wine-writing husband-and-wife team who have raised more than a few hackles in South African wine industry circles. It now belongs to an international businessman based in London and is best known for its sweet wines. Best sweet wine: NLH Riesling.

## Delheim Wines, Simonsberg ☆

*PO Box 10, Koelenhof 7605*

Established in 1941, this is a joint venture between two families and mainly specialises in red wines. Best sweet wines: SLH wines, NLH Edelspatz, a full-flavoured peachy botrytis wine from Riesling and Bukettraube; occasionally an NLH Riesling is also produced.

## De Trafford, Stellenbosch ☆☆☆

In 1997 this estate produced South Africa's first Vin de Paille ("straw wine"), a complete monster of a wine boasting over 16 per cent alcohol and firm acidity underpinning the voluptuous fruit.

## De Wetshof, Robertson ☆☆☆

NLH Riesling Edeloes is produced here in varying styles, sometimes light and silky, in other vintages, such as 1998, rich and tangy with bracing acidity.

## Klein Constantia, Constantia ☆☆☆

*PO Box 375, Constantia 7848*

Established in 1685 as part of the Groot Constantia estate by Simon Stiel, one of the pioneers of South African wine. The Jooste family replanted Muscat de Frontignan in 1982. About half the crop is picked early and sold off; the rest stays on the vines until raisined. Once picked, the grapes are fermented on the skins to 15 per cent alcohol, leaving about 100–120 grammes of residual sugar. The wine is matured in older oak for 12 months.

Researchers believe the original Constantia was not fortified, so this revived Vin de Constance is also unfortified. The wine has a rich, spicy, tangerine nose and flavours of marmalade, lime and stewed apricots. The finish is lively and clean.

In some years, such as 1992 and 1996, a botrytised Sauvignon Blanc is produced here at Klein Constantia. Again aged in oak, it has a spicy, smoky nose: a vigorous, creamy wine with a fine texture. Best sweet wines: Vin de Constance (Constantia), NLH Sauvignon Blanc.

### KWV International, Paarl ☆☆
*PO Box 528, Suider-Paarl 7624*

This was the giant cooperative of cooperatives which virtually ran the South African wine business in the years before democracy. It lost its constitutional status in 1995 but today, as a private company, it is still very much the biggest animal in the South African wine zoo. Past ascendancy means that its wines encompass most of the styles of the country. Best sweet wines: NLH wines.

### Lievland Estate, Stellenbosch ☆☆☆
*PO Box 66, Klapmuts 7625*

Established in 1981, this company specialises in new-wave wines but still manages to produce something spectacular in the botrytis dessert department. Best sweet wines: NLH wines.

### Nederburg, Paarl ☆☆
*Private Bag X3006, Paarl 7620*

Established in 1936, this company is owned by the Stellenbosch Farmers' Winery. Since it was first made in 1969, Edelkeur has become one of South Africa's most celebrated wines, a very rich and intensely sweet Chenin Blanc with up to 170 grammes of residual sugar. There is also a less rich NLH Riesling, a delicious appley wine often as good as Edelkeur, with about 95 grammes of residual sugar, and a Sauternes-style Semillon first made in 1997. Best sweet wines: M Eminence, NLH Edelkeur.

### Neethlingshof Estate, Stellenbosch ☆☆
*PO Box 104, Stellenbosch 7599*

Established in 1974, this is the retirement project of a German banker, Hans-Joachim Schreiber, and substantial investment is delivering excellent wines, notably ravishing NLH Riesling, intensely sweet but balanced with high, refreshing acidity. Best sweet wines: NLH wines.

### Perdeberg Cooperative, Paarl ☆
*PO Box 214, Paarl 7620*

This is another cooperative with an advancing reputation, particularly for wines made from the Chenin Blanc – known until recently in South Africa as the Steen. Best sweet wine: NLH Chenin Blanc.

### Robertson Winery, Robertson ☆☆
*PO Box 37, Robertson 6705*

This, too, is a cooperative making a name for itself in the dessert-wine market. Best sweet wine: SLH Rheingold.

### Simonsig, Koelenhof ☆☆

Frans Malan first made NLH Chenin Blanc in 1979, but the estate usually find that Bukkettraube is more affected by botrytis. In 1998 this wine was called Vin de Liza, and 25 per cent was barrel-fermented. The wine has honeyed and dried-fruit aromas and is sustained by firm acidity.

### Stellenzicht Vineyards, Stellenbosch ☆☆☆
*PO Box 104, Stellenbosch 7599*
Established in 1986, this winery is owned by Hans-Joachim Schreiber, who also owns Neethlingshof Estate (*see* entry), and is regularly gilded in national and international competitions. Best sweet wine: NLH Semillon.

### Trawal Wine Cellar, Olifantsrivier ☆☆
*PO Box 2, Klawer 8145*
This is a cooperative that used to sell most of its wine to other houses but which has been ploughing its own furrow during most of the 1990s. Best sweet wines: LH and SLH wines.

### Twee Jonge Gezellen Estate, Tulbagh ☆☆
*PO Box 16, Tulbagh 6820*
Established in 1947, this belongs to the Krone family, who have farmed here for two centuries. Best sweet wine: SLH Rheingold.

### Weltevrede Estate, Bonnievale (Robertson) ☆☆
*PO Box 6, Bonnievale 6730*
Established in 1974 and owned by the Jonker family (whence Lourens Jonker, chairman of the KWV), this is a well-respected company producing value-for-money wines. Best sweet wine: SLH Therona.

Other excellent late harvest wines are occasionally made by L'Avenir (Colombard), Bon Courage (Riesling), Fleur du Cap (Chenin Blanc), Morgenhof (Chenin Blanc), Spier (Bukettraube), Vergelegen (Semillon) and Zonnebloem (blended).

# Index